OBJECTS OF DESIRE

THE SEXUAL DEVIATIONS

OBJECTS OF DESIRE

THE SEXUAL DEVIATIONS

Editors

Charles W. Socarides, M.D.
Abraham Freedman, M.D.

Associate Editors

Kenneth Gould, M.D.
Selma Kramer, M.D.

INTERNATIONAL UNIVERSITIES PRESS, INC.

Library of Congress Cataloging-in-Publication Data

Objects of desire: the sexual deviations/editors, Charles W. Socarides, Abraham
Freedman; associate editors, Kenneth Gould, Selma Kramer.
    p. cm.
Includes bibliographical references and index.
ISBN 0–8236–3731–X
    1. Sexual deviation. 2. Psychoanalysis and homosexuality—Case studies.
3. Sexual orientation. 4. Gays—Case studies. 5. Lesbians—Case studies.
I. Socarides, Charles W., 1922– II. Freedman, Abraham.

RC451.4.G39 025 2002
616.89'17'08664—dc21

                                                    2002068819

Manufactured in the United States of America

To
The
Memory of
Selma Kramer, M.D.
Child Psychoanalyst
Teacher and
Friend

How much truth can the mind endure, how much can it dare to entertain? For me this has always been the real measure of value. Every acquisition, every advance in knowledge, is the outcome of courage, of sincerity towards oneself.

—Nietzsche

Table of Contents

Acknowledgments

We wish to express our thanks to the patients described within these pages whose courage and endurance in the quest for liberation from their sexual deviation have furthered our comprehension of the various forms of sexual deviation.

We owe a debt of gratitude to Dr. Margaret Emery, Editor-in-Chief, International Universities Press, and to our wives Claire Alford Socarides and Isobel Rigg Freedman, M.D., whose encouragement has made it all possible.

We wish to acknowledge the following publishing houses that have allowed us to reprint several articles which have appeared in their books following their presentation at the Discussion Group:

Oxford University Press, Oxford, London, New York, I. Rosen, editor, *The Sexual Deviations*, Third Edition, 1996, for "Advances in the Psychoanalytic Theory and Therapy of Male Homosexuality," by Charles W. Socarides, pp. 252–278.

Yale University Press, New Haven, CT, *The Psychoanalytic Study of the Child,* editors A. J. Solnit, P. B. Neubauer, S. Abrams, A. S. Dowling, Volume 52, 1997, for "The Analysis of a Prehomosexual (Transvestite) Child with a Twelve-Year Developmental Follow-up," by Georgie Babatzanis, pp. 159–189.

International Universities Press, Madison, CT, H. Blum, editor, *Psychoanalytic Explorations of Technique,* 1980, for an extract from "The Technical Significance and Application of Mahler's Separation–Individuation Theory," by Selma Kramer, entitled "A Note on the Resolution of Separation–Individuation Transference Phenomena in the Analysis of a Homosexual Woman," pp. 241–255.

Contributors

Georgie Babatzanis, is Supervising Analyst and Faculty member at the Toronto Child Psychotherapy Program; Past President of the Child Section, Toronto Child Psychotherapy Program, Toronto, Canada.

Jerome S. Blackman, M.D., F.A.P.A., is Professor of Clinical Psychiatry at Eastern Virginia Medical School, Norfolk, VA; Training and Supervising Analyst, New York Freudian Society, Washington, DC Psychoanalytic Institute.

Abraham Freedman, M.D., is Honorary Professor of Psychiatry and Human Behavior, Jefferson Medical College, Philadelphia and Faculty member, Psychoanalytic Institute of the Philadelphia Association of Psychoanalysis.

Kenneth S. Gould, M.D., is Clinical Professor Psychiatry, University of Medicine and Dentistry, New Jersey (Formerly Rutgers).

Ian Davidson Graham, M.D., F.R.C.P.(C), is a Training and Supervising Analyst, Toronto, Canada.

Selma Kramer, M.D., was Professor of Clinical Child Psychiatry, Thomas Jefferson University Medical School; Training and Supervising Analyst, Philadelphia Psychoanalytic Institute.

Zvi Lothane M.D., is Associate Clinical Professor of Psychiatry, Mount Sinai School of Medicine, New York, NY.

Houston Macintosh, M.D., is Teaching Analyst, Washington Psychoanalytic Institute.

Purnima Mehta, M.D., is a child, adolescent, and adult psychoanalyst; Faculty Member, Michigan Psychoanalytic Institute.

Alberto Montes, M.D., was a Member, American Psychoanalytic Institute and International Psychoanalytic Association.

Charles W. Socarides, M.D., F.A.C.Psa., is a Life Member, American Psychoanalytic Association, International Psychoanalytic Association; Fellow, American College of Psychoanalysts; Clinical Professor of Psychiatry, Albert Einstein College of Medicine, New York City (1978–1996).

Preface

The discussion group "The Sexual Deviations: Theory and Therapy" was initiated in May 1983 by Charles W. Socarides and Vamık D. Volkan, with permission of the Program Committee of the American Psychoanalytic Association. Our intention was to present clinical material by individual psychoanalysts that would shed light on etiology, course, symptoms, and therapy, as well as to describe new research findings on these conditions. The discussion group presentations became a launching pad for the further development of each author's ideas. We were especially eager to undertake this project for it is a matter of psychoanalytic history that few psychoanalysts have had the opportunity during their psychoanalytic careers to treat or report upon more than one or two patients with well-structured sexual deviations. Psychoanalysts have been confronted by the ego-syntonic nature of perverse symptoms—by the need for such patients to engage in perverse acts whenever they experience anxiety and to act out. Analysts have been similarly dismayed by the unyielding nature of a condition that brought instant pleasure instead of painful suffering to those afflicted. Thus, many psychoanalysts and psychoanalytic institutes have limited their goals to the alleviation of the associated symptomatology, or have pronounced such cases unsuitable for psychoanalytic treatment, and certainly "too difficult" for the neophyte psychoanalytic candidate. We owe a profound debt of gratitude to those in the past who persevered in their efforts to remove perverse symptoms and establish normal functioning; for example, William Gillespie, Robert Bak, Sandor Lorand, Gustav Bychowski, Phyllis Greenacre, Masud Kahn, Janine Chasseguet-Smirgel, Edward Glover, Renato Almansi, and, of course, Freud. This book would not have been possible without their earlier theoretical, clinical, and therapeutic observations that formed the foundation upon which we based our deliberations. In the shared experiences of our participants, we have attempted to gain sufficient knowledge on which to make some broad generalizations and explanations.

For the first ten years the Discussion Group was cochaired by Drs. Socarides and Volkan and on occasion by Salman Akhtar. Dr. Kenneth Gould coordinated the vast majority of meetings, which were held biannually over these years, for a total of thirty-two sessions. Our aim was to offer a forum for a wide discussion of these ineluctable and often mysterious disorders, to provide theoretical explanations for an often dismaying set of symptoms, and to explore therapeutic tactics or techniques for their alleviation. We feel that the success of our project may well be reflected by the continuation of this discussion group in an uninterrupted fashion. Companion volumes will report on other sexual deviations including pedophilia, voyeurism, sadomasochism, exhibitionism, and fetishism.

We wish to express our appreciation to the presenters of these papers as well as all the members of the discussion group, and especially to those "regulars" who have made this a sustained, informative, and gratifying experience, to mention only a few. Raymond Paine, Robert Dickes, the late Ruth and Theodore Lidz, Renato Almansi, the late Selma Kramer, Lothar Gidro-Frank, Georgie and John Babatzanis, the late George Zavatzianos, Cora Ann Dobbs de Fiero, Felix and Loretta Loeb, Sylvia Brody, Salman Akhtar, Carroll Weinberg, Houston Macintosh, Helen and Harry Wagenheim, Jerome Blackman, and David Goldman.

Finally, we wish to make it perfectly clear that the case material presented here by individual psychoanalysts in the areas of male or female homosexuality does not reflect the official position of the American Psychoanalytic Association, but is a product only of individual research, treatment, and opinion. We wish furthermore to thank the American Psychoanalytic Association for its permission to hold this discussion group in the spirit of psychoanalytic research and inquiry.

We hold that the resolution of any patient's psychopathology is accomplished through a determined pursuit and perserverance on the part of both patient and analyst. It informs us once again that what is decisive in the psychoanalytic treatment of deviant patients is not the patient's symptomatology per se, or his life history, but the nature of the spontaneously developing transferences, and the willingness and ability of the patient to follow the lead of the analyst in a mutual endeavor of tracing and understanding the genesis of his condition (the therapeutic alliance). It is our hope that our experiences with these remarkable and worthy patients will encourage others to pursue similar investigations. It is our belief that unconscious mechanisms are nowhere better revealed than in the study of these conditions. While these patients often present flawed and dramatic manifestations, these manifestations have arisen simply from abstract ideas, and while they express unacceptable impulses to many, they are largely a means to express fundamental wishes and anxieties whose understanding remains a fundamental task of all psychoanalytic inquiry (Freud, 1900).

The Editors

Reference

Freud, S. (1900), The Interpretation of Dreams. *Standard Edition,* 4&5. London: Hogarth Press, 1953.

Introduction

This book reports on the continuing investigation of sexual deviations by the clinical psychoanalytic method. The extent of the literature on this subject can be judged by the number of references at the end of each chapter.

Psychoanalysts and other biosocial and psychological scientists do not use the words *deviant* or *perversion* in a perjorative sense. *Deviant* means different from the usual and *perversion* means a turning from the usual course. The fact that there is a cultural prejudice against people to whom the terms apply when preceded by the adjective *sexual* does not make the words perjorative when used for scientific classification and study.

The first of two theoretical chapters by Socarides reviews the developmental psychology and psychopathology of male homosexuality and reviews recent advances in its treatment. The data underlying the theory are derived from years of experience in the psychoanalysis of many homosexual patients, probably more than have been treated by anyone else. It is a scientific, not a political, discussion of male homosexuality.

Dr. Blackman gives us a masterful description of the treatment of a borderline patient whose homosexuality was only one of many presenting problems. The patient's development had been hindered during childhood by poor parenting and sexual overstimulation. The reader can follow the vicissitudes of the case with its clarifying descriptions of the transferences and interpretations. The outcome of the patient's sexual orientation was not a therapeutic goal, but a shift to heterosexuality occurred in the terminal phase of the treatment. Sessions number 470 to 522 are given in detail and the reader is referred to sessions 497, 498, and 499 that took place at the time of the shift in sexual orientation.

Dr. Zvi Lothane's study of the Schreber case questions Freud's hypothesis that paranoid psychosis is a defense against homosexual drives. He cites hospital records that were not available to Freud and proposes that the psychotic regression was the cause of Schreber's gender identity confusion and bisexual wishes and behavior rather than the result of it. Schreber's fear of homosexuality, not a primary wish for homosexuality, followed the onset of the illness and evoked defensive formations which colored the clinical picture.

The second theoretical chapter by Dr. Socarides introduces the section on female homosexuality with a review of its causative process. This topic is less familiar to most psychoanalysts than the origins of male homosexuality, and the theory is clarified by clinical examples. This thereotical chapter is enhanced in another chapter in the same section by the review of the literature which Dr. Macintosh appended to his clinical description of the psychoanalysis of a homosexual woman. He lists all the factors that many authors have been described as causative, and specifies those that apply to his case.

Dr. Montes uses the psychoanalysis of a homosexual woman to explore the multiple functions of sexual object choice and he successfully demonstrates the defensive and compromise formation utility of the homosexuality. Before the treatment, his patient had a conscious wish to relate to men and become a married woman with children but unconscious conflicts dictated her homosexual orientation. The case demonstrates that although the patient had no choice in her unconscious selection of homosexuality, it does not mean that the homosexuality is inevitable; sexual orientation can change when, with psychoanalytic treatment, it is no longer necessary in the psychic economy.

Dr. Graham describes the psychoanalytic treatment of another homosexual woman who also had a conscious wish to have a close relationship with a man but was thwarted by unconscious conflicts. There were many levels of conflict. Issues of separation and individuation were reenacted with homosexual lovers and in the transference as were oedipal difficulties with the father. A preanalytic course of treatment with a woman therapist had both prepared the patient for analysis and provided a mode of acting out the conflicts in the transference rather than analyzing them.

The cases of Drs. Montes and Graham, with their similarities of unconscious conflict determining homosexual orientation, which frustrated the conscious desire for a heterosexual lifestyle, form a

strong argument for the availability of psychoanalytic treatment
with the possibility of change in sexual orientation.

Dr. Kramer gives us a brief but very illuminating description
of the analysis of a homosexual woman whose problems stemmed
from early development. Her case shows the value of using Mahler's
concepts of separation-individuation to understand the transference
and the psychogenetic material. Unlike the two previous cases, dissatisfaction with homosexual orientation was not a factor when this
patient sought treatment. However, after analysis of the problems
of separation-individuation, oedipal material became available as
the patient became more feminine in her appearance, thoughts, emotions, and dreams. This case shows that a pretreatment conscious
wish for heterosexuality was not a prerequisite for a shift in sexual
orientation as the analysis progressed.

Dr. Macintosh describes the psychoanalysis of a homosexual
woman with full details of her personal history and the course of
the analysis. The preoedipal and oedipal origins of her disorder are
amply illuminated. She came into treatment because of a severe
depression that followed the loss of her homosexual lover. Her homosexual relationships repeated the course of her ambivalent relationship with her mother who had died one year before the beginning
of the analysis. Although she was interested in men from adolescence, she was never able to sustain a romance and was too frightened by heterosexuality to achieve it. In the course of the analysis,
she did form a relationship with a man whom she married, but she
had to resolve her conflict over the fact that he had been the husband
of a woman she had liked. Dr. Macintosh tries to elucidate all the
possible formative factors in homosexuality that were active in
his patient.

Opening the section on transvestism, Babatzanis presents the
analysis of a prehomosexual boy, which began when he was age 8,
continued for three years, and afforded occasional contact for follow-up until he was 20. Treatment was begun because the child
liked to dress in female clothes, play at being a girl, and disrobe
and dance in the nude. We are given the details of this child's early
development and his behavior in the treatment. We learn that there
were strong heterosexual drives in childhood that were activated in
sexual play with his older sister. Guilt and conflict were relieved

by feminization. The choice of sexual orientation remained conflictual as the boy grew up.

Dr. Mehta undertook the treatment of a 3½-year-old boy who dressed in his mother's clothes and showed interest in being a girl. She worked with both parents as well as with the child and described how she had tried to prepare the parents for the child's treatment. A large part of the feminization was a defense against aggression. In the beginning of the treatment the child was encouraged to keep his transvestite behavior within the treatment situation. His aggression tended to increase as the transvestism abated. As his sexuality and aggression became more manifest in nursery school, it frightened the staff. Also, the pediatrician seems to have resented being left out of the treatment and sided with the nursery school. Although Dr. Mehta saw the increased phallic aggressiveness as a sign of desirable change, she was unable to persuade the parents to allow the child to continue in treatment, even in the face of the child's distress at not being allowed to see the therapist. However, she has continued to work with the parents and hopes that the child will resume treatment. She cites these problems in a recommendation that children of this age be in a therapeutic nursery school while under treatment so that there is continued cooperation of parents and others who have contact with the child.

Both cases of transvestism illustrate the defensive use of feminization against conflict over aggression.

The Editors

PART I

Male Homosexuality

CHAPTER 1

Advances in the Psychoanalytic Theory and Therapy of Male Homosexuality

CHARLES W. SOCARIDES, M.D., F.A.C.Psa.

Introduction

Sexual reproduction was antedated by asexual reproduction or fission; that is, one cell splitting into two identical cells. The word *sexual* is derived from biology and refers to a form of reproduction occurring between two cells that are different from each other. Their combined nuclear material results in completely new individual cells (germ cells differentiated as male and female). This event became the basis of the evolutionary differentiation of the sexes. Radó (1949) notes:

> Taken in its entirety, the male–female reproductive pair is an emergent entity, a biological organization of a higher order. Produced by evolutionary differentiation, male and female germ cells, coital organs and individuals are but so many component parts of this new entity. . . . The pattern of these early [alimentary] pairs is destined to exert a powerful influence on the individual's future sexual behavior. Sexual activity began solely as reproductive activity. It was later

Portions of this chapter, a revision and expansion of my chapter entitled "The Psychoanalytic Theory of Homosexuality with Special Reference to Therapy" published in Ismond Rosen's (1964, 1979) books on sexual deviation, are adapted or replicated from my diverse writings on male homosexuality over a thirty-five-year period (1968a,b, 1974, 1978, 1988; Socarides et al., 1973).

enlarged to sexual pleasure activity, with or without reproduction [p. 187].

Male–female sexual pairing is determined by several billion years of evolution, a product of sexual differentiation. Sexual activity was first based solely on reproduction and later widened to include sexual gratification; from one-celled nonsexual fission to the development of two-celled sexual reproduction, to organ differentiation, and finally, to the development of two separate individuals reciprocally adapted to each other anatomically, endocrinologically, psychologically, and in many other ways.

In man, heterosexual object choice is not innate or instinctual, nor is homosexual object choice; both are learned behaviors. The choice of sexual object is not predetermined by chromosomal tagging, but is outlined from birth by anatomy and then reinforced by cultural and environmental indoctrination. It is supported by universal human concepts of mating and the tradition of the family unit, together with the complementariness and contrast between the two sexes (Radó, 1949).

Everything from birth to death is designed to perpetuate the male–female combination, a pattern not only anatomically outlined but culturally ingrained and fostered by all the institutions of marriage, society, and the deep roots of the family unit. The term *anatomical outline* does not mean that it is instinctual to choose a person of the opposite sex (heterosexuality). The human being is a biological emergent entity derived from evolution, favoring survival.

In man, due to tremendous development of the cerebral cortex, motivation—both conscious and unconscious—plays a crucial role in the selection of individuals or objects that will produce sexual arousal and orgastic release. Massive childhood fears may produce a destruction of the standard male–female pattern. The roundabout method of achieving orgastic release is through instituting male–male or female–female pairs (homosexuality). Such unconscious fears are responsible not only for the later development of homosexuality but of all other modified sexual patterns of the obligatory type.

The term *standard pattern* was originated by Radó (1949) to signify penetration of the male organ into the female at a point before orgasm if possible and, of course, carries with it the potential for reproduction. Within the standard pattern, from which the foregoing characteristics are never absent, there are innumerable variations dependent on individual preference. Homosexuality is a modified pattern because it does not conform to the essential characteristics of the standard pattern. Other modified sexual patterns, also referred to as perversions or deviations, include fetishism, voyeurism, exhibitionism, and pedophilia. Individuals suffering from these conditions have in common the inability to perform in the standard male–female design and achieve orgastic release in a substitutive way. A homosexual, therefore, is an individual who engages repetitively or episodically in sexual relations with a partner of the same sex or experiences a recurrent desire to do so. If required to function sexually with a partner of the opposite sex, he can do so, if at all, with very little or no pleasure.

While Freud himself deplored the word *perversion* because it carried a moralistic connotation, he continued to use it free from its pejorative meaning and in a scientific sense. He used it to denote sexual arousal patterns that are unconsciously motivated, stereotyped, and derived from early psychic conflict. Perversions, unlike neurotic symptoms, brought pleasure, not pain. In 1905, he coined the term *inversion* for homosexuality and Ferenczi (1909) followed with his term *paraphilia* to encompass all the perversions. The term *sexual deviation* is a more acceptable one to many because it neither moralizes nor normalizes. Some behavioral scientists, especially those who believe that homosexuals can only achieve their proper civil rights through the normalization of this condition, insist that there are no sexual perversions and deviations, only alternative or different lifestyles, and that these conditions are merely a matter of social definition, some made permissible by society and others socially condemned. This is held to be especially true as regards homosexuality. It is my belief that the majority of psychoanalysts have no interest whatsoever in limiting the civil rights of obligatory homosexual men and women, especially since their disorder arises from unconscious conflict over which they have no control. Arlow (Panel, 1986) sums up as follows:

> As scientists, our interest is in understanding the psychodynamics and the genesis of those patterns of sexual activity that deviate in a

considerable degree from the more usual forms of gratification. While it is true that the term "perversion" in current usage carries the connotation of adverse judgment, the essential meaning is a turning away from the ordinary course. As such, the term "perverse" is an accurate one. . . . The origin and meaning of unusual sexual behavior is the subject matter of our scientific concern. The phenomenology of perversion should be approached from a natural science point of view, divorced from any judgmental implications [p. 249].

Psychoanalysts comprehend the meaning of a particular act of human behavior by delving into the motivational state from which it issues. In their investigative and healing arms, psychoanalytic and psychodynamically oriented clinicians continually ask three questions: What is the meaning of an event or piece of behavior or symptom? (cause searching); where did it come from? (end-relating, means to ends); and what can be done to correct things? (healing function). By studying individuals with similar behavior, we arrive at objective conclusions as to the meaning and significance of a particular phenomenon for that individual under investigation—thus is insight achieved. To form conclusions as to the specific meaning of an event simply because of its frequency of occurrence is to the psychoanalyst scientific folly. Only in the consultation room, using the techniques of introspective reporting and free association, protected by professional ethics, will an individual, pressed by suffering and pain, reveal the hidden meaning and reasons behind his or her acts, and ascertain that obligatory homosexuality is a roundabout method for achieving orgastic release in the face of conscious or unconscious fears. The basic principle for understanding whether certain sexual activities can be considered deviations or not was supplied by Freud (1915–1916) when he stated: "Let us once more reach an agreement upon what is to be understood by the 'sense' of a psychical process. We mean nothing other by it than the intention it serves in its position in a psychical continuity" (p. 40). Thus, whether or not homosexual acts can be termed *sexual deviations* or *perversions* can be justified by the study of the conscious or unconscious motivation from which they issue.

In considering the differences between normality and abnormality, Kubie's (1978) comments are invaluable. He concluded that stereotype and automatic repetitiveness are signposts of the neurotic process. Therefore, when we describe homosexuality as not simply an alternative lifestyle or normal act, we are not issuing a judgment of value but rather a clinical description of attributes of behavior common to neurotic action and absent from normal ones.

[The essence of normality is flexibility, in contrast to the] freezing of behavior into patterns of unalterability that characterizes every manifestation of the neurotic process, whether in impulses, purposes, acts, thoughts or feelings. Whether or not a behavioral event is free to change depends not upon the quality of the act itself, but upon the nature of the constellation of forces that has produced it. No moment of behavior can be looked upon as neurotic unless the processes that have set it in motion predetermined its automatic repetition irrespective of the situation, the utility, or the consequences of the act. This may be the most basic lesson of human conduct that has been learned from psychoanalysis. Let me repeat: No single psychological act can be looked upon as neurotic unless it is the product of processes that predetermine a tendency to its automatic repetition [Kubie, 1978, p. 142].

Since the predominant forces in homosexual patients are unconscious, they will not respond to experiences of pleasure or pain, to rewards or punishments, ''neither to the logic of events nor to any appeals to mind or heart. The behavior that results from a dominance of the unconscious system has the insatiability, the automaticity, and the endless repetitiveness that are the stamp of the neurotic process'' (Kubie, 1978, p. 143).

The ego syntonic nature of homosexuality requires clarification. A number of ego syntonic phenomena can be successfully analyzed at the present state of our knowledge. These include neurotic character traits, addiction, psychopathy, borderline conditions, psychotic characterology, and perversions. When one speaks of the ego syntonicity of homosexuality or any other deviant act, it is evident that we are dealing with two components: conscious acceptance and unconscious acceptance. The degree of conscious acceptance of a perverse act varies with a person's reactions to societal pressure and consciously desired goals and aspirations. The conscious part of ego syntonicity can be more readily modified than its unconscious component. Analysis of homosexual patients reveals that ego syntonic formations accepted by the patients are already the end result of unconscious defense mechanisms in which the ego plays a decisive part. In contrast, where the superego or id plays a decisive role, the end result is often an ego-alien symptom. The splitting of the superego promotes ego syntonicity. The superego is especially tolerant of this form of behavior because it may represent the unconscious acceptable aspects of sexuality derived from the parental superego. The split in the ego and the split in the object lead to an idealized object relatively free of anxiety and guilt. The split in the ego leads also to an ego, relatively free of anxiety, which is available for purposes of an incestuous relationship at the cost of renunciation of a normal one. A homosexual act differs from a neurotic symptom, first by the form of gratification of the impulse, that is, orgasm, and second by the fact that the ego's wishes for omnipotence are satisfied by the arbitrary ego syntonic action. We may conclude that a homosexual act differs from a neurotic symptom in that the symptom is desexualized in the latter; discharge is painful in neurosis, but it brings genital orgasm in the homosexual enactment.

Major Psychoanalytic Formulations

During the early years of psychoanalysis, the view of "neurosis as the 'negative' of perversion," as Freud put it (1905, p. 237) and of the pervert who accepted sexual impulses that the neurotic tried to repress, led to the general belief that homosexual patients could not be treated in analysis because they gratify their infantile wishes consciously, without interference from the ego or the superego. A successful analysis, it would seem, was only possible if the patient suffered from his symptoms, desired to eliminate them, and wished to cooperate in searching for the unconscious elements causing them. Since interpretation did not result in therapeutic change (i.e., the cessation of the homosexual act), the material elicited from the analysis of the homosexual patient was often considered by many to be of little or no value. If the patient repressed nothing, he had nothing for the analyst to uncover and decipher. As a result, many analysts were disinclined to treat homosexuality, or treated only the associated symptoms. Over time these obstacles were gradually overcome so that today they no longer pose serious problems. It became increasingly apparent that the homosexual had indeed repressed something: an unconscious conflict and aspects of his infantile sexuality. The part that was admitted to consciousness and was allowed gratification was connected to very strong pregenital fixation and helped eliminate the danger of castration. What was approved in the homosexual action was not identical with a component instinct and did not amount to a simple gratification of part of a polymorphous perverse activity of childhood. The component instinct had undergone extensive change and masking in order to be gratified by the homosexual action. This masking was conditioned by the defenses of the homosexual ego. Thus the homosexual act, like the neurotic symptom, did result from a conflict among various agencies of the mind. It represented a compromise and contained elements of both instinctual gratification and frustration, all the while satisfying the demands of the superego. Similar to a symptom, this instinctual gratification could then be seen as taking place in a masked form, its real content remaining unconscious.

Comprehension of the psychopathology of the homosexual has been dependent upon the status of our theoretical and clinical knowledge of psychiatric disorders in general. Theoretical propositions have often preceded their clinical validation and, conversely, clear-cut and accurate distinctions have been made decades in advance of a theoretical understanding of the structure of the phenomena described. For example, Freud's (1905) observation that in homosexuals there is an early intense fixation to the mother were to be explored and documented by a number of investigators over a seventy-five-year period (Fenichel, 1945; Klein, 1946; Panel, 1952; Socarides, 1974). The discovery of infantile sexuality and the view of "neurosis as the 'negative' of perversion" was of compelling significance in our approach to these patients during the early years of psychoanalysis, later giving way to newer information gained from advances in the formulation of ego psychology, improvements in analytic technique based on our understanding of the transference relationship, and more recently, research findings derived from psychoanalytic observational studies of the mother–infant relationship. Important contributions to this subject have been made by Stoller (1964, 1966, 1968a,b, 1975), Roiphe (1968), Galenson and Roiphe (1973), Volkan (1979), Mahler (1967, 1968), and Mahler, Pine, and Bergman (1975).

Freud (1905) clearly saw through the "inverts" assertion that they could never remember any attachment to the opposite sex,

realizing that in most instances they had only repressed their positive heterosexual feelings. He reviewed conceptions of homosexuality prevalent for centuries: it was innate, a form of degeneracy. Both
he believed to be untrue and of no scientific value, since homosexuals appear otherwise unimpaired and may distinguish themselves by
especially high intellectual and cultural development. Were homosexuality innate (hereditary or inborn), the "contingent" homosexual (i.e., the nonobligatory homosexual), would be much more
difficult to explain. Freud's assumption was that inversion is an
acquired character of the sexual instinct, and he tested this hypothesis by removing inversion by hypnotic suggestion, an event he said
would be "astonishing" (1905, p. 140) if the condition were innate.
He theorized that some experiences of early childhood had a determining effect upon the direction taken by the male invert's libido.
In "A Child Is Being Beaten" (1919), Freud stated that psychoanalysis had not yet produced a complete explanation of the origin of
homosexuality. Nevertheless, it had discovered the psychic mechanism of its development and had made essential contributions to
the statement of the problems involved. Foremost among these discoveries was his conclusion that in the earliest phase of childhood,
future (male) inverts passed through a stage of very intense but
short-lived fixation to a woman, usually their mothers, and later
continued to identify themselves with a woman and took themselves
as a sexual object. Proceeding from a "narcissistic object
choice"(1905, p. 146), they look for men resembling themselves
and whom they may love as their mothers loved them. Freud (1905)
underscored that the problem of inversion is highly complex in men.
However, in the case of women it is "less ambiguous" (p. 146)
because active inverts exhibit masculine characteristics, both physical and mental, with peculiar frequency and look for femininity in
their sexual object. He remarked, however, that a closer knowledge
of the facts might reveal great variety in female inverts.

In 1905, Freud noted that psychoanalytic research decidedly
opposes any attempt to segregate homosexuals from the rest of mankind as a group of special character, in that *all* human beings are
capable of making a homosexual object choice and that many have,
in fact, made an unconscious one. Libidinal attachments to persons
of the same sex play an important part in normal mental life and,
as a motive force of illness, an even greater part than do similar

attachments to the opposite sex. Freud believed that object choice independent of sex—freedom to range equally among male and female objects (as is found in childhood and in primitive societies in the early phases of history)—is the basis for a subsequent restriction in one direction or the other, and from which both the normal and the homosexual types develop.

In the ensuing decade, Freud (1910, 1919, 1922), along with Ferenczi (1914, 1916, 1926, 1955), developed the formulation of the essential developmental factors in male homosexuality. (1) In the earliest stages of development, homosexuals experience a very strong mother fixation. On leaving this attachment they continue to identify with the mother, taking themselves narcissistically as their sexual object. Consequently, they search for a person resembling themselves whom they may love as their mothers loved them. (2) The different types of narcissistic object choice were outlined: the individual searched for a person he has loved; what he himself is; what he himself was; what he himself would like to be; someone reminiscent of another who was once part of himself (Freud, 1914). A combination of these possibilities indicates the varieties of sexual object choice. (3) Clinical investigation of the genetic constellations responsible for this developmental inhibition—an overstrong mother fixation with the resultant running away from the mother and a transfer of excitation from women to men in a narcissistic fashion—led to the discovery in these cases of an early positive Oedipus complex of great intensity.

Long before the advent of ego psychology, Freud remarked that ego functions of identification and repression play an important part in homosexuality; and in homosexuals one finds a "predominance of archaic constitutions and primitive psychical mechanisms" (Freud, 1905, p. 146, fn 1915–1916). The lack then of a concept of ego psychology and development comparable to the already established phases of libidinal development presented difficulties for many years in the application of structural concepts to homosexuality.

Of considerable importance was Freud's (1920) comment that the late determinants of homosexuality come during adolescence when a "revolution of the mental economy" (p. 231) takes place. The adolescent, in exchanging his mother for some other sexual object, may make a choice of an object of the same sex. In his

(1910) work on Leonardo da Vinci, Freud pointed out that the absence of the father and growing up in a feminine environment or the presence of a weak father who was dominated by the mother, furthers feminine identification and homosexuality. Similarly, the presence of a cruel father may lead to a disturbance in male identification.

The concept of bisexuality has been interpreted as a genetic (inborn) characteristic of attraction to persons of both sex. This was not Freud's meaning. He did not believe that any specific genetic (chromosomal) factor was capable of directing the sexual drive into overt homosexuality. He always believed that there are a number of factors that determine sexual integration: of these the psychodynamic ones were the most important. The constitutional factors determined only the strength of the drive.

There have been numerous and varied contributions to the theory, origin, and meaning of homosexuality over the decades since 1910. Ferenczi (1914) divided homosexuals into passive homosexual inverts and object homoerotics; the latter remain masculine in their behavior and may pursue another man as though he were a female. Thus, he differed from the observation that role reversal is more the rule than the exception. Fenichel (1945) maintained that homosexual love is mixed with characteristics of identification and generally agreed that there is an element of identification with the object in all homosexual love. Homosexuality, in his opinion, proved to be the product of specific defensive mechanisms that facilitate the repression of both Oedipus and castration complexes. He noted that a homosexual will reject a part of his or her personality, then externalize it onto someone else who becomes the sexual object. The homosexual is seeking an image of himself in someone else. Anna Freud (1951) expounded the same views in considerable detail.

The idea that homosexuality was really a disguised form of psychosis was not borne out over the subsequent years. Homosexuality began to appear often during psychotic episodes where previously there had been no indication of its presence. In many others, however, homosexuality occurred without psychosis or disappeared during it.

Melanie Klein (1946) held that homosexuality was fundamentally concerned with the earliest phases of libidinal development.

The chief factors, therefore, in the production of homosexuality are anxieties around the oral and anal phases. These anxieties produce insatiable needs that bind the libido to oral and anal forms. Such binding leads to profound disturbances of the genital function. The object relationship of the genital phase became filled with the pattern acquired at the oral zone, including the unconscious fantasies and feelings of desire and fear. In many men this was interpreted as a fear of being devoured by the vagina. This is probably the most important factor responsible for psychosexual impotence in men. Similar unconscious fantasies may be responsible for the fear of the penis and for frigidity in women and therefore for the development of homosexuality. The Kleinian theoretical framework stressed the preoedipal, oral–cannibalistic fantasies as the basic psychological factor in the development of homosexuality. The Oedipus complex is a later development, and the emotional patterns elaborated in object-relations shifts during this period enter into the defenses against both heterosexuality and homosexuality. The Kleinian school believed that the emotional nature and intensity of the oedipal fantasies are determined by the earlier repressed oral fantasies and their unconscious anxieties.

Sachs (1923) clearly demonstrated the "mechanism" (p. 545) not the motive for perversion. He stated that we are not dealing simply with a fixation of the component sexual drive, as the dictum of the "neurosis being the 'negative' of perversion" (Freud, 1905) would let us assume. Sachs's theory (which I paraphrase here) was of considerable importance in noting that in homosexuality one preserves a particularly suitable portion of infantile experience or fantasy in the conscious mind while the rest of the representatives of the instinctual drives have succumbed to repression, instigated by their all-too-strong need for gratification or stimulation. The pleasurable sensations of infantile sexuality in general are now displaced under the conscious "suitable portion of infantile experience" (p. 540). This conscious suitable portion is now supported and endowed with a high pleasure reward—so high, indeed, that it "competes successfully with the primacy of the genitals" (p. 540). Certain conditions make the fragment particularly suitable: the pregenital stage of development on which the homosexual is strongly fixated must be included in it. The extremely powerful partial drive must find its particular form of gratification and this particular fragment had to have some special relationship to the ego that allowed it to "escape repression" (p. 540). In essence, there is a separation or split, in which the one piece (of infantile sexuality) enters into the service of repression and thus carries over into the ego the pleasure of a preoedipal stage of development, while the rest falls victim to repression; this appears to be the "mechanism of perversions" (p. 542).

It could be seen, therefore, that in homosexuality the instinctual gratification takes place in a disguised form while its real content remains unconscious. The infantile expression of sexuality simultaneously serves to reassure the patient and to help him maintain a repression of his oedipal conflicts and other warded-off remnants of infantile sexuality. Repression is facilitated in homosexuality through the conscious stress of *some other aspect* of infantile sexuality. Therefore, it could be stated that homosexuality is a living relic of the past testifying to the fact that there was once a conflict involving an especially strongly developed component instinct in which complete victory was impossible for the ego and repression was only partially successful. The ego, therefore, had to be content with the compromise of repressing the greater part of infantile libidinal strivings (primary identification with the mother, intense unneutralized aggression toward her, dread of separation, and fear of fusion; at the expense of sanctioning and taking into oneself the smaller part). For example, the wish to penetrate the mother's body or the wish to suck and incorporate and injure the mother's breast undergoes repression. In these instances, a piece of the infantile libidinal strivings has entered the service of repression through displacement and substitution. Instead of the mother's body being penetrated, sucked, injured, or incorporated, it is the partner's body that undergoes this fate; instead of the mother's breast, it is the penis with which the patient interacts. Homosexuality thus becomes the choice of the lesser evil. In this mechanism, two defense mechanisms—identification and substitution—play crucial roles. The male homosexual makes an identification with the masculinity of his partner in the sexual act. In order to defend himself against the positive Oedipus complex, that is, his love for his mother and hatred for his father, and punitive, aggressive, and destructive drives toward the body of his mother, the male homosexual substitutes the partner's body and penis for the mother's breast. Homosexuals desperately need and seek a sexual contact whenever they feel weakened, frightened, depleted, guilty, ashamed, or in any way helpless or powerless. In a patient's words, they want a "shot of masculinity." They then feel miraculously well and strengthened, thereby avoiding any tendency to disintegrative anxiety and enhancing their self representation. They instantly feel reintegrated on achieving orgasm with a male partner. Their pain and fear and weakness disappear for the time being and they feel well and whole again. The male partners whom they pursue are representatives of their own selves in relation to an active phallic mother.

Other contributions were made by Bibring (1940); Bergler (1943, 1944, 1951, 1956, 1959); Greenacre (1953); Arlow (Panel, 1952, 1954); Eidelberg (1954); and Litin, Giffin, and Johnson (1956).

In 1956, W. H. Gillespie presented his paper "The General Theory of Sexual Perversion" at the International Psycho-Analytic Congress in Geneva. His formulations represented the status of our theory and understanding of sexual perversion at that time. His paper was remarkably comprehensive, taking into account infantile sexuality and affirming that the problem of homosexuality, along with other sexual perversions, lies in the defense against oedipal difficulties. He underscored the concept that in sexual perversion there is a regression of libido and aggression to preoedipal levels rather than a primary fixation at those levels. He stressed the importance of ego behavior and ego-defense maneuvers as well as the importance of the Sachs's mechanism. He delineated the characteristics of the ego that make it possible for the ego to adopt a certain aspect of infantile sexuality, thereby enabling it to ward off the rest. It was shown that the superego has a special relationship to the ego that makes the latter tolerant of this particular form of sexuality. A split in the ego often coexists with a split in the sexual object so that the subject becomes idealized, "relatively anxiety free and relatively guilt free in part" (Gillespie, 1956, p. 402).

Over the years other analyst writers such as Fenichel (1945), Barahal (1953), Bychowski (1954), and Lorand (1956), began to show that there is a relationship of homosexuality to other perversions, especially fetishism. A review of these contributions is beyond the scope of this chapter.

In 1974, the Ostow Psychoanalytical Clinical Research Group, all experienced clinicians, reported an extensive study of over eight cases in detail and thirty-five vignettes of patients with perverse behavior, including homosexuality, over a four-year period. They concluded that perversion and homosexuality were two aspects of the same disorder for the following reasons: (1) the developmental arrest required for one appeared to favor the other; (2) both phenomena represented infantile fixations with respect to the object in homosexuality and to the aim in other perversions; (3) narcissism, infantilism, and acting out were common in both perversions and homosexuality; (4) homosexuality was sometimes used as a defense against other forms of sexual perversion predominant in heterosexual relations. This study adumbrated future developments in our psychoanalytic understanding by noting that there appeared to be gender disturbances, object-relations conflict, and severe disturbances in early ego development in these individuals: this forecast was to be expressed with conviction, reinforced by further clinical experience ten years later by one of the group, Arlow (Panel, 1986), in his assertion that "no matter what other factors pertain, perversions constitute problems of gender identity of male–female differentiation" (p. 248). The Ostow report (Ostow et al., 1974) made a great advance in theory and clinical study but did not suggest a comprehensive, integrated, and systematized theory of perverse development because theoretical constructs had not been made in the areas of the pathology of internalized object relations, concepts of narcissism, and knowledge of the earliest primary psychic development derived from infant observational studies.

As noted in *Psychoanalytic Terms and Concepts* of the American Psychoanalytic Association (Moore and Fine, 1990).

[T]he outcome of the oedipal phase was considered the essential explanation for the origin of homosexuality and heterosexuality. More recent studies, however, of sexual orientation in early childhood development have emphasized preoedipal determinants that result in the failure to progress from the mother–child unity of earliest infancy to individuation. Although some cases may present a predominantly oedipal or preoedipal configuration, most involve mechanisms stemming from multiple levels of fixation or regression [p. 86].

Classification

In the 1950s and 1960s, it became increasingly clear that one could not simply depend on dividing the homosexualities into reparative, situational, and variational types (Radó, 1949) or Freud's (1905) subgroups of homosexuality into absolute, amphigenic, and contingent. As a result of extensive clinical experience, I noted that the deeper understanding of homosexuality could only be established by a psychoanalytic classification that embodied multiple frames of reference: we would be unable to comprehend this condition simply by a knowledge of the process of symptom formation or defenses. Rather, as suggested by a panel (1960a) on nosology, and Rangell (1965) we must adhere to a multidimensional approach, which should include data derived from a number of sources: (1) the level of libidinal fixation or regression (instinctual framework); (2) the stage of maturation, fixation, or regression of the ego (developmental framework); (3) the symptom itself as an "end product"; (4) the process of symptom formation; and (5) an inventory of ego functions, including object relations. Specific forms of homosexuality had to be seen in relation to other forms. A comprehensive classification had to correlate and integrate many factors in a logical fashion.

Three contributions aimed at describing the origins of homosexuality set the stage for attempting this comprehensive classification of homosexuality: the first by Gillespie (1956), described above, the second by Greenacre (1968), and the third by this writer, Socarides (1968b, 1974, 1978). Summing up extensive clinical research in 1968, Greenacre suggested that:

> [O]ur most recent studies of early ego development would indicate that the fundamental disturbance is . . . that the defectively developed ego uses the pressure of the maturing libidinal phases for its own purposes in characteristic ways because of the extreme and persistent narcissistic needs. . . . Probably in most perversions [including homosexuality] there is a prolongation of the introjective–projective stage in which there is an incomplete separation of the "I" from the "other" and an oscillation between the two. This is associated with a more than usually strong capacity for primary identification [1968, p. 302].

In a 1967 paper, I suggested that the genesis of well-structured cases of homosexuality may well be the result of disturbances occurring earlier than had been generally assumed, namely in the preoedipal phase. I then divided the homosexualities into oedipal and preoedipal forms and described the characteristics of each (Socarides, 1974). In 1978 I sorted the homosexualities into oedipal form, preoedipal Type I and preoedipal Type II, and schizohomosexuality. I considered these the clinical forms of homosexuality, and situational and variational forms not clinical. It appeared increasingly evident that the classification system I had suggested for the homosexualities (1978) could well be applied also to the various forms of other perversions. My classification demonstrated that the same phenomenology in homosexual men may have different structures in different individuals.

The essential ingredient of any homosexual act is the unconscious and imperative need to pursue and experience sexual pleasure and orgastic release in a particular manner and with a specific, particular object. This act expresses, in a distorted way, repressed, forbidden impulses, and usually brings temporary relief, either partial or complete, from warring intrapsychic forces. The homosexual mechanism for the relief of unconscious conflict exists at any level of libidinal fixation and ego development, from the most primitive to the more highly developed levels of organization. The underlying unconscious motivational drives are distinctly different, depending on the level from which they arise. Oedipal homosexual activity arises from the phallic organization of development and must be differentiated from preoedipal homosexual behavior arising from preoedipal levels of development. We associate narcissistic neuroses and impulse disorders with the latter. The homosexual symptom can operate at an anal level, especially when it represents a regression from a genital or oedipal phase conflict. In the schizophrenic, the symptom may represent an archaic and primitive level of functioning, a frantic and chaotic attempt to construct object relations.

There is a wide range of clinical forms of homosexual behavior, including those derived from the very archaic, primitive levels to products of more highly differentiated stages (Socarides, 1978, 1988). Each case is hierarchically layered with dynamic mechanisms stemming from multiple points of fixation and regression. We can conclude that the clinical picture of the perverse homosexual activity itself does not necessarily correctly describe the origin of the particular mechanisms responsible for it. This requires a study of the developmental stages through which the individual has passed, the level of fixation, the state of object relations, and the status of ego functions.

In 1974 and 1988 I described the general criteria for each form of homosexuality: oedipal, preoedipal, latent, and schizohomosexuality. I detail the quality of object relations and degree of pathology in each case, as well as describe pathological grandiosity, disturbances in superego formation, and freedom from internal conflict; defenses in a primitive stage of development with splitting predominating over repression; degree of self-object differentiation; the nature and meaning of the sexually perverse activity; transference and therapeutic considerations; and criteria among perverse patients as regards the status of object relations; prognosis for recovery; meaning of the perverse act; degree and level of fixation; class of conflict; the Sachs's mechanism and ego syntonicity; tendency to regressive states; and degree of potential analyzable transferences. I further clarify the capacity of the orgasm to restore the sense of having a bounded and cohesive self. The status of ego functions other than object relations is carefully differentiated among each type and I describe the defenses present in each classification.

Psychoanalytic Technique in the Treatment of Homosexual Patients

Modifications

My technical procedures involve significant variations and departures from standard psychoanalytic technique and innovative procedures specifically designed for the alleviation of this disorder. As Anna Freud (1954) commented:

> Every discussion of therapeutic procedure in psychoanalysis derives added interest from the fact that it can never remain for long on purely practical grounds. In the history of psychoanalysis every advance and insight has been followed closely by an advance in technique; conversely, every technical rule has been considered valid only when rooted in a specific piece of analytic theory. Any doubt concerning the justification for a particular technique therefore, had

to be dealt with by inquiry into the theoretical assumptions which had given rise to it. . . . [One challenge, to standard technique] is due to the widening of the field of application of the analytic therapy to patients with character structures different from those for which the analytic technique was devised originally in this field. Eissler (1958a) has shown in a stimulating paper which deviations from our standard technique become necessary to meet deviations in the patient's ego structure and more than that—how technical experimentation in this respect may lead to new insight into abnormalities of structure. In this particular instance, theory profits from advances in technique [pp. 377–378].

Anna Freud expressed doubts as to whether "our standard technique equips us for the undertaking of character analysis as adequately as it has equipped us for the analysis of the various forms of hysteria and the obsessional neuroses." Perhaps the "various forms of perversion, fetishism, homosexuality, etc., which we now consider accessible to treatment justify deviations of technique" (pp. 381–382).

In what follows, I discuss my technical digressions against a backdrop of theoretical understanding, and justify them on the basis of the deviations in the patient's ego structure and the preoedipal origin for most types of homosexuality. It is my belief that when homosexual patients are treated in the manner to be described, unconscious anxieties of the preoedipal period (as well as those anxieties of the oedipal period) become manifest and can be dealt with in a modified psychoanalytic therapy.

It is necessary that the analyst provide the patient from the outset with an opportunity to admit the extent of his desolation to the paternal figure in the transference. Unconscious material revealing aspects of himself, which he abhors and wishes to change, may not appear for a long time. Eventually, the patient realizes that he or she is the victim of childhood events and early intrapsychic conflicts that have produced an interference in normal sexual development and functioning. As a consequence, the patient is forced to utilize roundabout methods for sexual arousal and sexual gratification, both to provide orgastic pleasure and to defend against deeper anxieties. The pathological form of sexuality for which a person seeks our help is, however, only one manifestation of a complex deeper disorder affecting all areas of development and functioning. The patient may fear the reawakening of hopes for heterosexuality, long suppressed, and express disbelief that anything can be done to remedy matters. Kohut's (1971) admonition to those who would treat narcissistic personality disorders should be well heeded in the treatment of homosexual individuals. He noted that therapists who do not enjoy putting a sympathetic and soothing tone in their voice will have a hard time treating preoedipal developmental arrests. One proceeds with correct empathy for the patient's feelings, ever mindful of his need for gratification through homosexual acts in order to ensure the development of both a relationship and a successful outcome. The patient's anxiety tolerance depends on his ability to identify with the therapist, who can both accept the patient's anxieties, his vulnerabilities and depressions, and pathological sexuality, as well as be a container for them.

Since the prognosis often depends on the patient's determination to change and the extent to which this determination can be awakened in analysis, it is important that no authoritative assertion of incurability be made regarding sexual practices. I make it clear from the outset that I view the obligatory performance of homosexual acts as a form of psychopathology, a disturbance in psychosexual functioning, a form of developmental pathology, and a consequence of preoedipal conflict. The essential task is the resolution of preoedipal conflicts in order to promote a process of developmental unfolding, in Spitz's (1959) words, "free from the anxieties, perils, threats of the original situation" and through this "transference relationship enable the patient to reestablish his object-relations or form new object-relations at the level at which this development was deficient" (pp. 100–101). The removal of these conflicts and obstacles makes it possible for the patient to progress along the road to heterosexual functioning as the need for perverse gratification becomes less obligatory. In time, it becomes neither tension relieving, fear reducing, nor a compensatory mechanism, and must then compete with newly established heterosexual functioning for pleasure and self-esteem. Thus, the treatment of all homosexual patients is the treatment of the preoedipal developmental arrest, which is the *fons et origo* from which the perverse activity emerged.

Obligatory homosexuals must be exposed to the information that neither homosexual nor heterosexual object choice is constitutionally determined, that is, hereditary in origin, biologically innate.

Both are learned behaviors, the perverse act constituting "abnormal learning" and the heterosexual act a normal form of sexual expression. It is vitally important that when the patient asks the analyst if the analyst was somehow not "born that way" (i.e., heterosexual), the analyst inform the patient that heterosexuals are not born that way either. It is well known that even when a patient announces at the beginning of therapy that he does not wish his homosexual perversion to be changed and that he is undergoing analysis simply for the treatment of "ancillary" symptomatology, psychoanalysis may well remove perverse activities (A. Freud, 1954).

Exceptions to my position that homosexual patients may be treated successfully and much of their suffering alleviated are found in situations similar to those described by others, for example Kernberg (1985), in the treatment of severe personality disorders. A poor outcome may be predicted in those patients who exhibit severe antisocial personality structure; are unwilling or unable to attend sessions; show severe disturbances in verbal communication with an inability to make connections in the analysis; have a severely defective superego so that they are unable to profit either from the therapeutic alliance or the positive transference; engage in chronic lying and withholding of information; or are severely drug dependent. The worst prognoses in my homosexual patients are for those who are in the most severe range of narcissistic pathology (borderline cases who at times lose reality), who demonstrate severe splitting of the ego with projection more prominent than repression, and a tendency toward paranoid thinking of an insistent and intractable nature. Such patients evidence psychosislike transference reactions, such as a chronic inclination to misunderstand others, and continually feel the analyst is letting them down. Under conditions of severe stress and environmental frustration of their unrealistic goals, they may retreat to a "malignant part" of the pathological grandiose self (Rosenfeld, 1949), a haven for revenge which is to be visited upon imagined depriving, powerful figures. These patients may remain in regression for extended periods of time, unaffected by interpretation and empathic responses.

Having defined the level of ego-developmental arrest, my overall strategy is to discover the location of the fixation point, to delineate ego deficits in the type of object relations dominating the patient's life. I make it possible for the patient to rediscover that part of development distorted by infantile or childhood traumas, conflicts, and deficiencies due to unmet needs and tensions. I eliminate compensatory reparative moves in the maladaptive process that have distorted and inhibited functioning, self-perpetuating defenses. With their removal I encounter head-on preoedipal conflicts, especially reenactments of rapprochement subphase conflict, separation and fragmentation anxieties, disturbances in self-cohesion, and castration anxiety of both oedipal and preoedipal origin. No matter the form of homosexuality, I routinely find anxieties relating to separation from the mother that are then relived and abreacted to in the course of therapy. For all patients, the essential task is the elucidation of the three great anxieties of the rapprochement subphase (Mahler et al., 1975, Socarides, 1985): fear of the loss of the object, fear of losing the object's love, and an undue sensitivity to approval or disapproval by the parents.

Any preodipal developmental arrest must be treated with supportive measures until the patient can begin full analysis. A longer psychoanalytic treatment may be necessary in order to first break through the developmental arrest and the pathological character structure activated in the analysis. Defenses in these patients may be immature, in a prestage of development, a prestage of defense (Stolorow and Lachmann, 1978, 1980). In addition, there has been interference with appropriate self–object differentiation and integration. The need to engage in homosexual activity is a manifestation of this arrest in development: it is a developmental necessity, at least for the time being, and not a resistance. In such cases, special techniques are necessary to promote the maturation of arrested ego functions. The aim of these techniques is to promote structuralization of ego functions sufficient for later exploration of the defensive aspects of the patient's psychopathology in terms of the instinctual conflicts they serve to ward off. Developmental imbalances can be reconstructed from memories and dreams in the transference and can be placed correctly in the specific developmental stages to which they belong. This approach of permitting idealizing transferences with borderline patients is not, however, without its perils; for in a borderline preoedipal Type II narcissistic perverse patient there is a tendency to fusion with the object and confusion between self and object, between analyst and patient. The subsequent ''failure'' of the object (analyst) to gratify the omnipotent and grandiose needs of the patient may be then responded to (if suitable interceptive interpretations are not made) with severe aggression, regressive paranoid feelings, and psychosislike transference reaction.

In order to facilitate the structuralization of the psychic apparatus, the analyst must promote gradually differentiated and integrated self and object representations within the therapeutic relationship. During this period, the analyst restricts interpretations to an empathic understanding of the patient's primitive arrested self and object representations, which the patient attempts to restore. This ensures the continuation of the positive transference, whether or not these ego deficiencies arise from the predominance of *aggressive* conflicts themselves in the earliest years of life (Kernberg, 1975) or were due to a lack of empathic response from early caretakers (Kohut, 1971). Neutrality and consistent understanding of archaic states promote differentiation and integration and contribute to the formation of the patient's new world of self and object representations. Once sufficient structuralization of the psychic apparatus has taken place, one may proceed with the analysis of transference manifestations of libidinal and aggressive conflicts as in any other psychoanalysis.

The bedrock of my therapeutic efforts rests on the establishment, consolidation, and maintenance of the therapeutic or working alliance (Greenson, 1967; Greenacre, 1971; Dickes, 1975), the condition of "basic trust" (Greenacre, 1969) that allows the patient to follow the lead of the analyst in searching for the meaning, content, and genesis of his condition.

These patients have failed to experience healthy ego functioning, have not achieved object constancy, and suffer from an inability to attain healthy object relations. The analytic situation offers them the opportunity for experiencing in depth "both the real and the unreal ways in which they deal with the world" (Greenson, 1968). When I make interpretations to these patients, my aim is not only to remove their unconscious anachronistic anxieties but also to help them experience appropriate ego functions and new object relations. In this manner, structuralization of the mental apparatus takes place not only through interpretation and assimilation but by a positive recognition of the patient's effective level of performance. To achieve this there must be a "real" nontransference relationship, all the while keeping an appropriate psychological and physical distance. Communication is designed to increase the development of object relations and restore internal self representations. In those patients with severe object-relations pathology (fusion between self and object) and in those with severe projective anxieties and tendencies or severe regressive episodes, the analysis proceeds for a long initial period in a face-to-face relationship. A unique indicator that a therapeutic alliance has been achieved is the patient's beginning awareness that he is not simply responding to an instinctual need in his perverse activities but is dominated by a tension that he can neither understand nor control. This indicator is especially true of the homosexual patient who has engaged in numerous face-saving rationalizations, including that of constitutional bisexuality to explain the need for same-sex partners.

Specific Tasks

In what follows, I describe four major tasks to be achieved for the successful psychoanalytic treatment of homosexual patients: (1) separating and disidentifying from the preoedipal mother; (2) decoding the manifest perversion; (3) providing insight into the function of erotic experience in homosexual acts; and (4) spoiling the perverse gratification. The delineation of these tasks fundamental for the treatment of all perversions in no way minimizes the importance of other tasks, either implicit with them or related to them: for example, promoting differentiation and integrating self and object representations; resolving castration anxiety of both preoedipal and oedipal phases; eliminating the ''narcissistic resistance'' to change; diminishing unneutralized aggression, and so on.

Separating from the Preoedipal Mother. A primary task in the treatment of all male homosexuals is to disclose and define to the patient the primary feminine identification with the mother that has led to the disturbance in gender-defined self identity, the core of the disorder. The ultimate purpose of this interpretation is to effect disidentifying (Greenson, 1968) from her (promote intrapsychic separation from her) so that a developmental step, previously blocked, a counteridentification with the father (analyst) may now begin to take place. In the female homosexual, our aim is to allow the female to make her own unique feminine identification separate from a primary identification with the hated, feared, and malevolently perceived mother. The female does not have the double task of making a disidentification from the mother and also making a counteridentification with the opposite sex. My aim is to aid the patient in successfully traversing separation–individuation phases and assuming an appropriate gender-defined self identity in accordance with anatomy. A consistent, disciplined, hopeful, and helpful attitude of the analyst toward the patient facilitates the identification with the analyst, a reopening of masculine identity in a new object relationships provided by the analysis, and extra-analytic experiences.

The patient is shown that the lifelong persistence of the original primary feminine identification has resulted in conscious–unconscious pervasive feelings of femininity or a deficient sense of masculinity. The patient is symbiotically attached to the mother, has fantasies of fusing with her (as elicited in dreams, fantasies, and in actual interaction with her), but is also intensely ambivalent toward her. A severe degree of masochistic vulnerability is manifest, especially in relation to the mother, to whose attitudes and behavior the patient is unduly sensitive. Early in therapy we encounter a deficit in body-ego boundaries accompanied by a fear of bodily disintegration, unusual sensitivity to threats of bodily damage by external objects explainable in part as a manifestation of castration anxiety, as well as threats of bodily damage involved with object loss and inability to successfully differentiate oneself from the body of the mother. Aggressive impulses threatening to destroy both the self and the object are commonly found in this phase of treatment.

I demonstrate to the patient through interpretation of dreams, transference and extra-analytic events, and sexual enactments, that perverse practices preserve identification with the mother, albeit in a disguised form. The patient attempts to relieve anxiety, tension, depression, paranoidal feelings, and other intense archaic ego states, including aggressive destructiveness, by pressing into service perverse enactments, making him feel secure because he has thereby reinstated the previously disturbed optimal distance from or closeness to the mother. (The term *optimal distance or closeness* refers to a psychological state in which the patient feels secure against both the loss of the mother and the preoedipal need she supplies, and against the wish for or dread of reengulfment.) These interpretations occupy much of the course of the early and middle phases of the analysis, as the patient endlessly engages in an obsessive repetition of a pattern of perverse enactments in order to relieve himself of intolerable anxieties, often made worse during this period of analytic investigation. While these acts represent flights from the mother, it is made clear that these perverse practices are simultaneously an attempt to maintain contact with her and constitute a reassurance against loss of self through merger in a somatopsychic fusion with her. They provide affirmation of one's individual existence through orgastic experience (Eissler, 1958b; Socarides, 1978; Stolorow and Lachmann, 1978, 1980; Lichtenstein, 1983).

To summarize what has already been stated: maturational achievements are unconsciously perceived and equated with intrapsychic separation and reacted to with anxiety and guilt of various degrees, which is then analyzed in a manner similar to that used with neurotic conflict. These anxieties relate to actual or fantasized threats or intimidations by the mother, and are placed in a genetic restructuring of the patient's childhood. Archaic conflicts and rapprochement crises ultimately lose their strength and disappear. The patient, after the phobic avoidance, is analyzed and the genital schematization fortified through the patient's acknowledgment of the ownership of his own penis and elimination of castration anxieties of both preoedipal and oedipal periods, is then able to begin to function heterosexually, at first with and ultimately without perverse fantasies. Such therapeutic progress requires months of analytic work and mutual dedication to the task.

Decoding the Manifest Perversion.   The perversion is an ego syntonic formation, the end result of unconscious defense mechanisms accomplished with the Sachs's mechanism. The attachment to the mother, hatred toward the father, and punitive aggressive destructive drives toward the body of the mother have undergone disguise as the homosexual substitutes the partner's penis for the mother's breast. (The female homosexual substitutes the fictive penis of her female partner for the abhorrent maternal breast; resulting in a masculine attitude on the part of the female partner or herself.)

Through decoding, the patient can perceive the disorder in its original form: archaic longings and dreads, primitive needs and fears arising from the struggle to make a progression from mother–child unity to individuation. One can now perceive what one seeks to rediscover in one's object choice and aims: the primary reality of narcissistic relations with different images of the mother and later with the father. The male homosexual perceives that his fear of engulfment due to a lack of separation from the mother or dread of fusing with her forces him to seek salvation from her by running toward men. Ironically, he does not seek femininity in approaching men but is attempting to regain lost masculinity so cruelly denied him in the earliest years of childhood. (The female homosexual is attempting to find her lost femininity in the body of the partner through resonance-identification.) Preoedipal Type II narcissistic homosexuals realize that they are in addition warding off threats to self-cohesion and fears of fragmentation and desperately need to experience emotions through the response of their self-objects, their sexual partners.

We should not overlook a unique function of all perversions, including homosexuality: each dramatically restores the sense of having a bounded and cohesive self through the production of orgasm, which reinforces an "incontrovertible truth" (Lichtenstein, 1983) of the reality of personal existence separate from the mother. Therefore, orgasm in perversion has an "affirmative function" (Eissler, 1958b; Lichtenstein, 1983).

Providing Insight into the Function of Erotic Experience.   As an analysis progresses it becomes increasingly clear that it is not the fixated neurotic experience per se (the instinct derivation—its polymorphous perverse derivative) that is regressively reanimated in the patient's homosexuality, but rather it is the early function of the erotic experience that has been retained and regressively relied on (Stolorow and Lachmann, 1978, 1980; Socarides, 1979). In this way, through erotization, the patient attempts to maintain structural cohesion and implement the stability of threatened self and object representations.

The patient's erotic experiences are understood as providing two functions: a warding-off function to forestall the dangers of castration, fragmentation, separation anxieties, and other threats; and a compensatory function consisting of intrapsychic activities that help maintain and decrease threats to the self and object representations. Through erotization, anxiety and depressive affects are also eliminated (Socarides, 1985); depression is turned into its opposite through a "manic defense" (Winnicott, 1935), a flight to antidepressant activities, including sexuality.

Spoiling the Perverse Gratification.   Perverse patients, unlike neurotic individuals, suffer from a widespread impairment of both libidinal and ego development throughout the major phases prior to the oedipal period. In these patients we are confronted at the outset with the seemingly insurmountable task of stimulating sufficient neurotic conflict that can then be analyzed. It is my intention to bring about this conflictual situation. To this end I have adopted Kolansky and Eisner's (1974) phrase, "spoiling the gratification of a preoedipal developmental arrest followed by analysis" (p. 24) to connote therapeutic activity which, although leading to discomfort and anxiety in relation to previously held ego-syntonic areas of immaturity, results in the conversion of an addiction or impulse neurosis or perversion into a condition similar to a neurosis. "Spoiling" is accomplished through the analytic comprehension of the defined psychopathology resulting from the failure to make the intrapsychic separation from the mother, educating the patient as to the nature of specific vulnerabilities, and uncovering and decoding the hidden meaning and content of perverse acts and underlying fantasy system. This is accomplished with tact, without injury to pride, as traumas to these individuals are so early and severe that narcissistic defenses are held onto tenaciously. It would be a narcissistic manifestation on the therapist's part to fail to acknowledge the difficulty or perhaps the impossibility in some instances of the patient ever giving up a specific need. On the other hand, we must keep in mind the *relativity* of the *need* for perverse gratifications. Such needs are determined by other needs, are not absolute or independent, but dependent for their existence, intensity, and significance on the total functioning of the individual. Kolansky and Eisner (1974), referring to such needs in impulse disorders and addictions, point out the distinctions between the phrases *cannot do* and *will not do* and *do not want to do*, and note that the analyst must question the *cannot* before the *do you want to*. The same can be said for the phrase *need for immediate gratification.* Is it a "need" like breathing is a need or is it a "wish" for gratification such as the wish for candy? There is a back-and-forth movement as to the relevant strength of "need for gratification" at various points in treatment.

Lest I be misunderstood, I equate "spoiling" to uncovering conflict and comprehending the meaning of symbols. For example, uncovering a homosexual's obligatory need to swallow another man's penis and semen is decreased when it is revealed to be a search for his own lost masculinity through the incorporation of the masculinity and body of another male, who also feels similarly deficient. It leads to relief rather than frustration as the patient is no longer a "slave" to the imperativeness of a homosexual desire, nor driven by total reliance on a partner as a means of sexual arousal. It is an attempt to find lost masculinity rather than a desire for femininity. This interpretation has a profound effect on most homosexual patients, diminishing shame and guilt on an unconscious level, regular accompaniments, both conscious and unconscious, to homosexual practices. In such instances, "spoiling" leads not to frustration but to an increase in self-esteem, a release from importunate tensions and obligatory performances, and sets the stage for previously blocked, new possibilities of sexual arousal and release.

"Spoiling" perverse gratifications in order to stimulate neurotic conflict that can then be analyzed does not mean that a perverse patient remains without sexual pleasure during the analysis. Prohibitions against perverse activity should not be engaged in, as indicated by the rule of *non prohibere*. This rule, however, should not be misconstrued by the patient (and the analyst) as representing passive permission to persist in patterns of self-destructive, antisocial, perverse behavior, or an inadvertent permissiveness which may precipitate acting out of perverse impulses. It is not a policy of indifference on the part of the therapist which would tend, according to Arlow, to perpetuate already established patterns of overt perverse behavior (Panel, 1954). The patient's increasing knowledge of the psychological conflicts responsible for the perversion and the analyst's position that the perversion is an end product of deep intrapsychic trauma or need, reinforced by continuous analysis of the motivational forces leading to each individual perverse act, militate against such misunderstanding. This therapeutic approach not only reduces the patient's feelings of failure when perverse practices continue for a lengthy period of time, but lessens countertransference reactions during periods of severe acting out.

Once the perverse act is fully understood by the patient to be a symptom, that is, a compromise formation, a necessity in order to avoid more painful and damaging anxieties (a measure taken by the ego to ward off dangers and at the same time compensating for them), the patient may more actively join the analyst in seeking to modify the enactment of perverse needs. There may be a partial disbelief on the part of the patient that these activities may be modifiable; but ultimately the patient's belief in that possibility becomes a strong as that of the analyst. Modification of perverse practices should be first suggested by the patient, analyzed fully before they are attempted, and undertaken only when a full knowledge of the underlying structure of the symptom is known and understood by both patient and analyst.

A Survey of Treatment Results

In 1960, Edward Glover devoted considerable attention to the problem of therapy of male homosexuality. The Portman Clinic Survey in England reached the following conclusion: "Psychotherapy appears to be unsuccessful in *only* a small number of patients of any age in whom a long habit is combined with psychopathic traits, heavy drinking, or lack of desire to change" (p. 236).

Glover divided the degrees of improvement into three categories: (1) *cure*, the abolition of conscious homosexual impulses and development of full extension of heterosexual impulse; (2) *much improved*, the abolition of conscious homosexual impulse without development of full extension of heterosexual impulse; and (3) *improved*, increased ego integration and capacity to control the homosexual impulse.

In conducting focal treatment (brief therapy aimed at the relief of the homosexual symptom), Glover commented on the significance of social anxiety present in these patients. This social anxiety, despite apparently rational justification, however, is based largely on a projected form of unconscious guilt. The unfortunate punitive attitude of society enables the patient to project concealed superego conflicts onto society and the law.

Glover felt that almost from the outset the therapist must decide whether to conduct the treatment through the regular and prolonged course of analysis or through focal therapy of the symptom. In following the latter course, he would soon find that having uncovered some of the guilt, he would then strike against a core of sexual anxiety, and, in particular, the multifarious manifestations of the castration complex. At this point, the history of the individual's familial relations, traumas, frustrations, disappointments, jealousies, and so on, would come to the surface or should be brought to the surface.

It is necessary to demonstrate the defensive aspects of the homosexual situation, for only by uncovering the positive aspects of his original relation to women (mother, sister) and by demonstrating the anxieties or guilts (real or fantasized) associated with a hostile aspect of these earlier relations, can a path be cleared for the return of heterosexual libido.

An unpublished and informal report of the Central Fact-Gathering Committee of the American Psychoanalytic Association (1956) was one of the first surveys to compile results of treatment. It showed that of fifty-six cases of homosexuality undergoing psychoanalytic therapy by members of the Association, they describe eight in the completed group (which totaled thirty-two as cured; thirteen as improved, and one as unimproved). This constitutes one-third of all cases reported. Of the group which did not complete treatment (total of thirty-four), they describe sixteen as improved, ten as unimproved; three as untreatable, and five as transferred. In all reported cures, follow-up communications indicated assumption of full heterosexual role and functioning.

A research team consisting of nine psychoanalysts and two psychoanalytically trained psychologists published the findings of a nine-year study of male homosexuals (Bieber et al., 1962). The team psychiatrist and seventy-seven respondents to a five hundred-item questionnaire were members of the Society of Medical Psychoanalysts, whose roster consisted of faculty and graduates of the Psychoanalytic Division of the Department of Psychiatry of New York Medical College. The research sample consisted of 106 male homosexuals and a comparison group of one hundred male heterosexuals, all in psychoanalytic treatment with members of the Society. The data obtained were analyzed statistically in consultation with statistical experts and the clinical applications were carefully analyzed and evaluated. The results of treatment were as follows:

> Of the 106 homosexuals who started psychoanalytic therapy, twenty-nine were exclusively heterosexual at the time the volume was published. This represented 27% of the total sample. Fourteen of these 29 had been exclusively homosexual when they began treatment; 15 were bisexual. In 1965, in a follow-up study of the 29, I was able to reclaim the data on 15 of the 29. Of these 15 men, twelve had remained exclusively heterosexual; the other three were predominantly heterosexual, but had occasional episodes of homosexuality when under severe stress. Of the twelve who had remained consistently heterosexual, seven had been among the 14 who had been exclusively homosexual when they started treatment. Thus, seven men who started treatment as exclusively homosexual had been exclusively heterosexual for at least six or seven years [Englehardt and Kaplan, 1987, p. 424].

During a ten-year period from 1967 to 1977, I treated psychoanalytically fifty-five overt homosexuals: thirty-four of these patients were in long-term psychoanalytic therapy of over a year's duration (average 3.5 years). The number of sessions ranged from three to five per week. In this group there were only three females. The remainder (eleven) were in short-term analytic therapy (average six to seven months) at two to three sessions per week. Three were female.

In addition, full-scale analysis was performed on eighteen latent homosexuals in which the symptoms never became overt, except in the most transitory form. Thus the total number treated in long-term analysis, whether overt or latent, was sixty-three. In addition, over three-hundred-fifty overt homosexuals were seen in consultation (average one to three sessions) during this ten-year period.

I can report that of the forty-five overt homosexuals who underwent psychoanalytic therapy, twenty patients, nearly 50 percent, developed full heterosexual functioning and were able to develop love feelings for their heterosexual partners. This includes one female patient. These patients, of whom two-thirds were of the preoedipal type and one-third of the oedipal type, were all strongly motivated for therapy.

In addition, similar positive therapeutic results occurred during the period from 1977 to 1988 in which I treated over fifty more overt homosexuals in psychoanalytic therapy. I also report a seven-year follow-up of a patient who achieved full heterosexual function and the ability to love his opposite-sex partner (Socarides, 1978, pp. 497–529).

Most recently, a report by Macintosh (1994) reveals that in response to a survey of 285 psychoanalysts who reported having analyzed 1,215 homosexual patients, 23 percent changed to heterosexuality from homosexuality, and 84 percent of the total group received significant therapeutic benefit.

During the early development of psychoanalysis, reports of favorable outcome in the treatment of homosexuality rarely appeared; the outlook was pessimistic. Starting in 1944, Bergler published extensive studies confirming his finding that with suitable treatment, homosexuality could be reversed (1944, 1959). Bychowski (1945, 1954, 1956), Lorand (1956), and other workers including Gershman (1967), Ovesey (1969), Bieber (1967), and Socarides (1969) also published significant material to this effect, including psychoanalytic, psychotherapeutic, and group therapy.

Concluding Remarks

In this chapter I have expanded and refined my earlier findings as regards the origins, symptoms, course, pathology, meaning, and function of obligatory male homosexuality. Significant progress has been made in two areas: a classification of the various types of homosexuality, as well as the general and specific techniques that should be employed in order to achieve a satisfactory result. The specific therapeutic tasks I describe should become a vital aspect in the treatment of any homosexual patient of the preoedipal type.

I wish to close by citing an earlier comment of mine:

> One's compassion for the plight of the homosexual, his responsiveness as a patient, and his value as a human being in interaction with the scientific challenge and fulfillment posed by his intra-psychic conflicts, leads to a mutuality of gratitude and satisfaction between patient and psychoanalyst, which well justifies the commitment to the attempted alleviation of this important and serious disorder [Socarides, 1979, p. 275].

References

American Psychoanalytic Association (1956), *Report of the Central Fact-Finding Committee*. New York. Unpublished.

Barahal, H. S. (1953), Female transvestism and homosexuality. *Psychiat. Quart.,* 27:390–438.

Bergler, E. (1943), The respective importance of reality and fantasy in the genesis of female homosexuality. *J. Crim. Psychopathol.,* 5:27–48.

———— (1944), Eight prerequisites for psychoanalytic treatment of homosexuality. *Psychoanal. Rev.,* 31:253–286.

———— (1951), *Counterfeit Sex.* New York: Grune & Stratton.

———— (1956), *Homosexuality: Disease or Way of Life?* New York: Hill & Wang.

———— (1959), *1000 Homosexuals: Conspiracy of Silence on Curing and Deglamorizing Homosexuality.* Patterson, NJ: Pageant Books.

Bibring, G. L. (1940), On the oral component in masculine inversion. *Internat. Zeitschr. Psychoanal.,* 25:124–130.

Bieber, T. (1967), On treating male homosexuals. *Arch. Gen. Psychiatry,* 16:60–63.

———— Dain, H. J., Dince, P. R., Drellich, M. E., Grand, H. G., Gundlach, R. H., Kremer, M. W., Rifkin, A. H., Wilbur, C. B., & Bieber, T. B. (1962), *Homosexuality: A Psychoanalytic Study of Male Homosexuals.* New York: Basic Books.

Bychowski, G. (1945), The ego of homosexuals. *Internat. J. Psycho-Anal.,* 16:114–127.

———— (1954), The structure of homosexual acting out. *Psychoanal. Quart.,* 23:48–61.

———— (1956), The ego and the introject. *Psychoanal. Quart.,* 25:11–36.

Dickes, R. (1975), Technical considerations on the therapeutic and working alliances. *Internat. J. Psycho-Anal. Psychother.,* 4:1–24.

Eidelberg, L. (1954), *A Comparative Pathology of Neurosis.* New York: International Universities Press.

Eissler, K. R. (1958a), Notes on problems of technique in the psychoanalytic treatment of adolescents: With some remarks on perversions. *The Psychoanalytic Study of the Child,* 13:223–254. New York: International Universities Press.

———— (1958b), Remarks on some variations in psychoanalytic technique. *Internat. J. Psycho-Anal.,* 39:222–229.

Englehardt, H. T., Jr., & Kaplan, A. L., Eds. (1987), *Scientific Controversies: Case Studies in the Resolution and Closure of Disputes in Science and Technology.* New York: Cambridge University Press.

Fenichel, O. (1945), *The Psychoanalytic Theory of Neurosis.* New York: W. W. Norton.

Ferenczi, S. (1909), More about homosexuality. In: *Final Contributions to the Problems and Methods of Psycho-Analysis.* New York: Brunner, 1955, pp. 168–174.

—— (1914), The nosology of female homosexuality (homoerotism). In: *Contributions to Psychoanalysis.* New York: Brunner, 1950, pp. 296–318.

—— (1916), *Contributions to Psychoanalysis.* Boston: Badger.

—— (1926), *Further Contributions to the Theory and Techniques of Psycho-Analysis.* London: Hogarth Press, 1950.

—— (1955), *Final Contributions to the Theory and Techniques of Psychoanalysis.* London: Hogarth Press.

Freud, A. (1951), Homosexuality. *Bull. Amer. Psychoanal. Assn.,* 7:117–118.

—— (1954), Problems of technique in adult analysis. In: *The Writings,* Vol. 4. New York: International Universities Press, 1968, pp. 377–406.

Freud, S. (1905), Three Essays on the Theory of Sexuality. *Standard Edition,* 7:123–243. London: Hogarth Press, 1953.

—— (1910), Leonardo da Vinci and a Memory of His Childhood. *Standard Edition,* 11:58–137. London: Hogarth Press, 1957.

—— (1914), On narcissism: An introduction. *Standard Edition,* 14:67–105. London: Hogarth Press, 1957.

—— (1915–1916), Introductory Lectures on Psychoanalysis. *Standard Edition,* 15. London: Hogarth Press, 1961.

—— (1919), "A child is being beaten." *Standard Edition,* 17:175–204. London: Hogarth Press, 1955.

—— (1920), Psychogenesis of a case of homosexuality in a woman. *Standard Edition,* 18:145–172. London: Hogarth Press, 1955.

—— (1922), Some neurotic mechanisms in jealousy, paranoia and homosexuality. *Standard Edition,* 18:221–232. London: Hogarth Press, 1955.

Galenson, E., & Roiphe, H. (1973), Object loss and early sexual development. *Psychoanal. Quart.,* 42:73–90.

Gershman, H. (1967), Psychopathology of compulsive homosexuality. *Amer. J. Psychoanal.,* 17:58–77.

Gillespie, W. H. (1956), The general theory of sexual perversion. *Internat. J. Psycho-Anal.,* 37:396–403.

Glover, E. (1960), *The Roots of Crime: Selected Papers on Psychoanalysis,* Vol. 2. New York: International Universities Press.

Greenacre, P. (1953), Certain relationships between fetishism and the faulty development of the body image. In: *Emotional Growth: Psychoanalytic Studies of the Gifted and a Great Variety of Other Individuals,* Vol. 1. New York: International Universities Press, 1971, pp. 9–31.

———— (1968), Perversions: General considerations regarding their genetic and dynamic background. In: *Emotional Growth: Psychoanalytic Studies of the Gifted and a Great Variety of Other Individuals,* Vol. 1. New York: International Universities Press, 1971, pp. 300–314.

———— (1969), The fetish and the transitional object. In: *Emotional Growth: Psychoanalytic Studies of the Gifted and a Great Variety of Other Individuals,* Vol. 1. New York: International Universities Press, 1971, pp. 315–334.

———— (1971), Notes on the influence and contribution of ego psychology to the practice of psychoanalysis. In: *Separation-Individuation: Essays in Honor of Margaret S. Mahler,* ed. J. B. McDevitt & C. F. Settlage. New York: International Universities Press, pp. 171–200.

Greenson, R. R. (1967), *The Technique and Practice of Psychoanalysis,* Vol. 1. New York: International Universities Press.

———— (1968), Disidentifying from the mother: Its special importance for the boy. In: *Explorations in Psychoanalysis.* New York: International Universities Press, 1978, pp. 305–312.

Kernberg, O. F. (1975), *Borderline Conditions and Pathological Narcissism.* New York: Jason Aronson.

———— (1985), *Severe Personality Disorders: Psychotherapeutic Strategies.* New Haven, CT: Yale University Press.

Klein, M. (1946), Notes on some schizoid mechanisms. *Internat. J. Psycho-Anal.,* 27:99–110.

Kohut, H. (1971), *The Analysis of the Self.* New York: International Universities Press.

Kolansky, H., & Eisner, H. (1974), The psychoanalytic concept of the preoedipal developmental arrest. Paper presented at the American Psychoanalytic Association, December.

Kubie, L. (1978), Distinction between normality and neurosis. In: *Symbol and Neurosis: Selected Papers of L. S. Kubie,* ed. H. J. Schlesinger. New York: International Universities Press, pp. 115–127.

Lichtenstein, H. (1983), *The Dilemma of Human Identity.* New York: Jason Aronson.

Litin, E., Giffin, M., & Johnson, A. (1956), Parental influence in unusual sexual behavior in children. *Psychoanal. Quart.,* 25:37–55.

Lorand, S. (1956), The theory of perversions. In: *Perversions: Psychodynamics and Therapy,* ed. S. Lorand & M. Balint. New York: Random House, pp. 290–307.

Macintosh, H. (1994), Attitudes and experiences of psychoanalysts in analyzing homosexual patients. *J. Amer. Psychoanal. Assn.,* 42:1183–1207.

Mahler, M. S. (1967), On human symbiosis and the vicissitudes of individuation. *J. Amer. Psychoanal. Assn.,* 15:740–764.

———— (1968), *On Human Symbiosis and the Vicissitudes of Individuation,* Vol. 1. New York: International Universities Press.

———— Pine, F., & Bergman, A. (1975), *The Psychological Birth of the Human Infant: Symbiosis and Individuation.* New York: Basic Books.

Moore, V. E., & Fine, B. D., Eds. (1990), *Psychoanalytic Terms and Concepts.* New Haven, CT: American Psychoanalytic Association/ Yale University Press.

Ostow, M., Blos, P., First, S., Geru, G., Kanzer, M., Silverman, D., Sterba, R., Valenstein, A., Arlow, J. A., Loomis, E., & Rappaport, E. (1974), *Sexual Deviations: Psychoanalytic Insights.* New York: Quadrangle/ New York Times.

Ovesey, L. (1969), *Homosexuality and Pseudohomosexuality.* New York: Science House.

Panel (1952), Psychodynamics and treatment of perversions. Reporter: J. A. Arlow. *Bull. Amer. Psychoanal. Assn.,* 8:315–327.

———— (1954), Perversions: Theoretical and therapeutic aspects. Reporter: J. A. Arlow. *J. Amer. Psychoanal. Assn.,* 2:336–345.

———— (1960a), An examination of nosology according to psychoanalytic concepts. Reporter: N. Ross. *J. Amer. Psychoanal. Assn.,* 8:535–551.

———— (1960b), Theoretical and clinical aspects of overt male homosexuality. Reporter: C. W. Socarides. *J. Amer. Psychoanal. Assn.,* 8:552–556.

———— (1986), Identification in the perversions. *Internat. J. Psycho-Anal.,* 67:245–250.

Radó, S. (1949), An adaptational view of sexual behavior. In: *The Psychoanalysis of Behavior. Collected Papers of Sandor Radó,* rev. ed., Vol. 1. New York: Grune & Stratton, pp. 186–213.

Rangell, L. (1965), Some comments on psychoanalytic nosology with recommendations for improvement. In: *Drives, Affects, Behavior,* Vol. 2, ed. M. Schur. New York: International Universities Press, pp. 123–157.

Roiphe, H. (1968), On an early genital phase. *The Psychoanalytic Study of the Child,* 23:348–365. New York: International Universities Press.

Rosen, I., Ed. (1964), *The Pathology and Treatment of Sexual Deviations.* Oxford: Oxford University Press.

———— Ed. (1979), *Sexual Deviation,* 2nd ed. Oxford: Oxford University Press.

Rosenfeld, H. A. (1949), Remarks on the relation of male homosexuality to paranoia, paranoid anxiety, and narcissism. *Internat. J. Psycho-Anal.,* 30:36–47.

Sachs, H. (1923), On the genesis of sexual perversion. In: *Homosexuality,* ed. C. Socarides. New York: Jason Aronson, 1978, pp. 531–546.

Socarides, C. W (1967), In: *Homosexuality,* ed. C. W. Socarides. New York: Jason Aronson.

———— (1968a), A unitary theory of etiology of male homosexuality: A case of preoedipal origin. *Internat. J. Psycho-Anal.,* 49:27–37.

———— (1968b), *The Overt Homosexual.* New York: Jason Aronson, 1974.

———— (1969), The psychoanalytic therapy of a male homosexual. *Psychoanal. Quart.,* 38:173–190.

———— (1974), Homosexuality. In: *American Handbook of Psychiatry,* 2nd ed., Vol. 3, ed. S. Arieti. New York: Basic Books, pp. 291–315.

———— Ed. (1978), *Homosexuality.* New York: Jason Aronson.

———— (1979), The psychoanalytic theory of homosexuality with special reference to therapy. In: *Sexual Deviations,* 2nd ed., ed. I. Rosen. Oxford: Oxford University Press, pp. 243–277.

———— (1985), Depression in perversion: With special reference to the function of erotic experience in sexual perversion. In: *Depressive States and Their Treatment,* ed. V. D. Volkan. New York: Jason Aronson, pp. 317–334.

———— (1988), *The Preoedipal Origin and Psychoanalytic Therapy of Sexual Perversions.* Madison, CT: International Universities Press.

———— et al. (1973), Report of the Task Force on Homosexuality of the New York County District branch of the American Psychiatric Association. Homosexuality in the male: A report of a psychiatric study group. *Internat. J. Psychiatry,* 11(4):460–479.

———— Volkan, V. D., Eds. (1991), *The Homosexualities: Reality, Fantasy, and the Arts.* Madison, CT: International Universities Press.

Spitz, R. (1959), *A General Field Theory of Ego Formation.* New York: International Universities Press.

Stoller, R. J. (1964), A contribution to the study of gender identity. *Internat. J. Psycho-Anal.,* 45:220–226.

———— (1966), The mother's contribution to infantile transvestite behavior. *Internat. J. Psycho-Anal.,* 47:384–395.

———— (1968a), Further contributions to the study of gender identity. *Internat. J. Psycho-Anal.,* 49:364–368.

———— (1968b), *Sex and Gender.* New York: Science House.

———— (1975), Healthy parental influences on the earliest development of masculinity in baby boys. *Psychoanal. Forum,* 5:234–240.

Stolorow, R. S., & Lachmann, F. M. (1978), The development of prestates of defenses: Diagnostic and therapeutic implications. *Psychoanal. Quart.,* 47:73–102.

———— ———— (1980), *Psychoanalysis and Developmental Arrest: Theory and Treatment.* New York: Jason Aronson.

Volkan, V. D. (1979), Transexualism: As examined from the viewpoint of internal object relations. In: *On Sexuality: Psychoanalytic Observations,* ed. T. B. Karasu & C. W. Socarides. New York: Jason Aronson, pp. 189–222.

Winnicott, D. W. (1935), The manic defense. In: *Collected Papers: From Pediatrics to Psychoanalysis.* New York: Basic Books, 1958, pp. 129–44.

CHAPTER 2

Shift from Homosexual to Heterosexual Orientation During the Termination Phase of Analysis

JEROME S. BLACKMAN, M.D., F.A.P.A.

The entire subject of homosexuality is controversial today. The etiology of homosexualities is controversial. Any treatment directed at any type of homosexuality is controversial.

The following case may be helpful as a contribution to the intense ongoing discussion. What is homosexuality, how does it arise, and can it be modified or changed in any way through child-rearing techniques or psychoanalytic treatment?

The theoretical arguments regarding these questions are contentious, so I will first discuss the patient, his psychopathology, salient history, and what I consider to be nodal points of his psychoanalysis. These data will highlight matters for theoretical discussion. For in-depth study, I have included an Appendix containing a more detailed recording of the interactions in sessions #470–522 (the termination phase).

The Case

Cory was a 29-year-old, single, white law student who first consulted me because he was drinking, beating up his gay lover, having trouble studying, and experiencing anxiety. He impulsively engaged in anonymous oral sex almost nightly in a local park pickup spot.

Although he felt his homosexual activity was normal, he worried about his promiscuity and AIDS. The few years he spent in once-a-week therapy in New York had, he thought, helped him tone down his promiscuity. Before treatment he had gone to bath houses, had group sex, given golden showers, engaged in S&M and even worked as a homosexual prostitute for a few months in Copenhagen.

Cory's relationships were so extractive and narcissistic when I first evaluated him that I doubted his treatability with analysis. His impulsivity, drinking, and promiscuity suggested impairments in reality testing, judgment, and self-preservation. I wondered briefly during the initial evaluation whether he was psychotic, but over a period of sessions it became clear that his integrative capacity was quite good, his abstraction ability was good, his reality testing regarding the world around him was excellent, and his observing ego operated at a sufficient level. He expressed a fervent desire to be relieved of pain and was interested in an analytic approach to help him with this, although he was not interested in changing his sexual orientation. I agreed that change in sexual orientation need not be a goal, but recommended we not exclude any topic from free associations, including Cory's sexuality. Cory was agreeable, although he feared I might be a "follower of Socarides." He was surprised, although pleased, that I would not identify myself as anyone's disciple.

Cory had been involved with Gustav, a Viennese musician, for almost three years and wore a wedding ring indicating that he and Gustav were symbolically married. Sexually, Gustav was a "bottom" and Cory was a "top." Their arguments centered around control, introduction of other men into the relationship, which they both did, and Cory's drinking. At other times, Cory berated Gustav for not working and Gustav would respond that Cory was "sucking" on him and his uncle, who helped support the two. Their fights could escalate to a point where they got physical. Nevertheless, they expressed "love" for each other and seemed to care about each other's welfare to a certain extent.

Psychoanalysis as treatment did not seem indicated at first. I suspected Cory might need medication because of his ego weaknesses (in impulse control and affect tolerance), and this later turned out to be the case. Besides that, Cory was going to law school on loans, and was concerned about affording treatment even twice a week, as I recommended. (He independently worked out his loan structures to afford it.) He had been in therapy for over a year when he expressed a desire for analysis. With some trepidation, I decided to give analysis a try because of the possibility of better resolution of his conflicts. His ego strength had improved, and his motivation was high. I treated him in psychoanalysis for three years after that, during which time his ego strength and ego functions improved. The resolution of his intrapsychic conflicts seemed inextricably involved in his change of orientation to heterosexuality.

Past History

Cory had had no medical difficulties. He claimed his penis was unusually large, and this made him a favorite of many homosexual men.

He was raised by his mother and father. He was the youngest of six, having three brothers and two sisters. His father was alcoholic until Cory was 16. At that point, his father started taking his mother to ballet and opera, although the family lived in a trailer park. His father had a low-level bureaucratic job.

His mother went to work when he was 11, but before that had been home with the children. By his description, she was limited in her capacities to soothe, as well as overwhelmed by the number of children. Cory's father had violent fights with her when drunk. The father at times locked the mother out of the house for hours in the snow. Also, the father beat Cory's older brothers severely with belts and sticks. Cory was spared because of his mother's protection. His mother told Cory he was conceived as part of a bargain for the mother made with the father to get the father to stop drinking. However, the father did not hold to this bargain until 17 years later.

Throughout his upbringing, Cory was sexually overstimulated. He remembered when he was four witnessing his 26-year-old sister seduce his 16-year-old brother. He witnessed another teenage sister having sexual intercourse with multiple boys while he was in grade school. In addition, his older brothers often held him down and beat him. A couple of his brothers raped him anally while he was in grade school, although his memory for those traumas was somewhat vague as to time and age. One of these brothers persisted in a mutual fellatio relationship with Cory throughout grade school, and even into high school. Cory still had periodic sexual thoughts about his brother. I did not know until much later in his treatment that a different brother, Todd, had been kind to Cory and not sexual, but that Todd had been killed in a motorcycle accident when Cory was in college.

Cory had been convicted of assault on Dawn, a high-school girl, when he was 16. The assault occurred while they were having drunken sexual intercourse in her parents' bedroom: he suddenly began beating her with his fists. He now felt embarrassed and guilty about that incident. He had also been arrested for homosexual solicitation when he was 19, and convicted. He had not been put in jail for either of these offenses, but had a record. He worried about his ability to get jobs after law school because of these convictions.

Mental Status Examination

Cory did not present any evidence of primary or secondary psychotic symptoms. He was bright, articulate, and slightly effeminate. He was attractive and tall and dressed nicely in a masculine fashion, but swished a bit when he walked. His voice was slightly high pitched, dropped when he got angry, and we eventually analyzed that he associated masculinity with violence.

He had never attempted suicide, but had thought of it when in despair. His tension tolerance was weak. When not having anonymous sex in the park, he would often masturbate between two and five times a day.

Initial Diagnosis

(1) Borderline personality organization with impulsivity, dependency, and addictive features, work inhibition, and psychopathic traits (Kernberg, 1975).
(2) Homosexuality, preoedipal Type I, with some features of Type II (Socarides, 1988).

Course of Treatment

In Cory's initial sessions, he described his problems with studying and his anxiety. An initial resistance was his fear I would criticize him for being gay. When I pointed out that he experienced me as critical because of his own self-criticism, he confirmed that he had sometimes "screwed girls as a front, to not face my homosexuality."

He saw his homosexuality as "rebellious" and claimed that he saw law as masculine and psychology as feminine (he had majored in psychology in college). This statement created a bit of castration anxiety in me; contrarily, Cory's lack of affective expression led me to ask him if he actually believed what he was saying about gender. He laughed, saying it sounded like "pop psychology"; his "true rebellion" was that he "hated working." At times, though, he overworked to prove that he was not lazy.

In the following session (#13), Cory reported hitting Gustav while drunk. Cory wished "to be someone's wife and live in leisure." He caught himself making excuses for having hit Gustav, but eventually admitted that he had been manipulating Gustav because of his own laziness.

Cory's oral conflicts were connected to his difficulty with studying, his irresponsibility, and his sense of entitlement throughout his analytic work. A second theme that arose rather quickly and also continued was that of self-destructiveness.

Cory's regression into beating up Gustav worried me, but perhaps not as much as his minimization of the impulsiveness involved. I was even more worried Cory would get himself killed through his wild sexual activity, and felt some desperation myself about whether I would be able to treat him. These feelings tipped me off that he might also be feeling desperate.

I said to him in session 15 that his drinking showed a desperate need to be independent, but also provoked the whole world to take care of him, including me. Nevertheless, he might get himself killed before he could be helped. He agreed he was desperate and worried about his self-destructiveness. He remembered Aaron, a wealthy gay man to whom he had attached himself upon moving to Boston at age 22. He had lived with Aaron for a couple of years. Aaron introduced Cory to gay men in many different countries, who entertained them royally. Regarding his alcoholism, Cory stated that, because he could enliven a party, he felt he was a different type of alcoholic from his father.

In a session a week later, he revealed a fantasy of "marrying a woman who lives in Los Angeles." Cory disliked living in the Norfolk metropolitan area. He complained of homophobia, lack of culture, and provinciality. He loved Boston, Los Angeles, and major cities in Europe, and in fact seemed quite cosmopolitan and worldly.

In session 20, Cory wanted to get his therapy over quickly. Although I associated his statement with some sort of fear of sexual transgression, the resistance closer to the surface seemed to concern passivity conflicts. I pointed out that if he shortened the therapy, he would not have to allow himself to be treated by me. He had a plethora of associations about "hating giving in," his "wish to be a wife," and his "irritation" with me for not being more reassuring to him. When he complained, he whined in an effeminate voice, which I interpreted as a defense against the hostility.

In the following session, he reported giving thought to my interpretation that he defended against hostility by becoming effeminate. With Gustav, he did the same thing, and they tortured each other.

Some months later, Cory got mad at Gustav for giving him gonorrhea (which was treated). Cory responded by "picking up a good-looking homosexual boy" to sodomize without a condom. His life-threatening behavior, which occurred periodically, made me feel I was not a very good analyst. I considered that my feeling of inadequacy might be a concordant identification with Cory, and formulated that Cory's behavior was a narcissistic defense. I interpreted to him that his fantasies of incorporating the beautiful boy's penis during anal sex (concomitant with Cory doing the penetrating) seemed to improve his self-esteem. He immediately concurred, stating that his problems with continuing alcoholism and studying made him feel inadequate. He now thought his relationship with Gustav was doomed by both of them. In fact, Gustav eventually moved out.

About two weeks later, Cory asked me to give him a fraudulent bill with extra sessions on it to manipulate a bank officer into loaning him money he would use for travel. I adamantly refused to do this, and told him such manipulation was extractive, dishonest, destructive to me, and dangerous to him. He contritely said that he was poor and having financial difficulties because he wanted to go to Paris over Christmas, and that I did not understand. He also complained that my confrontation about his dangerous homosexual activity was "homophobic and condescending." He associated how nobody had ever taken care of him financially.

At this juncture, I thought of discharging Cory from treatment. He was browbeating me, projecting onto me, losing track of reality, and continuing to act out. However, I also realized that I felt retaliatory because he must be fighting with me. I therefore proposed to him the idea that his complaining seemed to have the unconscious meaning of provoking me into a fight. He agreed, and added that he wanted to blame me because he was sensitive about homosexuality. However, he was still angry I had not "helped" him with the money, and did not know if he wanted to be in treatment with me. I suspected he again was manipulating me, but in any case, a therapeutic alliance was not developing. I said if he felt uncomfortable with me, and we could not analyze it, I would help him find another therapist or he could choose one of his own.

In the following session, he decided he would stay in treatment with me, confessed to more unprotected, anonymous sex the night before, and despaired about drinking. I insisted he take disulfiram and a benzodiazapine to give himself some control over the drinking, which interfered with his judgment and reality testing about sex. In the session following, he said that he "took to heart" my confrontation about his judgment and reality testing problems. He realized he was weak and that sexual activity was a bad way to manage his weakness. He felt the medication gave him something "concrete and tangible" that helped him, and it reduced his anxiety so he could study somewhat better. He now revealed a masturbation fantasy of "a penis in a vagina" without people attached. He associated: "While I'm fucking a man in the ass, I sometimes imagine having intercourse with a woman." He then remembered "getting fucked by my brother" and dreams where he was either having sex with a woman who is taken away by a man, or sex with a man who is taken away by a woman.

Cory took disulfiram and chlordiazepoxide for several weeks, gradually tapered them off, and was able to stop drinking. He regressed periodically after that, but the intensity and chronicity seemed to have been relieved. He talked for weeks about his weakness in controlling himself. I interpreted to him that this (ego) weakness had become sexualized; that is, it had taken on a symbolic meaning of being "unmanly." His urge for a sexual contact with a man was thus designed to relieve tension and repair the sense of weakness (Blackman, 1991a). He responded with thoughts of how his father had "fucked with my mind." I linked a joke he had made to me earlier, in legal jargon, that in homosexual activity he was "the fuckor, not the fuckee."

Starting in session 78, about ten months into his treatment, Cory began complaining that I did not give him enough interpretations. This complaint persisted throughout the psychotherapy phase, another few months, and reappeared throughout his analytic work, which lasted another three years. His pressure on me was understood to be an identification with adults who had raped him and the father who had brutally criticized and manipulated him. Separation dynamics also partly explained his demandingness: he wanted to make me part of him, control me, beat me up like a teddy bear and throw me away, or hold me tight, symbolically, for support. One unique demand was his request for a précis of each session during the last five or ten minutes. For the first year (in psychotherapy), I decided to provides ego support (integration and secondary process) by giving him an integrative review of interpretive work from the session. During the second year, while he was using the couch, I tapered this off, and eventually addressed his unconscious seductiveness as a compromise formation.

After his first year of treatment, on returning from summer vacation, Cory wanted to enter analysis. I thought if he could tolerate the regression and the intensity, I could no doubt do more to help him. On the other hand, I feared him regressing and becoming suicidal or psychotic because of his unstable self–object constancy and ego strengths. The dilemma was solved by his literally jumping on the couch and in a playful way demanding that I analyze him. I pointed out to him that he would have to come four times a week, and that my technique would be somewhat different. He said he wanted to get better and would get loans to cover it, and essentially, that is what happened.

During his first session on the couch (#85), he angrily accused me of being afraid that he would develop AIDS through his promiscuous sexual activity. Although I was aware periodically of parental and defensive sibling countertransferences, I still felt that his blaming me was due to projection that was interfering with his reality testing. So I confronted the projection by telling him he was the one who needed to fear AIDS, not me. He replied that he knew he should fear AIDS, but was angry and looking to fight with me. He was angry because he had lately been stopping himself from indulging in promiscuous sex. He quipped that I sounded "hostile." I interpreted that he confused hostility with my aggression in confronting his defense. He replied he was "filled with rage" and he was attacking me because I was handy. He associated being mad at his mother for abandoning him, his father for threatening him, and his brother for raping him. His affective tone was intense and rageful.

As I had feared, Cory regressed after this session. He called me at home, feeling he would explode. He could not concentrate, sit still, or study. He felt disorganized; his mind was on fire. I called in a prescription for Trilafon 2 mg twice a day and told him it might help him with reduction of affect so that he could think.

In the next session, he said that the Trilafon had made him feel somewhat better the prior night, and he could think more clearly. I advised him to take it for a few more weeks and then taper it off; he was relieved because he did not want to take medication. However, he was angry at me for being on the telephone when he came in, even though he was fifteen minutes late, and when I clarified this self-centered attack on me, he admitted he was still trying to get a rise out of me.

Over the next month or two, Cory's rage and the defenses against it were the central focus of our work. His angry provocativeness was understood as an identification with his rapist-brother, where he was symbolically raping me. After we saw that he used anger as a way of separating himself from fond feelings toward me to guard against fear of losing his identity, he remembered his mother leaving him alone in the house when he was obstreperous at 3 or 4 years of age. She would leave for what seemed like hours to go to the neighbors.

Some time later, in a particularly worrisome bit of acting out, Cory took two old Trilafons with a couple of beers. This got him tipsy. I confronted the rebellious hostility toward me symbolized in this, as well as the self-punitive aspect of hurting himself. We continued understanding the transference acting out of his separation problems from his mother. Taking medication symbolized incorporating me, but doing it without asking symbolized rejecting me.

In another session, when he insisted I speak and give him more interpretations, I pointed out that if I spoke he could feel close, but since I was doing the talking, he could simultaneously feel distance. He understood this and sadly commented that his problems were "serious." When he still felt like attacking me, he said he knew he should study more, but it was "an insult to my grandiosity." He associated how his mother wanted him to do well in school, and how he rebelled and kept distance from her by not doing so. He did not have any further episodes of mixing medication with alcohol.

Gradually, as Cory consciously curtailed his symptomatic sexual behavior, he brought in more analyzable material, including transference. Cory got angry because his father told him he should quit school, and then reported a masturbation fantasy, "My father and I are having sexual intercourse with a woman simultaneously. We're both inserting our penises into her vagina while we are all standing up." His association to the fantasy was somehow getting love from his father through physical means.

Sadomasochistic sexual fantasies allowed symbolic ways of keeping control while obtaining love and dependency gratification. In session 203, after not drinking for months and keeping sexual activity to a minimum, he began experiencing more and more pain. When I explored this, he began remembering Todd, the brother who loved him, and the motorcycle accident that killed him. Cory began crying, screaming, and cursing, and at one point fell off the couch onto the floor (cf. Waugaman, 1987). He felt "an elephant is sitting on my chest." He was afraid he would never get over the pain.

A couple of weeks were taken up analyzing the ramifications of his relationship with Todd. Cory defensively retreated from object relatedness after Todd's death. His homosexual behavior symbolically searched for Todd. He punished himself for Todd's death. Unsafe sex relieved guilt over displaced oedipal rivalry, which he had acted out two years after Todd's death by having sexual intercourse with Todd's widow. I also interpreted this latter behavior as Cory's defense against grieving over Todd. Throughout these weeks, Cory cried bitterly, often with rage, but was able to recoup and function between sessions, indicating improvement in his ego functioning. The alliance improved as he developed more trust and object-relatedness toward me. Positive transference seemed to contribute to his positive feelings toward me, associated with some of his warmer interactions with Todd, who had also protected him.

Oedipal aspects of the transference began to appear with some clarity in session 269, when Cory reported he had stopped verbally attacking women. He credited my prior interpretation that his sarcastic comments toward women provoked punishment toward himself in a way he wished his mother had punished his father for his father's brutality. Cory momentarily wished "to find a woman, feel comfortable, get married, and have children." He feared he could not, and then revealed that he had seen my wife and me at the opera. He imagined talking to her, and noticed that she is younger than I am. When he imagined that she was 16 when I married her, I sensed my own discomfort with the incestuous implications. Following my formulation that he was blaming incestuous activity on me to defend against guilt over his own oedipal strivings, I asked Cory if he imagined I was a child abuser. He responded that he wondered if I also had engaged in premature sexual activity, like he and his brothers. When he heard my shoulder crunch (I have a bit of arthritis) he joked, "You're too old for that young girl!"

Sensing his obvious oedipal competition, I said destroying himself by provoking retribution from women or by engaging in unsafe sex relieved him of guilt about competing for my "young wife." He associated to his mother favoring him, and recalled how she had packed him up to leave his father when he was 5, telling him he would be her man from then on. The two of them had apparently gone some distance out of town in her car, when she changed her mind and returned to his father. He was bitterly disappointed, and feared his father would kill them.

Negative oedipal dynamics also emerged. In session 374, for example, he reported "feeling horny." I explored what he meant by this, and he clarified a wish for a penis in his rectum, which would mean "someone to take care of me." He wished for me to fill his "void" with medications. He reported masturbation fantasies about women. He associated to feeling competitive with men, followed by wishes to run away and suck or be feminine. As a child, he sometimes dressed as a girl. When I confronted his periodic invasions of me—assumptions or questions about my personal life and marriage—he referred to "the power of the pussy" associated with his invasive mother.

Later, in session 411, he reported a masturbation fantasy: "I'm having 69 with a woman on top, at the same time another man is penetrating her vagina doggy style." He visualized possessing a "vagina-mouth" to compete with his mother for his father's attention, giving him "power of the pussy." I linked this fantasy with his prior interest in my wife, and interpreted that he seemed competitive with her. He concurred, saying he got more attention being feminine, and further associated to his old visits to Baths International for anonymous sex.

Toward the end of his third year of treatment, Cory reported anxiety over his upcoming job interviews. They reminded him of getting beaten up on the playground as a boy. He also wanted to stay in treatment with me, which came into conflict with his plan to go to Los Angeles in a year. Since he had recently had unprotected sex, I interpreted that if he got sick and could not practice law, he might have to stay in town for me and his parents to take care of him. Thereby, he also outcompeted my wife for my attention, got me to take care of him as his mother had not, and forced me as a cold, demanding father to change and be sympathetic. Although Cory was unsure my interpretation was connected with him leaving, he then imagined I could prescribe medication for him to take to Los Angeles. When I interpreted how symbolically he wished to take something of me with him, he realized he would miss me and might be acting up to hold onto me.

In the middle of his fourth year of analysis, Cory needed to decide whether to stay in the Norfolk area to continue his treatment or move to Los Angeles to pursue his career in entertainment law. He disliked the Norfolk metropolitan area, which he considered provincial and homophobic. In Los Angeles, he judged he could adapt himself as a gay man, find a suitable partner, and avoid de facto discrimination.

In addition, Cory was feeling better. He wondered whether he really needed further treatment after he finished up with me in the next five or six months. He contacted several Norfolk-area law firms to inquire about entertainment law positions. Not only was entertainment law unavailable, but he got the cold shoulder from the law firms. This was due to some persistent effeminate mannerisms and the fact that his grades in law school were less than exemplary. In contrast, he had gay friends in Los Angeles, through his years of traveling with Aaron. Moreover, his job interviews in Los Angeles went fabulously. He eventually got job offers from two law firms, although not his first and second choices. He had no offers in the Norfolk area whatsoever.

Ironically, during the termination phase of his analysis, his sexual orientation changed from homosexual to heterosexual, and the comparatively less accepting atmosphere in Norfolk would no doubt have been less of a problem for him (see below and Appendix). Nevertheless, the work situation seemed impossible. Particularly after the shift in sexual orientation, he became desirous of continuing treatment longer, in order to have time to work through the resulting complications in his feelings. I agreed with him that more analytic work might be necessary. On the other hand, the reality of his work situation did not seem to allow him to continue treatment in the Norfolk area. He was also excited about the job possibilities in Los Angeles, which paid extremely well and let him into the field where he wanted to practice law.

As we embarked on the last phase of his treatment (session #471), Cory reported that he was tired of "being selfish, manipulative, and violent, and thinking that sticking my penis here, there, and everywhere is normal, and that being wild, drinking, and outrageous behavior is normal." He felt he was changing. He toyed with not paying me but feared I would kick him out. I asked, "Do you think I'm a prostitute?" He said he did not think so rationally, but he might feel this way. I interpreted his projecting onto me and generalizing protected him from anxiety about being close and trusting me. He responded, "If you've been screwed as much as me, you wouldn't trust either. I want to put you in my pocket. You be my auxiliary brain and you tell me what to do." His further demands that I guide him led me to clarify that his reexperiencing anxiety about trusting me arose after he decided to leave town. He answered, "I want proof that you're there, listening and understanding. I find your voice soothing. I dream of your voice. If you don't talk, you've disappeared. That's childish!"

In session 496, Cory verbalized fantasies that he was my penis. He thought his interest in men's penises had developed in lieu of identifications with me. Specifically, he imagined sucking on my penis or brain. He then asked me, "Why do I sexualize it?" Thinking of his shame over oral dependency wishes and castration anxiety, I asked him if he felt less embarrassed seeing everything as sexual. He responded, "I would be your penis. I don't like the work part. I associated work with my father. . . . Sexualizing is comfortable. I've had experience with it. It's not like being friends. . . . If someone wants to be my friend, then I think of them sexually. . . . If I expose my friendly wishes, and it gets cut off . . . I'm not embarrassed or disappointed at a bar. I can just say, 'Wanna fuck?' "

In the following session, he expressed direct gratitude because I had been able to change an appointment time to accommodate his exam schedule. He reported the following dream:

> I'm having a party in a room attached to the house that I used to live in. There's a room beyond and a garden. My friend had decorated it like with Tiffany lamps. I liked the gaudiness.
> I'm going to have a floor show in the room in front. My mother, father, sister and brother are going to the show. I have a garden party and a show. I'm in the room showering, talking to someone I don't know, who was weird. I had dreamed it before, but now it was really happening. I saw my family members coming through the garden and they didn't see me. As they arrive, I'm showering for the party with other people. This was disturbing.

His associations centered on wishing to torture his family by parading before them a future beautiful house and possessions. He thought wealth would express his hostility toward women in the professions, as well, and then stated with a sigh, "My overall wish is to be a man! No, a woman!" He had oscillated similarly for a couple of years, and we had analyzed aspects of his bisexual fantasies. As I was listening to him, the conflict seemed rather pointed. My next intervention derived from my preconscious integrated impressions about his conflicts and his sense of humor. I said to him, with some irony, "I have the solution for you." He asked, "What is it?" and started laughing. I said, "Why don't you be gay?" He laughed harder and commented that that was probably what his gayness was all about, anyway, a bit of being a man and a woman. He immediately associated that he could become rich and not care about anybody, but have "nice things." I said the dream indicated conflict over having nice things. He associated Nietzsche's theory of "an effeminate, priestly class—they become meek, mild priests. Real men get what they want!" Then he toyed with the idea of becoming altruistic, which I interpreted as a rationalization against the embarrassment over his hunger. He admitted wishing for a rich man like Aaron.

Session 498 (immediately following) was pivotal in his thinking about his gender identity. I had again rearranged the time of his session at the end of the work day because of his examination schedule. He thanked me for staying late and then said, "I have a strange idea: I'm straight!" His masturbation fantasies had shifted to women: "It makes sense! I go to bed with a woman and get married!" He associated my staying late with a recognition that I genuinely cared about him and said he wanted to identify with me: "I want my own kids." He felt he did not have to "suck on your penis or brain." He commented that he had dated and had sex with women in college, but at graduation "plunged into the gay world for ten years."

Confirming a concern I was beginning to develop listening to his thoughts, he said, "Maybe I think it would make you happy. I'm sort of entrenched in the gay world, but I guess that's not really a problem." Although I was concerned he might be developing a transference cure, I decided to refrain from commenting. His exposition of thoughts and feelings was dramatic and I was impressed that he seemed to be integrating prior insights from his treatment. Cory thought he could settle down with one person and that sexual attraction to other men or women would be "like seeing a nice painting." He felt exultant that he could be a "real husband and father."

There seemed to be some shift in his conscious masturbation fantasies. Excitedly, he said, "I've been masturbating with a mirror lately, and I noticed: I'm a man! I guess a vagina goes with it. I've been thinking about . . . being buddies with men." He then paused and expressed anxiety because of "disproving those who say being gay is innate. They say it's not a choice. What if it *is* a choice?" He felt he did not need rich lovers "or their penises," because he could have his own material possessions. He could have his own woman and not just fantasize about a woman with a man. He said, "Lately, in my fantasies, it's just me and a woman, not rape." He contrasted deriving admiration from a man with having them "suck on my dick." Essentially, he recognized that sublimated admiration could be satisfactory. He pondered, "Why have I repressed my heterosexuality for so long?" He reconsidered his old belief that homosexuality was "natural." He now felt, "I don't want my penis to go away!" He could get closeness with men in more sublimated ways, "colleagues, pals, clients."

Although I was somewhat skeptical of this dramatic shift, wondering whether he was only presenting a split-off aspect of his self-image, I began to think that the change was more integrated when he expressed ambivalence: "Could I live up to this ideal? Of not having things through sex?" Sensing his ambivalence, and seeing that he was asking me for reassurance, I formulated that he was defensively becoming passive and seducing me. I intervened by saying, "Why are you asking me for reassurance?" He replied that he was leaving town. He wanted to take a piece of me with him, and was afraid the work we had done would "deteriorate." On the other hand, he felt he would be successful because he had already surpassed the people that he had suffered with growing up. He then considered whether family life would tie him down. He had advantages in the gay world and more freedom. He considered that he could be heterosexual in Los Angeles, married to a wife who was interested in his ambitions. He would not have to practice in a rural town as his father had advised. As he continued experiencing pleasure in this reintegration of his identity, he commented, "I think of all the petty jealousy I had, trying to be like my father and brothers, thinking that if women did not succumb to my will, I was a failure as man." He could see himself as considerate, flexible, and still masculine.

As I considered whether this change in his orientation was genuine, split-off or transferentially designed to please me in an "as if" way, I wondered if the shift was a defense against affects associated with termination. The material in the next 23 sessions (see Appendix) confirmed that the shift was an integrated result of treatment, but was enhanced by Cory's identification with certain perceptions and fantasies about my life being gratifying as a heterosexual, and affected by residual transference gratifications that he had pleased me/father. I saw that my neutrality regarding his conflicts over sexuality caused him to believe, correctly, that I did not favor homosexuality over heterosexuality, and that to the extent that he could integrate his (id) wish for a wife and children with his ego functioning, I was not averse to helping him.

In session 500, Cory again expressed frustration and sadness about ending treatment. He presented two dreams:

1. I'm in L.A. and I meet a woman. She's a self-assured person. I want to go out with her, I ask her and she accepts.
2. I have intercourse with Dawn (the girl I had beaten up), and there's nothing weird about it.

He felt "weird" having dreams of sex with women. He associated to his father criticizing him and missing college friends. He then mentioned that he had masturbated last night with a fantasy of giving fellatio to a boy he knew in college, but the activity was "not exciting." He preferred thinking of sex with larger-breasted women. I felt that the recurrence of the homosexual fantasies was defensive against feelings of loss of me and defensive against loss of his father's love (which occurred when his father criticized him). I pointed out the contiguity of his homosexual fantasies occurring after these painful thoughts. He immediately thought homosexual fantasy protected him from grief. He cried as he thought he would miss me, and wished I had been his father.

He asked me, "Have any other patients as gay as I am gone straight? Is it possible?" Following on my formulation about his transferences and splitting mechanisms, I commented that he seemed to wish that I would be proud of him for changing to heterosexuality, and that this would make him special to me. He immediately responded that he hoped his shift in sexual orientation would "give you pleasure." I asked, "A pleasure your father did not have?" He responded, with vehemence, "I didn't get a fucking thing from my father!"

My concern about possible splitting of his self-image into hetero- and homosexual aspects, with him having just presented the heterosexual aspect as a defense against grieving, came up again in the following sessions. In session 501, he reported that his most recent HIV test was negative. He first felt I should be proud, but then imagined he would pick up AIDS during unsafe sex to hurt me. His impish rebelliousness and his tone of voice here sounded like an adolescent autonomy conflict. I discussed with him the possibility that hurting me and getting me angry might ease his painful feelings of being separate from me and help him feel more intact.

He agreed, and added that he was experiencing some guilt over anger toward me. I then interpreted that he was turning anger on himself by thinking of becoming HIV+. Cory then revealed "a romantic wish to find a beautiful woman, sail around the world, and live off the fat of the land."

A few sessions later, Cory reported shame over becoming sexually stimulated by looking at his niece's boyfriend. He again imagined his homosexual stimulation would make me angry and hurt me. He reported the following dream:

> I'm on a tall ship. We're going somewhere, and something is happening. I'm going to have sex. It's not worked out. I'm leaving. There's an old black man who stopped me and asked to go to bed. I think, that's ludicrous! I had somehow forgotten that I had a connecting ship or a plane flight to China and there wasn't time. Then I was screwing this guy, thinking: This is boring and gross—feces—I got upset that I was missing the flight while I was doing this.

I suspected the "black man" symbolized me because of my surname. The traveling in the dream no doubt had something to do with separation. There were many conflicts in this dream that I realized we would not get to analyze in their entirety. Since he would be leaving in a few weeks, I tried to give my intervention "multiple appeal" (Hartmann, 1939) and focus on termination. I simply said the dream seemed to indicate Cory's ambivalence about ending treatment. He responded that he felt some insecurity about his sexual identity, although he was enjoying feeling masculine. He still recognized "sexual" interest in men without shirts at the beach. However, he had already analyzed that this "sexuality" masked competitive feelings he had with them. He did not make the connection between the black man in the dream and me, but focused rather on his growing disgust with homosexual activity. I suspected that he may have been projecting homosexual wishes onto me, thinking that I wanted him to go to bed with me, and that he could not separate from me by becoming heterosexual. I was not sure of this formulation, and did not bring it up. Further, I did not think interpreting his heterosexuality as a defense against self–object fusion would help him; the current compromise formation seemed adaptive because it integrated his (id) wishes for a positive oedipal resolution of obtaining his own wife and children.

I felt vindicated in my caution when in session 505 Cory reported working out with male friends and enjoying the sublimated relationship. Although he had a fleeting thought of getting fellatio to tone down his anxiety about heterosexual intercourse, he recalled a dream from the prior night: "I'm in the mountains skiing with women and with my old college girl friend, Sandy. I have a fear that I have to climb something large, get off and climb down." He associated to sexual stimulation by the idea of a man with a woman. I clarified that he must be in that fantasy, and he responded he felt like he was both the man and the woman. "I'd like to make love to the mirror-image of myself!"

He expressed jealousy that women could "have men in the way I can't." This was connected to his fear of extreme rage at his mother, which he associated with skiing in the mountains. He revealed embarrassing but stimulating fantasies of "a slut who had lots of men" and a virgin nun being raped in a movie. He associated skiing trips to Switzerland with Aaron and their lobster dinners. He wondered what "screwing a man in the ass" had to do with rape fantasies toward women. I interpreted the thought of penetrating a man as a displacement, avoidance, and discharge of his guilty wish to violently rape a woman, with which he agreed. He looked forward to loving sex with a woman, which he thought would be "novel."

A few sessions later, he reported a very long dream where a knife gash in his face brought him to a hospital to see an ER surgeon against his will. He insisted on a plastic surgeon, but the plastic surgeon refused to see him. Cory pulled out the yellow pages to throw angrily, and was then asked by the surgeon if he was in control of himself. He wanted his face sewn up and was afraid he would be sedated instead.

He associated the dream with leaving me, feeling that in some ways he was still not completely fixed; the gash in the face went through "to the brain." He associated plastic surgery with wanting more psychoanalysis and again brought up the possibility of continuing treatment in Los Angeles. He would be able to afford it better, and competitively, with some humor, said, "I want to make more money than you do, and be more famous."

In session 513, Cory reported graduating, having a party for his family and a few old friends. He felt guilty that his father was proud of him, because he wanted to say to his father, "Fuck you."

He felt guilty about anger at his mother and girl friend, and his response to all of this was to get drunk and obtain fellatio from a man in the park. I formulated that this regression was not only a response to saying goodbye to his mother and father, but probably to me as a transference representation of both. I interpreted to him that this old method of destroying himself not only relieved guilt over outdoing his father and separating from his mother, but also was unconsciously designed to hurt me, deprive me of the narcissistic gratification he imagined I wanted as his father, and again make himself sick so he would not have to leave me. He cried bitterly and concurred, adding that he wanted to ''show you and myself just how damaging my family had really been to me!''

In session 517, Cory imagined he should not waste his time coming to see me because he was feeling stronger, with better control and stability in his heterosexual identification. He was isolating affect, which I brought to his attention, and then he revealed ''hatred'' toward me because I did not convince him to stay in Norfolk. I interpreted that his wish to not come rejected me before I rejected him. He responded that I was not ''tangled'' with him as he had been with his mother. When I clarified that his identification with the aggressor guarded him further against grieving about losing me, he cried briefly, again, and admitted fondness toward me.

In session 521, he again tackled the dynamics of guilt over outdoing his father, which had led him into homosexual activity. I mentioned his recent fantasies of making more money than me, outdoing me, which had led him into regressive homosexual defensive activity. He joked that if he could not go to Los Angeles, he could remain my son and get my love and attention. Cory had begun this session by complaining about his back. At the end of the session when he got up from the couch, he again complained of his back. I interpreted that perhaps if his back hurt enough, he would not be able to get off the couch. He laughed, and said he was already off the couch—our session tomorrow would be his last.

In his final session, Cory noted the changes that had occurred during his analysis, particularly his improvement in ego strength and the shift in his sexual orientation. He was excited in preparing to work in Los Angeles and meet a woman. He felt sadness leaving me, wished that he could stay around to do some more work, and would miss our interactions. He was glad, however, that I had not put "hooks" in him. He felt that perhaps our work might have been sufficient for his purposes. He was aware that he could seek further analysis in L.A.

As he left, we shook hands. He said, "You have changed my life!" and asked if he could keep in touch. I said certainly, but made no specific request of him. I wished him the best.

Follow-up

Four months after completing his treatment, Cory bumped into me at the opera in Norfolk. He was visiting his parents, and was glad to see me. Just after that, he dropped me a letter from overseas in which he described his new girl friend, Shirley, with whom he was traveling: professional, attractive, and loving. He was feeling competitive at work, and enjoying his sex life with his girl friend. They had common interests in art, travel, and wishes for a family.

A communication from him four years later indicated that he and Shirley had broken up after about two years. He dated other women, but got together with Shirley again, and after a year of more courtship, they had just become engaged. A Christmas card from Cory after eight years revealed his joy in the fourth year of their marriage; Shirley was pregnant.

Discussion

When I first met Cory, helping him to change from homosexuality to heterosexuality was the furthest thing from my mind. His homosexual behavior, feelings, and fantasies seemed pathologically entwined in his self-esteem regulation, social functioning, and defensive activity. His identity seemed to have consolidated around homosexuality over the ten previous years, although he had had a period of bisexuality before that.

Because of the entrenchment of his homosexual orientation in his personality, and its enormous secondary elaboration into his social activities and even professional development, I thought his homosexual orientation was there to stay.

A couple of years of prior treatment in Boston had helped him to settle on a lover (Gustav), and to tone down his promiscuity.

However, promiscuous sexuality was handy for him, easy and familiar, and even toward the end of his analytic work with me, there
were still many episodes of quick gay pickups for orgastic discharge.

This case may be less unusual than one might think. Cory's
history was traumatic, and shocking, but the analytic literature is
replete with examples of similar cases of "borderline" childhood
(Masterson, 1971; Blum, 1974). Although childhood sexual trauma
does not necessarily result in homosexuality (Meers [1975] describes a type of hyperheterosexuality in sexually traumatized ghetto
youth), the preoedipal Type II homosexuals (Socarides, 1988) tend
to have had extraordinarily overstimulating and frightening backgrounds.

To complicate matters, it is well known that some people ob-
sess about ego-dystonic homosexual fantasies or activities. In those
patients, the compromise formations causing the obsessional fantasies are analyzable over a period of time, leading to relief from the
homosexual preoccupations. More recently, there has been a focus
on entrenched homosexual men who seem to need a brief psychotherapy approach to focus on particular conflicts. These patients
may utilize some analytic insight without any notion of their shifting
in sexual orientation.

Cory's shift in sexual orientation was remarkable since he had
been a proactive homosexual man, apparently consolidated in his
identity. Surprisingly, Cory turned out to be analyzable (with modifications of technique for the first two years) and he dramatically
shifted his sexual orientation.

Another remarkable feature was Cory's considerable object
hunger, in spite of his narcissism and anxiety about mistrust. The
object hunger and his suffering both led him to continue treatment,
where many other patients probably would have requested less contact, persistent medication, and more distance from the analyst.

The Appendix contains transcriptions of my notes from about
twenty sessions before and after his "conversion," which occurred
between sessions #497 and 499. The notes afford a more in-depth
look at specifics of the analytic work that immediately led up to the
change, and what happened afterwards. The theoretical questions
include (1) how much of the shift was due to analysis of his conflicts; (2) how much was due to what Socarides calls "decoding the

perverse symptom," and (3) how much was due to Cory's attempts to identify with me or please me.

Further, did Cory's homosexuality represent a regression from and a substitution for whole-object relations? When I first saw him, he was narcissistic and had only part-object relationships. He seemed to improve in this area during his treatment, suggesting that the homosexuality was a modifiable compromise formation that included regression as a defense.

Those who have studied homosexuality offer quite varying opinions regarding the etiology and treatability of the condition. Although Socarides has come under attack from gay theoreticians, his proposed nosology of homosexual types (1988) into schizo-homosexuality, preoedipal homosexuality Types I and II, and oedi-pal homosexuality, remains the most comprehensive attempt to distinguish diagnostically between clinical presentations. Socarides describes psychotic individuals as suffering with ego defects in inte-gration, abstraction, and reality testing. He further separates the preoedipal types by the severity of the conflicts surrounding separa-tion-individuation (Kramer and Akhtar, 1988) and ego strength. Oe-dipal types have traversed those early infantile phases and the etiology of their conditions is more akin to neurotic development (Freud, 1926).

Socarides's formulations regarding the origin of homosexuality follow the studies of Stoller (1968), Mahler (1968; Mahler, Pine, and Bergman, 1975), Kernberg (1975), Money and Ehrhardt (1972), and Volkan (1987). Intrapsychic dynamics *causing* the development of homosexuality, although not pursued by Freud (1905, p. 146) were clearly and succinctly demonstrated by C. Brenner and other members of the Kris Study Group (1975), and have more recently been delineated by Dickes (1983, 1991), Siegel (1988, 1991), and Levine (1990, 1991). John Frosch has described eloquently the dy-namic relationships between homosexuality and psychosis (1981, 1983, 1991), and Freedman (1991) has elucidated the identification processes so crucial in understanding homosexuality.

My own contribution to the topic (1991a) revolves around my discovery that ego weaknesses (in affect tolerance, impulse control or containing primary process thinking) can take on gender symbol-ism, with weakness becoming unconsciously equated with feminin-ity. The homosexual man's interest in incorporating a penis then becomes a concretely acted out attempt to find ego strength (Socarides, 1974; Goldberg, 1993).

Regarding treatment, Loeb (1991) details successful psychoanalysis of an oedipal homosexual man. Rich (1991) describes managing the dangerous "cruising compulsion" also addressed by Calef and Weinshel (1984). Ira Brenner (1991) further explicates the dynamics in homosexual men who unconsciously wish to develop AIDS. Successful psychoanalytic treatment of homosexual men, initially reported by Socarides (1969), has more recently been described by Myers (1991), R. Stolorow and Trop (1991), and Volkan and Greer (1991).

Isay (1985, 1986, 1987), Roughton (1997), and Friedman (1997) maintain that homosexuality is immutable. They have alleged that "straight" psychoanalysts, influenced by homophobic pressures, both intrapsychically and environmentally, have been too ardent in "labeling" homosexuality as an illness to be treated. These authors theorize that homosexuality represents a different line of development heavily influenced by innate, though vague, biological factors. Countering such criticisms, Macintosh's (1994) elegant study clearly shows that psychoanalysts as a group are extraordinarily ecumenical and neutral regarding anyone's *need* to change sexual orientation. Furthermore, the therapeutic approach used by the majority of psychoanalysts reflects no professional or personal investment whatsoever in the eventual sexual orientation of an analysand.

Although one could leave these controversies as being about experts who agree to disagree, there is a profound issue that would thereby be ignored. Cory, during his analysis, revealed that he had fervent wishes to be heterosexual, have a wife and children, *if he were able*. He felt, however, that this was an impossibility because he was sexually stimulated in relation to males. To me, that set of thoughts represents intrapsychic conflict. Therefore, if ego functions and object relations are sufficient, psychoanalysis would be the treatment of choice. If one viewed his homosexuality as immutable and biological, the best he could do would be to adapt to a compromise formation that left his own wishes and desires unintegrated with his functioning.

It is not scientific to establish an entire theory of mental functioning based on one case. This is a criticism that has become popular of late in attacking psychoanalytic theory and practice. However, it may be that if more cases like Cory's can be studied, included within the breadth of case material already available from the practices of many psychoanalysts, the various theories we utilize in our therapeutic work can be given an even more rigorous test.

In the case of Cory, the factors that led to his homosexuality were many. First, he had developed severe oral deprivation, apparently because of a somewhat emotionally nonattuned, unsoothing mother. He apparently had difficulty establishing an identity separate from hers, since separateness brought with it the fears of his violent, alcoholic father hurting or killing him. His identification with his mother in the most primitive sense (having a vagina in fantasy, to gain the "power of the pussy"), therefore served the purposes of obtaining oral soothing, preventing loss of life, and protecting him from castration by the father.

The failures in separation and in soothing, in my opinion, seem to have left him with ego weaknesses (Socarides, 1978; Blackman, 1991b). By the time he was 4, he had witnessed frank sexual activity in the trailer, and I feel these experiences further weakened his developing capacities for containment of primary process and impulse control, by frequently producing in him a state of emotional disequilibrium. Add to these developmental problems the rape by his brothers during latency, and the picture so often seen in sexually abused children appears: ego damage and object-relations delay (Green, 1978; Blackman, 1991b). In addition, the intense, chronic rage created by these traumas leads to the development of the defense constellations of turning passive to active (at times provoking punishment), undoing of superego fairness, projective blaming, and generalization, to name a few. Fantasies of becoming a "pretend girl," à la Cory, serve a large variety of defensive and drive-related purposes.

As abstract thinking develops, various intellectualizations may take hold, such as the belief that all homosexuality is normal. Moreover, orgastic discharge can be used as a tranquilizer, as Cory used it. That type of masturbation in gay or straight adolescents may signal psychopathology (Marcus and Francis, 1975), although moderate masturbation is usually not considered pathological.

Arguendo, Cory received modified classical psychoanalytic treatment. I looked to establish a frame and a reality-based working alliance. I addressed resistances coming from the id and the ego that threatened to destroy the analytic alliance. To further enhance the alliance, during the psychotherapy phase, I also supported his ego by making suggestions to help him control impulses that were both self-destructive and destructive to the treatment.

Later, I investigated the defensive and drive-related meanings of his various problems, including his work inhibition, his anger, his difficulty establishing friendships, and finally his conflicts over his sexual identity. In the process, material from all psychosexual levels eventually came into the work, both as a focus and as they operated as regressive defenses. Separation–individuation pathology was handled analytically, utilizing some ideas about the "bipersonal field" (Langs, 1976) and the "intersubjective" experience (D. S. Stolorow and R. Stolorow, 1989; R. Stolorow and Trop, 1991; Jacobs, 1991). Identity issues were interpreted along the lines established by Mahler et al. (1975), Blos (1962), and Erikson (1968).

At no time was pressure brought to bear on the patient regarding his sexual orientation. Prejudices and distortions of his were dealt with analytically. Occasional self-disclosures, for example that I was married and had a child, and that I taught at the medical school, although apparently supportive, seemed to operate as confrontations of several of his prejudicial feelings (that married life was boring, or that having "2.5 children" was stultifying). Further, my "analytic" interventions no doubt had the "supportive" effect of eventually indicating to him that I did not share his biases regarding relationships or marriage.

Finally, although I did not in any way encourage him to be gay or straight, I did not discourage or object to his wish to get married and have children, and I did not agree with him that such an outcome was impossible. My impression is that some of my attitudes regarding these issues had some effect on him, though quantitating them is difficult. The detail in the Appendix, which follows, will allow the reader to consider how the analytic process effected Cory's change in sexual orientation.

References

Blackman, J. (1991a), Instinctualization of ego functions and ego defects in homosexual men: Implications for psychoanalytic treatment. In:

The Homosexualities and the Therapeutic Process, ed. C. Socarides & V. Volkan. Madison, CT: International Universities Press,
pp. 148–158.
———— (1991b), Intellectual dysfunction in abused children. *Acad. Fo-
rum,* 35(1,2):7–10.
Blos, P. (1962), *On Adolescence.* New York: Free Press.
Blum, H. P. (1974), The borderline childhood of the wolf man. *J. Amer.
Psychoanal. Assn.,* 22:721–742.
Brenner, C. (1975), Alterations in defenses during psychoanalysis. In: *Kris
Study Group of the New York Psychoanalytic Institute,* Monograph
6. New York: International Universities Press.
Brenner, I. (1991), The unconscious wish to develop AIDS: A case report.
In: *The Homosexualities and the Therapeutic Process,* ed. C. Socar-
ides & V. Volkan. Madison, CT: International Universities Press,
pp. 251–276.
Calef, V., & Weinshel, E. (1984), Anxiety and the restitutional function
of homosexual cruising. *Internat. J. Psycho-Anal.,* 65:45–54.
Dickes, R. (1983), Review of *Homosexuality,* by C. W. Socarides. *Psychoanal. Quart.,* 52:285–288.
———— (1991), Observations on the treatment of homosexual patients. In:
The Homosexualities and the Therapeutic Process, ed. C. Socarides & V. Volkan. Madison, CT: International Universities Press,
pp. 9–27.
Erikson, E. (1968), *Identity: Youth and Crisis.* London: Faber & Faber.
Freedman, A. (1991), Identification processes in the therapy of male oedi-
pal homosexuality. In: *The Homosexualities and the Therapeutic
Process,* ed. C. Socarides & V. Volkan. Madison, CT: International
Universities Press, pp. 159–190.
Freud, S. (1905), Three Essays on the Theory of Sexuality. *Standard Edition,* 7:123–243. London: Hogarth Press, 1953.
———— (1926), Inhibitions, Symptoms, and Anxiety. *Standard Edition,*
20:75–172. London: Hogarth Press, 1959.
Friedman, R. (1997), Review of *Affirmative Dynamic Therapy with Gay
Men,* ed. C. Cornett. *Psychoanal. Quart.,* 65:827–829.
Frosch, J. (1981), The role of unconscious homosexuality in the paranoid
constellation. *Psychoanal. Quart.,* 50:587–613.
———— (1983), *The Psychotic Process.* Madison, CT: International Universities Press.
———— (1991), Homosexuality and psychosis. In: *The Homosexualities
and the Therapeutic Process,* ed. C. Socarides & V. Volkan. Madison, CT: International Universities Press, pp. 29–45.
Goldberg, A. (1993), Sexualization and desexualization. *Psychoanal.
Quart.,* 62:383–399.

Green, A. (1978), Psychiatric treatment of abused children. *J. Amer. Acad. Child & Adol. Psychiatry,* 17:356–371.

Hartmann, H. (1939), Psychoanalysis and the concept of health. In: *Essays on Ego Psychology.* New York: International Universities Press, pp. 1–18.

Isay, R. (1985), On the analytic therapy of homosexual men. *The Psychoanalytic Study of the Child,* 40:235–254. New Haven, CT: Yale University Press.

——— (1986), The development of sexual identity in homosexual men. *The Psychoanalytic Study of the Child,* 41:467–490. New Haven, CT: Yale University Press.

——— (1987), Fathers and their homosexually inclined sons in childhood. *The Psychoanalytic Study of the Child,* 42:275–294. New Haven, CT: Yale University Press.

Jacobs, T. (1991), *The Use of the Self. Countertransference and Communication in the Analytic Situation.* Madison, CT: International Universities Press.

Kernberg, O. (1975), *Borderline Conditions and Pathological Narcissism.* Northvale, NJ: Jason Aronson.

Kramer, S., & Akhtar, S. (1988), The developmental context of internalized preoedipal object relations—Clinical applications of Mahler's theory of symbiosis and separation-individuation. *Psychoanal. Quart.,* 57:547–576.

Langs, R. (1976), *The Bipersonal Field.* New York: Jason Aronson.

Levine, H., Ed. (1990), *Adult Analysis and Childhood Sexual Abuse.* Hillsdale, NJ: Analytic Press.

——— (1991), The narcissistic imperative and therapeutic alliance in the opening phase of the analytic treatment of male homosexuals. In: *The Homosexualities and the Therapeutic Process,* ed. C. Socarides & V. Volkan. Madison, CT: International Universities Press, pp. 97–108.

Loeb, F. (1991), The psychoanalytic treatment of an oedipal male homosexual. In: *The Homosexualities and the Therapeutic Process,* ed. C. Socarides & V. Volkan. Madison, CT: International Universities Press, pp. 191–206.

Macintosh, H. (1994), Attitudes and experiences of psychoanalysts in analyzing homosexual patients. *J. Amer. Psychoanal. Assn.,* 42:1183–1208.

Mahler, M. S. (1968), *On Human Symbiosis and the Vicissitudes of Individuation.* New York: International Universities Press.

——— Pine, F., & Bergman, A. (1975), *The Psychological Birth of the Human Infant.* New York: Basic Books.

Marcus, I., & Francis, J. (1975), *Masturbation from Infancy to Senescence.* New York: International Universities Press.

Masterson, J. F. (1971), Treatment of the adolescent with borderline syndrome. *Bull. Menninger Clin.,* 35:5–18.

Meers, D. (1975), Precocious heterosexuality and masturbation: Sexuality and the ghetto. In: *Masturbation from Infancy to Senescence,* ed. I. Marcus & J. Francis. New York: International Universities Press, pp. 411–438.

Money, J., & Ehrhardt, A. (1972), *Man and Woman, Boy and Girl.* Baltimore: Johns Hopkins University Press.

Myers, W. (1991), The course of treatment of a case of photoexhibitionism in a homosexual male. In: *The Homosexualities and the Therapeutic Process,* ed. C. Socarides & V. Volkan. Madison, CT: International Universities Press, pp. 241–250.

Rich, H. (1991), Homosexual cruising compulsion. In: *The Homosexualities and the Therapeutic Process,* ed. C. Socarides & V. Volkan. Madison, CT: International Universities Press, pp. 227–240.

Roughton, R. E. (1997), Review of *Becoming Gay: The Journey to Self-Acceptance,* by R. Isay. *J. Amer. Psychoanal. Assn.,* 45:293–298.

Siegel, E. (1988), *Female Homosexuality: Choice Without Volition—A Psychoanalytic Study.* Hillsdale, NJ: Analytic Press.

———— (1991), The search for the vagina in homosexual women. In: *The Homosexualities and the Therapeutic Process,* ed. C. Socarides & V. Volkan. Madison, CT: International Universities Press, pp. 47–74.

Socarides, C. W. (1969), Psychoanalytic therapy of a male homosexual. *Psychoanal. Quart.,* 38:173–194.

———— (1974), Homosexuality. In: *American Handbook of Psychiatry,* Vol. 3, 2nd ed., ed. S. Arieti. New York: Basic Books, pp. 291–315.

———— (1978), *Homosexuality.* New York: Jason Aronson.

———— (1988), *The Preoedipal Origins and Psychoanalytic Therapy of Sexual Perversions.* New York: International Universities Press.

Stoller, R. (1968), *Sex and Gender,* Vol. 1. New York: Science House.

———— Herdt, G. (1982), The development of masculinity: A cross-cultural contribution. *J. Amer. Psychoanal. Assn.,* 30:29–59.

Stolorow, D. S., & Stolorow, R. (1989), My brother's keeper: Intensive treatment of a case of delusional merger. *Internat. J. Psycho-Anal.,* 70:315–326.

Stolorow, R., & Trop, J. (1991), Homosexual enactments. In: *The Homosexualities and the Therapeutic Process,* ed. C. Socarides & V. Volkan. Madison, CT: International Universities Press, pp. 207–226.

Volkan, V. (1987), *Six Steps in the Treatment of the Borderline Personality Disorder.* Northvale, NJ: Jason Aronson.

———— Greer, W. (1991), Transitional phenomena and anal narcissism controlling the relationship with representations of the mother and the father: The transference in a case of latent homosexuality. In: *The Homosexualities and the Therapeutic Process,* ed. C. Socarides & V. Volkan. Madison, CT: International Universities Press, pp. 109–142.

Waugaman, R. M. (1987), Falling off the couch. *J. Amer. Psychoanal. Assn.,* 35:861–876.

Appendix:
Termination Phase Sessions (#470–522)

The sessions described below begin in February. Cory had been in treatment almost four years and would be leaving town in June. The material at the time of the shift in sexual orientation is detailed in Sessions 497, 498, and 499.

470.   Cory presented a dream:

> I'm on an airplane. It gets hijacked. I knew it would be flying in the clouds. Men hijacked it. They got on the plane. It landed in a field where my parents live. They didn't notice. It went into a hangar. I was getting off the plane and I had to urinate. There was a bed in the bathroom. But a place to hide under the bed. I was hiding from the hijackers. I *enjoyed* the whole thing and somehow felt sexual attraction to the hijackers.

Cory associated to unprotected sex. He had good job interviews, but flunked an exam. His use of alcohol was self-destructive. He argued with an administrator at the law school. He wanted attention.

I commented that his failing and drinking symbolized his yelling to the world that he was in pain. He responded, "I really, really, really can't drink." While drunk, he had picked up a man at a bar who robbed him. In the dream, getting on planes was "going down in flames": failing exams. Gustav, who was HIV+, had started getting infections, and could bring him down.

Cory wanted me to "say some incantation" to relieve his "desperately lonely feeling." He felt no one cared about him—he might as well kill himself by getting HIV or getting mugged. Sex and drugs relieved his loneliness. To relieve guilt, he told friends he was in bad shape. He thought how he drove people away.

I told him there were questions about (1) what led him to still obtain relief in self-destructive activity; (2) what was interfering with his concentration; and (3) what interfered with his acceptance of an "establishment" identity by graduating.

He focused on becoming professional. His recent job interviewers had taken him seriously, which "freaked me out," because "I'm too fucked up." He taunted me to free associate.

I responded that he was trying to get me to help him avoid his own coerciveness: that his concentration "problem" was a symbolic way of avoiding work and getting me to do it for him.

Cory responded: "I wore my mother down until I would just take whatever I wanted. I guess I'm doing that with you, too. I don't want to do unpleasant things all the time! I wish to magically have everything, but not work for it. It's tedious, and boring. I want you to make it easy for me here. It's okay for me to go into law, but I'd rather go to Europe, eat, and do nothing, even though that's boring."

At this point, Cory flipped over on the couch and looked at me. When I said he seemed "curious," he laughed and said, "Fuck you!" I clarified that his behavior was rebellious, stubborn, and grandiose. He flipped back over.

Cory joked that he was nice except when he saw me. He connected drinking to "I hate having to be nice all the time. Are you that rigid?"

Feeling that he was still rebelling by turning the tables, I commented, "You're still at it." Cory said, sarcastically, "Any more compliments? Can we go faster?"

Cory seemed to fight integrating my interventions, I thought due to aggressivization of his integrative function causing defensive stubbornness. I commented, "You don't seem to want to listen to anybody, and would rather avoid your conflicts."

Cory said he would rather kill himself than become "an obedient parasite." He didn't want to become professional, "a good old boy." He preferred "to shock people," to drive everybody away; then he felt alone.

Cory complained, "You don't talk to me. You're like my family. You don't notice I'm getting fucked up the ass."

471. Regarding his antiestablishmentarianism, Cory recognized he had been rationalizing in believing that "being selfish, manipulative,

violent, and thinking that sticking my penis here, there, and every-where, being wild, drinking and outrageous behavior is normal! I'm changing."

He found himself becoming more "diligent and respectful," but "stuck between two worlds. In my new world, people trust each other. But my old friends used drugs and got into assault and went to jail. I'm not the first Cinderella in the world, but I don't like judgments." Los Angeles would be the "new world," where he felt like a fish out of water, because "in the old world, when it came to fucking and getting fucked, nobody was better at it than me."

Cory again demanded I talk. I asked if he was trying to irritate me. Cory responded with sarcasm, "I can be anything I want. You wouldn't ignore your own son!"

He toyed with not paying me, but feared I would kick him out. I felt somewhat insulted and then thought he was projecting and devaluing me because of his pain. So I asked, "Do you think I'm a prostitute?" He immediately said he did not think so, rationally, but that he felt this way. I interpreted his projecting onto me and generalizing protected himself from anxiety about being close and trusting me.

Cory responded, "If you've been screwed as much as me, you wouldn't trust either. I don't think I need guidance, but I want it! I want to put you in my pocket. You be my auxiliary brain and you tell me what to do in the new world." His father could not show him "a damn thing," except to "rob, steal, drink, use drugs, and fuck." He derided his upbringing as "a soap opera." He then at-tacked me: "You let me drift off course!" I interpreted that he was looking for guidance because he did not trust me. Cory wanted proof I was "there, listening, and understanding." He added, "I find your voice soothing. *I dream of your voice.* If you don't talk, you've disappeared. That's childish!"

Cory began crying. I responded, "You're doing good analytic work." Cory replied, "I want to fuck it up, so I can become a lawn mower. I want to cry more." He thought not studying was "rebel-ling against myself."

I interpreted further that by not studying, he deprived himself and expressed anger that I was not a better father to him. He re-sponded, "No one has ever been there."

472.   Cory had called me at home between last session and today, because he was fighting studying. I had reassured him we would continue working on it. In session, he now feared he had a brain disease; I interpreted that that might be easier than admitting he was not studying. He added he had "self-destructively" smoked pot.

He "wished for oblivion: You don't get it! I don't trust you or anybody. A joint or a blow job gets rid of the pain, but the price of getting rid of it . . . I don't think marijuana is so bad."

I pointed out he was rationalizing/minimizing his drug abuse. Cory confirmed, "It puts me into oblivion." He noted he had previously "rebelled" by telling his parents he went to sex clubs.

He saw "a reality need to settle in and study. It finally sunk in." His last anxiety attack had occurred when "I called you when I flunked that course. I hadn't even realized I hadn't studied enough."

He revealed that yesterday he had "sex" with a "sweet boy." He could have robbed the guy, but wanted the "mutual caressing." He started to have anal sex without a condom. He paused; I allowed myself a countertransference response by telling him that his sexual behavior was dangerous. Cory said, "There are ways I feel you are steering me. Like away from pot, and away from sex with random strangers. I want to leave the old world, but there are some things I like. Your life must be utterly boring! You don't do anything impulsive or dangerous or passionate or illegal. Why not do something dangerous and new? Hop in the sack with someone you don't know! Smoke a joint! Get into oblivion! Make some jokes! Think differently, do something unexpected. That would be fun." He was sure I had a predictable, boring life. In comparison, "traveling, fucking somebody new, I can never tell what's going to happen."

I thought Cory was projecting and turning passive to active, so I interpreted that managing danger and living through it made him feel "big, powerful, and like you can survive." Also, since he did not feel stable, he unconsciously attempted to destabilize me with jolting criticisms. Cory corrected me: his "jolting" me was done consciously.

473.   Cory "obsessed" over blond, "normal" boys, that is, not homosexual. He still had difficulty studying. I interpreted that he symbolically wished to magically absorb their normal brains to

avoid the deprivation of studying. He imagined the boys had helpful professional fathers.

Regarding the previous session, he thought mastering danger made him know who he was. He associated "carrying a bubble of dangerousness since childhood. It's awful to go through this!''

474.   He was studying better, but angry his parents went to the ballet without him. He wondered if I thought they were weird. He felt they tried to hurt him.

I inquired about his wish for my opinion. He said, ''You understood what I went through as a kid. It wasn't pleasant for you either, to hear about it. I'm not being like a jealous kid who wants to climb in bed between my parents. *They are mean!* My mother would blame me for being spoiled, and I wanted to say to her, ''Was that before or after I got fucked up the ass when I was 5 years old!'' Yesterday, about the boys' brains, ''It's really a wish to incorporate, somehow, normalcy! Maybe innocence, since I never had it.''

By way of empathy, I mentioned the *Songs of Innocence* by William Blake, with which he was familiar.

Cory wanted to be like a ''normal'' gay ''friend,'' who had once driven Cory home after drinking. To sever ties with his family, Cory would go to Los Angeles to work.

He wished he had been an innocent boy: ''I want positive attention from a man that I never got, as opposed to rape and abuse. Also, I wish to identify with him.'' But his identity was ''tied up with danger and violence and the underworld. That's not the whole story. Why I continue to create a dangerous world for myself and then live through it (like risking getting HIV and getting raped) must be to master it.''

I said he saw himself as ''the guy who surmounts all this.'' He concurred. He had known abuse. He said, ''If I got HIV, I'd have an illness, to show outwardly how ill I feel inside. People'd understand how much I'm suffering.''

Cory wanted professional identity. He now reported a dream about his brother, Todd, who had gotten killed on a motorcycle ten years prior: ''I was working for him and oddly enough, I'm going to bed with women. I was screwing these girls. I was doing construction work. I was feeling I was content, secure, and he was proud and liked my work.''

Todd and he had watched pornography together. He remem-
bered that Todd and another man had once picked up two girls.
When Cory walked in, one girl left and had sex with Cory. Later,
Todd threw him on the ground.

Cory thought the dream represented the pride and love he
wanted from Todd. Cory was closest with Todd. Cory's older
brother "loved to fuck me," and his mother "loved to fuck me,
but differently."

When Cory beat up Dawn, her father beat up Cory. Cory told
Todd and Todd beat up that father. Cory described Todd as "my
protector."

Cory asked me to interpret something, but I said nothing. He
continued, "How hurt I was, I thought it would hurt you. I'd be
glad. If I slammed your hand in the door of a car, I'd be glad.
Somebody would understand the pain. You said to me that you
understood it was not a lot of fun."

475.   Cory, crying, complained I was "mean" to him yesterday. I
interpreted his transference to me from the mother and father who
never understood him. He then recalled "telling my mother for
years that my father didn't love me. She would always say, 'He
feeds you!' "

I clarified his gratitude yesterday, followed by angry mistrust
toward me. Cory recalled his father being generous to everyone
else: "I can't show that I'm smarter than my father. My father
thinks I'm calling him stupid when I disagree, and flies into a rage.
I was constantly afraid I would be thrown out and be homeless, in
the streets. My parents let people come into my bedroom and abuse
me when I was just a child!"

I connected these memories with his fear that I would throw
him out.

476.   Cory reported the "bad news": he had unsafe homosexual
sex and snorted cocaine with his brother. The "good news": he
had "significant insights." He was competitive with his father and
never loved him. Neither Sandy [his girl friend from college] nor
Gustav wanted him: "I want love from people who don't want to
give it. I wished for love from my father, and if I couldn't get it I

felt it was my fault because I was unlovable. I wound up feeling that my wish for my father to love me was unreasonable.''

Regarding Gustav, "I became unlovable and abusive myself as an adult. I went from feeling unlovable to making myself unlovable.'' He asked me to talk. I interpreted that he tried to prove he did not need his father's love, but at the same time tried to evoke it. Asking me to speak indicated similar conflicting feelings toward me.

Cory agreed. He had called Gustav for "sadomasochism,'' because "I'm uncomfortable to think of a mutual, caring relationship with a man. It's safer to think everything is sadomasochistic and extractive.''

At a bar, he picked up a "big Navy sailor,'' didn't want sex but felt obligated. His pickups were "stray animals. I take them home and feed them and then do their bidding. But I screwed him in the ass without a condom.''

477.   Cory's car was towed. He had throat pain, probably from cocaine. He had gone to the doctor and got antibiotics. He thought cocaine use was masochistic—it hurt him. He described his father as a sadist and his mother as a masochist. He recalled a friend who "likes to be kicked and spat on and shat on. My love relationships are sadomasochistic. Now I have a parking ticket.''

Cory thought "one part of me punishes the other parts of me.'' Drugs and unsafe sex were punishments. I inquired what he was being punished for, and he said, "Faults I thought my father would not love me for. My weaknesses. My rage and my guilt.''

Cory then claimed he was "horny,'' and when I explored his use of the term, he said, "receptive to oral sex.'' The thought of a retarded girl being raped by 17-year-old boys made him feel "awful,'' for unclear reasons. He was back to having trouble studying.

I interpreted that studying made him lonely, and to relieve the tension, he fantasized oral sex. He thought being raped would get "love from someone. Something makes me do these things and I can't seem to stop it! It's like a monster. I don't even feel you can help me. It's like the parking tickets. It's painful. I'd rather be dead. I feel like I'm beyond repair.''

I commented that this was a familiar feeling. He responded, "Like in childhood.''

478.   Cory felt women were "catty, oriented to details that don't mater," whereas men were "harder, more easy going, less petty."

He felt like one of the guys by becoming an attorney. Alternately, he might "end up with Gustav et al., who are essentially women."

Women liked soap operas but men "cut through the bullshit and get to what matters." Women were "mushy and not courageous," whereas men would "look at what's important." Men "like to talk about women who love to fuck." Men were strong and "bad company."

479.   Cory saw me as a "sadist and women are masochists," because they "passively let life happen to them. Men and women can both be masochistic. Underhandedly I'm sadistic, and I enjoy it."

He had been sadistic to both Dawn and Gustav. He commented, "I guess that discounts my theory of the difference between men and women! They were both masochists."

Cory reported "feeling a little different already," not needing S&M in his relationships with traffic court, family, and friends.

He saw sex as "to rape or be raped." However, he desired "mutual sharing, not mutual torture." He was jealous of Sandy's boyfriend. He then revealed recent masturbation fantasies: "I'm fucking somebody's wife in front of him. The man is enticing me to fuck his wife. He is cooperating, and he is involved sexually. The woman is giving him a blow job, and then I'm giving him a blow job."

Cory commented, "I'm fertile with my imagination." Because of his "wish to have children," he envied women's childbearing ability: "I want to do it without anyone else involved." Contrarily, "It's nothing deep. It's just that if I were a woman, I could go to the sperm bank."

He associated, "I would just be a man with a vagina." I interpreted that he could then have children and still have a penis. Cory laughingly imagined telling Sandy, "You can be the bridesmaid." I interpreted Cory's wish to be a weak woman as protective. He laughed: "I have the fertile imagination! You give up the goddamn seed!" I clarified, "In the fantasy, first you fuck the guy's wife and then he cooperates. Then you wish to be a woman." Cory interrupted: "I don't want to be a man as a woman. I envy women, especially the big ugly ones with nice men. Somehow I wish to be a masochist: after I torture them, they would torture me.''

I contrasted these fantasies as defensive, and explored their meaning. Cory said, ''I don't like women. Being one would be being what I don't like. But I do like women.

''*I have this grandiose fantasy I could be both.* I do. To be a woman but not without a penis. I would be a pretend woman. Then I'd fuck with a man and get sensual pleasure like a woman. But I don't like being fucked in the ass.'' He ''could fuck women now. I might get over it. I liked getting fucked as a kid. I was having power over them, sort of back-handedly. I wanted to be a man-woman. Liking a woman bothers me. It's a conflict.''

480.   Cory complained of school debt. He passed an exam. He was becoming closer with other students. He associated to a masturbation fantasy: ''I imagine a man on top of me, but I don't have any labia. I guess I wish to be in place of a woman with a man.''

Although Cory was aware of my neutrality regarding his sexual orientation, he stated, ''You probably think it's not good for me to aim at this, but a goal of my life and of my therapy has been to be with a man, on my own. He would have the same IQ level, and he would not be from a fucked-up background. I want to be with a man and I want to go both ways. The rectal sphincter easily accommodates a penis, and it's not painful. I've had my arm up someone's ass. Fucking and being fucked is probably sadomasochistic, but it's only masculine and feminine in a stereotypical way. I'm not in anguish about it. I am interested in the origins of my sadomasochistic impulses. It is weird that I like to rape people. . . .''

Cory thought he had changed socially in class. He no longer said, ''odd things to turn them off.'' I interpreted that he veered away from his sadomasochistic fantasies by focusing on his progress in relationships. Cory responded: ''I'm a full-fledged S&M. Lotions, photos of nude men, and masturbating. I don't want straight pornography. I want penises and mouths and anuses. I want an S& M prostitute.'' Cory then recalled, ''When I was a prostitute in Copenhagen, one of the customers was a sadistic German. I let him tie me up and beat me. Why did I do that?''

I answered, ''There must have been some satisfaction in it.'' Cory responded, ''I didn't feel like a woman.'' I said perhaps the physical suffering may have proved he was not a *sissy* woman.

Cory's father and brothers thought he was a sissy. Cory had tried to prove to them "and to the world" that he was "a man." He felt no need to be a sadist unless he wanted to be—he wanted control, but "I don't mind a yearly foray into the S&M games I like."

He could act like his mother, "to please" his father. In high school, he had not exposed homosexual feelings "because I wanted attention from the boys that I didn't get from my father." He argued that his homosexuality was present before wanting boys, and proferred his theory that he was homosexual "by the age of 2. No. By 18 months I was already patterned."

I remarked that children try to establish an identity separate from their mothers at around 18 months of age. Cory stated, "I want to have an idea that my homosexuality was there when I was born. That justifies it. That way it would not be environmental. That way the homosexuality is not my fault."

481.   Cory was thinking about his identity conflict: gay man versus career. "I want children and I want to raise them myself," but he felt "gay. I don't think I could change that. If I could, I would, but I can't. It's a feeling I've had for all my life. But I've also felt like a piece of shit all my life and I don't like that either."

I clarified he was experiencing homosexuality as more conflictual. Cory responded with a "fantasy as a teen that I would get therapy and be straight." His father didn't love him because he was gay. That made his father hostile and his mother protective. He would feel better if his homosexuality did not come from problems with his father.

I asked what difference it made if his homosexuality were congenital or developmental? He didn't like to "think developmental, because that means your development is fucked up." He had trouble thinking of sex with only one man. It was settled: he was gay, any conflicts were external. "If I were going into interior decorating, it would just be easier."

Cory then observed, "I never wanted to talk about it here. My orientation, my sexuality. It's more natural to discuss drinking and concentration."

He worried that the rest of his life would be a waste. He rationalized: "My urges to fuck around are because I'm horny, lonely, bored and maybe a touch of pathology.'' He might think about his sexuality if he did not know the outcome already. He joked, ''I know it as well as I know the palm of my hand.''

For him, closeness, love, and sex were different with men and women. ''I don't feel the same when I look at men or masturbate. On their back or knees, they are receptive. I don't like hair. The body does make a difference with men. I don't like tall, big-breasted women. I like petite, boyish-looking ones.''

482.   I apologized to Cory for having missed an appointment with him yesterday due to my illness, especially since he had to drive to the office to find out. There had been no way of contacting him, unfortunately. He was ''pissed off'' and suspicious of my explanation, since I had gotten over it ''so quickly.'' He had a series of dreams last night:

> I am in Todd's [the dead brother's] house, talking with his widow. I am talking to her about all sorts of things.
>
> You are there, and you are giving me an appointment. You are writing down in your appointment book what we are going to talk about every day. As you go to write down the appointment times, I look over your shoulder into your appointment book, and your next patient, who is jealous, comes up behind me and starts rubbing his penis up my buns.
>
> It is a long dream where I am on a bus. I am driving, but it's more like a very big bus or a Winnebago. Inside are all these couples, both gay and straight, people I know from my past and my present, particularly from the school. I am the odd man out, though, and I have no one.

He associated that I was the father who didn't protect him from his brother's raping him. He now recalled a fourth dream: ''I am in Professor Z's office, we are at work. Maybe it is there that you were giving me appointment times and the other boy rubbed his penis on me and came on to me. And then it changed into the house we lived in which at the time was in a new neighborhood.''

Cory thought he did not want to talk about living in L.A. He was bored in Norfolk. Los Angeles was ''crazier, wilder, and more interesting.'' He derided a life ''with a wife, 2.5 children, and a station wagon in suburbia.'' He would die from boredom. When I interpreted these as rationalizations because of his anxiety about family life, Cory stuck to his intellectualizations. He then wondered why he was talking about this with me.

I answered that the first dream suggested I symbolized his dead brother, spurred by my absence yesterday. Todd had shown affection to Cory and not sexually abused him. I linked my being "gone" to Cory's masturbating excessively and wishing to "go fuck"—meaning "masturbating in someone else's mouth." He responded that calling Gustav today symbolically replaced his brother. We agreed that his interest in homosexual activity concretely provided him with male attention to stem his grief over Todd, the father/brother who protected him, when I was, similarly, "gone."

483. Driving home from a quick blow job in the park, Cory was arrested on a DWI and thrown in the drunk tank. He initially refused an inhalant alcohol test, but did accede to it later. He was brought to an ER for a blood alcohol level, which made him feel humiliated. He planned to get himself an attorney.

He vaguely enjoyed being thrown in jail, like a game, so he was upset when he couldn't get out of jail right away. I suggested that perhaps the connection with the car had something to do with Todd's motorcycle death.

Cory associated to seeing his other brothers lately. They used to do what he had just done: get drunk, get tickets, and "wind up in the clinker." I interpreted that he behaved masochistically (1) due to identification with his brothers' bad behavior, and (2) due to identification with his loved brother's accident as a way of keeping Todd alive within him (defense against grieving).

Cory agreed, cried, and said he usually feels nothing about Todd. We interpreted together that his life-threatening behavior made him feel alive, as well.

484. Cory got his third choice of jobs. He felt he should have gotten his first choice, and I confronted this as a grandiose defense. Cory responded that there were some sour grapes. He felt closer to classmates, but still worried about his "self-destructive stuff," though "I'm not obligated to risk my life to feel alive."

485. Cory was furious with his mother for giving him a credit card and then complaining how he used it: "It galls me. I'm strapped

for money, she gives me no help, and then invades." He paid her the money back. He complained that his parents "piss away" money.

I clarified that when his father did not give money to Cory, Cory felt hurt. Cory complained that his father never gave, and that his mother "gives with suction cups: she's controlling and manipulative."

He reported "safe" sexual activity last night, to prevent "anger lashing out of me." He would retaliate at his parents by becoming professional and personally capable. I interpreted, "I think your tender feelings get locked away by anger."

Cory stated, "I have emotion about painting, sculpture, and movies. It comes out of me in a spurt. But like a steel plate, I lock it away. I can fake feelings up to a point, but I'll withdraw into a shell so I can say 'so what,' tomorrow." He paused and then stated he didn't trust me, associating to a man in Europe who threatened to stab him. Moreover, "How could I trust someone like my mother, who gives me her credit card and then sticks it up my ass!"

I said Cory seemed to feel raped by his mother. He responded, "I felt raped as a kid, being fucked up the ass. I don't clearly remember all of it or beating up Dawn and going to court about it. I was drunk when I beat her up in her parents' bed." I said I still wasn't clear about that incident. He explained, "We were having intercourse in the missionary position. All of a sudden I punched her in the face and she started crying. She didn't fight back. I'm very embarrassed about this.

"My father held a gun to my mother's head for hours, daring her to move. He dragged her around the house by the hair. He locked her out of the house. She'd sit outside patiently in the rain or snow until he passed out. I guess she was masochistic. My mother is now a sadist. She gets back at him."

I interpreted that Cory's current-day sexual activities shielded him from feelings about his parents. He then remembered crying underneath his bed. At age 3, he hid in his toybox. "I have pictures. I remember the open doorway to my parents' bedroom. For 25 years they lived in a dream. I expect the whole world to torture me. But I won't be caught unawares."

I now interpreted Cory's doing dangerous things was an attempt to master his fear of being caught unawares. Cory responded, "It took hours to get mugged in Boston. I wanted trouble." I said,

"Hm-hm," and Cory responded, "I hate when you 'la de da' me. I want to feel good. I could blubber here, but I'm not going to. Maybe I'll go to bed with a guy or smoke a joint."

486. Cory was fifteen minutes late. He complained his upcoming job was not in a good neighborhood. I confronted his grandiosity, considering he had failed examinations. Cory recognized his success, then fantasized he would walk to work, although he had been advised to drive to their security area.

487. Cory said his mother had told him he was unwanted. She had agreed to get pregnant with a sixth child (Cory) if her husband stopped drinking. She began showing; then the father began drinking again. She complained she could not renege, and later stopped his father from "killing" him. Cory's sister would protect him if Cory was a "pussy—a girl."

I connected his childhood suffering and his wish to be saved with his recent acting out. He wanted me to be a better parent, and save him, while he isolated affect and got drunk as defenses and acted out his wish for protection.

Cory felt upset. He called me later, after crying for two hours. He had a (transference) reaction that I didn't care about him after I had commented that his feelings were painful. He feared I had brushed him off, which reminded him of his mother. I said I had not. He was relieved.

488. Cory felt better today. He faced his drinking and carousing as defenses against sadness over disappointment that his father could not offer love to him.

489. Cory was feeling much better. He clarified the remaining dates of his treatment with me. Regarding his loans, he said, "Mrs. Smith is trying to fuck me. I feel her penis coming close to my ass, but I am not going to let her." He made derogatory remarks about her to a secretary he thought shared his hostility. I said she could crucify him.

He associated making himself the butt of jokes, adding that when people ridiculed him, he felt loved. When he teased me about my baldness, he noted he hoped to provoke a sadistic response from me so he would feel loved.

490.   Cory did well on an exam. He was pleased because he had studied sufficiently. He was having anxiety attacks. In the car, driving to his parents' house, he masturbated to orgasm for relief.

On the way to my office, he had imagined praise from co-workers rather than sex with men, to repair his self-esteem.

He fantasized talking to a 12-year-old boy in my waiting room, imagining something sexual. He said he must be "sexualizing some wish for affection," instead of doing "for some child what was not done for me."

I wondered if his "sexual fantasy" about a child incorporated his wish to have a child. He then expressed a plan of raising a child born to an artificially inseminated lesbian who gives him and a gay lover the child to adopt. He wanted a male child only. This wish plus his plan to avoid marrying a woman indicated, I interpreted, avoidance of females. Cory confirmed he didn't like women, based on his mother.

As Cory was leaving, he asked me for Xanax. Since it was too late to start discussing his request, I hesitated. When he questioned my reluctance, I told him I was hesitating because I needed to get home. He responded, "Well, honesty is the best policy." He left immediately and said he would discuss medication with me to-morrow.

491.   Cory started by asking me, "What's a reaction formation?" I inquired about the basis for his question and he responded that he first felt grateful to me for being honest yesterday. Then he thought, "I wanted to rip your fucking head off!" Cory felt guilty and suspected that was why he felt grateful. He was "nice" to boys sexually, but remembered "my envy of boys who had their heads screwed on straight. I wanted to twist them off!"

I clarified that his feelings were intense, and he responded: "Toward women I'm neutral, except ones like Mrs. Smith." How-ever, he was "abused" by "bigger and more powerful" boys. He was envious of boys who were "not fucked up," and wanted to "fuck them up," literally and figuratively.

With children, he was "overly nice . . . I'm envious and angry at the base. It disgusts me, but I could have sex with children." Cory associated, "My father and brothers are sick puppies." I commented, "Now that statement is a reaction formation." Cory remembered Todd teasing him "mercilessly" and "I was sort of happy when he died. I felt I had caused his death, though. . . . I wished they would all die, and he did. I'm a person who wants to kill and destroy. . . ." I said, "Children." He responded, "Maybe I shouldn't have children. I have my father and my brothers in me."

I clarified his disgust at identifying with them. He responded he had "destructive fantasies before I had asked you for medicine. Why do I want to fuck the whole world? It makes me feel like I'm my father and my brothers."

Cory had been crying in the session. He likened his anger to "popping a zit." His emotions had been "taking up a lot of room. Somehow it all got sexualized. I was being fucked. It hurt. I didn't like it. But I had somebody's arms around me, so if I wanted to like and be liked, I guess it had to be sexual. So my anger is squelched by love for boys, huh? I feel guilty and ashamed and nervous. I want to get rid of it with alcohol or have an orgasm. Is that a reaction formation?"

Cory wanted me to say his violence wasn't his fault. He thought, "I have grandiose fantasies that I will help people. I really want to cut them up. That's why lawyers are assholes."

Cory paused. I commented that this had been an important session. He queried, "How do I get rid of all this venom?" I said it was curious that he referred to himself as a poisonous snake. He responded, "Women are seduced by venomous snakes. Then they in turn seduce us, like Adam. He was destroyed!"

Cory continued, "So that's why I want little boy children, to torture them. Is my homosexuality based on this? No!" He wanted a man unlike Gustav, although, "I love to torture him."

Cory felt drained. He expressed anger at people who "made me feel this way." When people were close or nice to him, "the more I want to rip their head off." He mistrusted people. "I imagine everybody is like me, with reaction formations to destructiveness when they are nice."

492. Cory was angry at Mrs. Smith for "mishandling" his loans. He felt "manipulative and controlling," with Gustav, but more so

with women, "certain boys, and boyish men." He felt depressed over these "horrible wishes."

He felt guilty he was a bit behind in paying my bill due to processing delays. But, "I'd rather put the screws to you, and neither they nor I will pay you." Maybe his insistence that the loan company pay me was a reaction formation, "because I feel people owe me things."

He would have preferred Mrs. Smith to be "nurturing." He did not see his parents. He wanted to get rid of his anger. I pointed out that he avoided his parents to anger them. He responded, "Would they kill someone and get away with it? Would they? I want a more torturous death for them. Would you? What's normal? Is this like a cancer growing? . . . You want to leave, I think. You're bored. I'm angry. I'm bored."

His anger did not "magically disappear because I unlocked Pandora's box. It's a pit of snakes, seething. I don't get close to people. I'm afraid they'd castrate me, kill me, and get me disrupted. It's worse when people get nicer. I want to hurt them and then I feel guilty. And then I get protective toward them.

"Mrs. Smith and my mother dick me around. Mrs. Smith had wanted to be a lawyer, too. So it gratified me to dick her over. I'd like to dick you over too. Why do I want to do that? I also want to dick all my friends at school. *I really want to keep distance but everything is all dicks.* Maybe it's because I was screwed as a kid. It's all wrapped up in penises.

"I have trouble getting close, because I get angry as a defense. Sometimes I think you want to screw me over, like I do. Also, my evil intentions bother me. I really want to choke and decapitate people."

Regarding my changing an appointment time for him, Cory said, "I think it was probably good for you. You wouldn't want to just help me, it would be too much like my mother. Usually I feel stifled and I don't care."

I pointed out, "A way of staying away from wanting to care." He said, "Yeah, I want to pull away and stop you and be bored, but in reality I'd like to be interested."

493.   He was uncomfortable seeing a teenage boy at the beach he fantasied "going to bed with." Cory wanted to hurt himself, "but not due to guilt. I think it's for being gay."

Cory thought of a professor, and about his final paper. Suddenly, he got angry and was frightened of this. I interpreted that anger was hard to handle when it alluded to me (the "professor"). He felt guilty to be hostile to someone who "didn't deserve it, so I deflect it onto myself."

During masturbation, his fantasies were not titilating. He could not find anybody "attractive" to pick up, and took out a lesbian friend. He stopped at the park last night. He got a blow job because he was "horny and lonely." He described a "certain kind of emptiness." The sex "takes away the pathology; it was familiar."

A classmate became "a buddy and friendly." Cory liked being friends, and said he preferred that to "a hundred acquaintances."

His description of the friend suggested displacement of improved object relatedness and of positive transference to me. But, I considered Cory might be splitting off a hostile self-image. I therefore said he seemed to avoid embarrassment over the blow job. He responded he wanted "to rip out the homosexual part of myself. It's because it's hated by society. I'd give my left nut to be straight. Sometimes I think I could live a straight life."

"Now I have an invasive wish to know what you just wrote down." I interpreted that his "invasion" covered up a wish to be friendlier with me. The idea of closeness threw him into a "hostile rage." He associated closeness with "getting fucked. My mother manipulated my life." He complained psychoanalysis was "the slowest way to my problems." He felt a Jung or Horney approach would be quicker because he could "get in and get out."

494.   He skipped class: "self-destructive," and avoidance of being "trapped." He recalled his brother "sitting on me and punching me." He hid in the toybox, or lay in bed, pretending not to breathe, "so various people having sex would not see me."

He felt trapped in his session. He complained about his tuition, that he was not learning anything but that he was partly at fault.

He did not want to graduate: "I don't want change in my life, now that I'm making friends." School was "a fucking waste of time." I said perhaps he also felt that way about his treatment. He responded, "It is like you are invading me and wasting my time. I realize there are people in my life who are trying to help me, but I want to go home to my house, lock the door, eat pizza, and be left alone.''

I commented on his anger, and Cory continued, "I'm wasting my time. I get my shit stirred here and then I feel helpless. I want to crawl in a hole and die. That's how I really feel. Do you like that?'' I pointed out that besides expressing himself, he was attacking me. He said, "How do you like *that?*'' He associated to his sexual activities.

I interpreted that closeness with me stimulated anxiety over being sexually overstimulated as a child, which made him want to hide from me, as he had as a child. He agreed.

495.   Cory said he had gone to class and the professor "didn't want to screw me. He just wanted to help and teach me.'' Cory then reported working for two hours on a paper last night.

He needed permission from Mrs. Smith to use his loan to pay me. Getting permission was being "a pussy.'' He said, "It's my mother trying to fuck me. Put your dick back in your pants! You don't have one! If you did, not on me!'' I said these people with dicks were women.

He exploded: "My sister! The ultimate petty, bureaucratic bitch! For a while I thought I was her child. I'm rebellious against my sister. I think women are either loving and friendly or total bitches.'' Cory then criticized my language. I interpreted his identification with his sister and his projection of his self-image onto me. He associated self-destructiveness.

496.   Cory thought, "You are my penis. Then I think I want a penis from a man instead of identifying with them.'' He thought of a professor who made jokes about "gays and presidents.'' Some people did not guess Cory was gay, because "I'm more aggressive. I don't want to analyze my homosexuality. I don't have time. I feel stifled. But I envy guys that are well adjusted. I can play at being in the world. They don't have the slightest idea about me.''

I clarified that Cory took pride in fooling classmates. He said this was true. "I can't rely on anybody else. People let me down. Over the weekend, I missed being here. The reality was I was capable of relying on people but I was not able to admit it.

"I think I want to suck on your penis. Maybe that's sucking on your brain. Why do I sexualize it?" I interpretively asked him, "Is it less embarrassing to sexualize it?" He responded, "I would be your penis. I don't like the work part. I associate work with my father, and it's painful. I don't get my penis from my father. Why do I sexualize it? I like sex. Do I pay for the attention? Sexualizing is comfortable. I've had experience with it. But it's not like being friends. I want to be friends, but I feel imposed upon if somebody wants to be my friend. What are they after? Then I think of them sexually. But if I expose my friendly wishes, and it gets cut off. . . . I'm not embarrassed or disappointed at a bar. I can just say, 'Want to fuck?' "

He had made contact with some old buddies from college.

497.   I had changed this appointment time for him because of a conflict with his classes. He expressed gratitude to me about this. His DWI charge was dropped. He then reported a dream:

> I'm having a party in a room attached to the house that I used to live in. There's a room beyond and a garden. My friend had decorated it like with Tiffany lamps. I liked the gaudiness.
>
> I'm going to have a floor show in the room in front. My mother, father, sister, and brother are going to the show. I have a party in the garden. I do both, have a garden party and a show.
>
> I'm in the room showering, talking to someone I don't know, who was weird. It had happened. . . . No, I had dreamed it before, but now it was really happening: I saw my family members coming through the garden and they didn't see me. As they arrive, I'm showering for the party with other people. This was very disturbing.

Cory wished to have a beautiful house to torture his family and friends with his success. Cory wanted to be like me: "have nicer things in my life." He hated women in the professions.

He compared Alan Alda as the Hawkeye Pierce character in *M*A*S*H* to Frank, the petty physician. Frank was more female, Hawkeye Pierce more male. Alan Alda was not gay, but "a whole man."

Following this, Cory stated with a sigh, "My overall wish is to be a man! No, a woman!" I spontaneously responded to him, with some irony, "I have a solution for you: Why don't you be gay?'' Cory laughed, "Is that what this is all about? Yeah, being gay is, I guess, a little bit of being a man and a little bit of being a woman, the way I think about it. Well, if I become a lawyer, I don't care. Now I have a crappy car and furniture, but I'll have nice things. It's not important.''

I interpreted that the dream indicated conflict over his wish to have nice things. He thought of Nietzsche's theory of "an effeminate, priestly class—they become meek, mild priests. Real men get what they want!'' Cory thought maybe he wanted to be "altruistic.'' I interpreted that his rationalizations about altruism avoided exposing his embarrassing hunger. He then thought he had wanted a rich man his own age, like Aaron.

498.   See pp. 55–56 of the text of this paper (above).

499.   Cory worried about telling a woman in the future about his homosexual past: the whole sordid story? I said that his past was past, and was his own business to a certain extent. He considered this, then thought that he could mention to her that he had a period of homosexuality which was resolved in analytic treatment. He recognized that "spilling the whole story would be a way of trying to get a woman to 'feel' for me.''

He thought sex with a woman was "cleaner,'' sex with a man was "dirtier and more brutish.'' He felt heightened sexual stimulation by women.

500.   Cory mentioned finishing treatment with me. He presented two dreams: "(1) I'm in L.A. and I meet a woman. She's a self-assured person. I want to go out with her. I ask her and she accepts. (2) I had intercourse with Dawn (the girl I had beaten up), and there's nothing weird about it.''

He felt "weird'' having dreams of sex with women. He recalled at his parents' house recently, his father criticized him. He then recalled a third dream:

> I'm at a strip mall near where I grew up. I had to go to the bathroom. Then, I'm getting a blow job from my nephew in the 69 position. I didn't want to. A woman walked by, saw us, and frowned. I feel guilty getting a blow job and not giving. I thought my penis was big.

A boy I loved at college—I had him upside down with his crotch in my face. He had on women's tights, like aerobics clothes. It was a pleasure. I was kissing his inner thigh. I got a warm, fuzzy feeling. He was close. I took out his penis and put it in his mouth. My hand was in a glove. It was like a pacifier. It wasn't sexual, just a warm, wonderful feeling. He had to go, so I went to the car with him. There was Dawn, and I was jealous. I think she's not good looking. I saw a couple, a woman and a man. He was kissing her, a sexual feeling to him or to her. I was confused. Then I call Sandra (my other girl friend from college) while having a fantasy of marriage. I think we'll live happily ever after.

Cory associated to cheating a bit during a game with friends. He teased a woman, who complained he was "condescending." Cory felt "freakish" not knowing "the answers to being a man."

Cory still had "feelings" toward men, though different. He thought, "If it's my nature, I'll be gay. If it's not, I don't want to be."

Last night he masturbated first imagining giving a blow job to a boy he knew in college, but it was "not exciting." Then, he started "thinking of sex with women, normal. Even with breasts. I liked women in college and in high school."

I pointed out that homosexual thoughts appeared after remembering how his father demeaned him, and after thoughts of loss of the college buddy and his fraternity brothers. He thought homosexual activity protected him from rage at his father and grief over his lost friends. He had witnessed sexuality as a kid. He used to like to compete with women, but thought he could be a man.

He asked me, 'Have any other patients as gay as I am gone straight? Is it possible?'' I felt Cory was projecting aspects of his own functioning onto me, so I commented, "It sounds as though you want me to be a proud parent and you hope that changing from homosexuality to heterosexuality might be unusual." Cory responded that he wanted his change in orientation "to give you pleasure." I commented, "A pleasure your father did not have?" He commented, "I didn't get a fucking thing from my father."

501.   Cory's HIV test was negative. After saying I should be proud of him, he imagined getting a blow job so he could turn HIV positive to hurt me. I interpreted that hurting me would separate him from

me, as he had wanted to do with his mother. The separation would ease his anxiety of fusion with her; but to relieve his guilt over separating, he would simultaneously hurt himself.

Cory then associated, "I have this romantic wish to find a beautiful woman and sail around the world, living off the fat of the land."

502.   Cory complained that his finances were not being handled well by the school, and apologized for this. He attacked Mrs. Smith, who was delaying him. He then presented the following dream:

> I'm in a western town (two rows of buildings). It's like the movies. I'm courting Madonna. I'm with her, then there are mountains, and my old girl friend, Sandy, is hiking with me, going around. We're in the house, trying to come back to town, where Madonna is. There's a path, narrow, high up and then dropped. At the end there's a funnel. There's not enough room to go through, to get to town.

Cory associated this dream with fame and wealth. Madonna was not his type. He wanted a female to have children with. He fantasized, "I could hook up with famous people and maybe write a song or a book. I would get people to like me." The dream-funnel reminded him of a house near the house he grew up in. Recently, ordering take-out food, he felt a waiter took care of him.

Cory had helped a man in a parking lot, "doing nice things for people I hardly know." He associated helpfulness with a "homosexual feeling, unformed." He had a yearning he identified as "sexual," for a dinner party guest he found "with it and together." He looked at the man's crotch, and thought, "I really want his brain."

Cory wanted a law career, a wife and children. However, he was "afraid I'll end up like your suburban life." I explored his antipathy to suburbia. He said, "I'll get lost in the shuffle. Twenty years from now maybe I'll have a professional wife and a son who's grown, and I'll be nothing. Maybe I'm envious of the staid, normal, suburban life, maybe that's why I put it down.

"I want to identify with you, but I'm afraid I can't or I don't want to. I don't want suburban, the quiet life, uncomplicated, quiet, familial, and professional. There'd be no turmoil! No knock down, drag out fights! I can't imagine having passion and strong will once a year. There's always tension in homosexual relationships. Men are headstrong, women are always subservient, or at least sometimes.''

503.   After seeing an explicit gay movie, Cory wished for a blow job, and had ''fantasies of the ten best blow jobs I'd ever had.''

I interpreted that moving back in a gay direction guarded against his grief about giving up homosexuality. His immediate association was, ''Homosexuality is a lot easier, from a practical standpoint''; that is, the relationships he had throughout the world, and the ease of hooking up, superficially, with homosexual people.

504.   Cory met a man who claimed to have ''screwed a girl'' in Cory's house. Cory found this story vaguely sexually exciting. He was ashamed he became sexually stimulated looking at his niece's boyfriend. He felt ''angry, and happy to hurt you with a possible setback.'' He then reported a dream:

> I'm on a tall ship. We're going somewhere, and something is happening. I'm going to have sex. It's not worked out. I'm leaving. There's an old black man who stopped me and asked to go to bed. I think, that's ludicrous! I had somehow forgotten that I had a connecting ship or a plane flight to China and there wasn't time. Then I was screwing this guy, thinking: This is boring and gross—feces—I got upset that I was missing the flight while I was doing this.

He thought of a homosexual student friend coming out. He asked me if he, himself, was identifiable as ''gay.'' I mentioned he thrust out his pelvis when he walked, appearing to mock women walking in high heels. We had briefly discussed this years previously. He now said, ''You're right about the way I walk.'' He realized he could walk in a masculine fashion, if he thought about it.

The dream, I said, seemed to indicate his ambivalence about stopping treatment. He responded he felt insecure, although he went rollerblading with male friends and helped a girl. He said, ''I enjoy being a man.'' But he reported interest in young men on the beach ''without shirts,'' which he first described as a ''sexual'' attraction. He then realized he felt ''competitive, like I should work out, to get more muscular and masculine.''

He expressed a wish for a blow job from a particular man. I asked him what the point of this would be. He said, ''I told him I had thought I was gay, but I was wrong. He was weak. I feel like the Ayn Rand story, *The Fountainhead.* The strong, heroic character is arrogant and antisocial. I'm living the Nietzsche philosophy. Even Kinsey found only 2 percent were exclusively homosexual. I've always thought to please people and be mediocre was heterosexual.''

505.   Cory enjoyed working out with male friends. When one man mentioned sex with a woman, Cory got horny, wanted a blow job, and realized, ''Women scare me.'' He was uncomfortable with masculine men; with gays, he was ''in charge, in control.'' He recalled a dream from the prior night. ''I'm in the mountains skiing with women and with Sandy. I have a fear that I have to climb something large, get off and climb down.''

Cory was terrified of heights, and associated mountains with women. He thought the pass was high and narrow and he was afraid. He was afraid a man might strike him. With gay men, he had felt more masculine because he was in charge. He worried women would compare him with other men.

The idea of a man with a woman turned him on. I interpreted that he was projecting himself onto that fantasy somehow. He responded, ''I'm both. I'd like to make love to the mirror-image of myself!'' Laughing, he said, he was more familiar with himself!

He confessed a fear he would not get an erection with women. He had not always with men, either. He recalled a college ''slut'' had agreed to have sex with him, but he didn't get an erection. He was drunk, another girl was present, and he had been troubled by fantasies: ''There were lots of men before me. Liberated and free. My sister was a nympho, but I think she was desperate.''

I said he seemed to have something to prove with that girl. He responded that he had had an erection once with seventeen different men and had nine orgasms in one night. This made him feel superior. He also felt superior with men because his big penis made men ''Ooh, ahh.'' On the contrary, women ''rarely mention my size.'' Men mentioning his size made him more comfortable and ''proud.'' With women, he felt more self-conscious. He was afraid of an urge to ''make love violently with a woman.'' He imagined throwing a woman in bed and inserting his penis without lubrication, ''the way gay men like it.'' He felt a woman ''won't put up with that.''

In the dream, he was afraid in the mountains (woman) he would let loose his fury. He was jealous that women "can have men in the way I can't." On the other hand, the fantasy of a "slut who had had lots of men" turned him on. I clarified that he seemed to wish to "rape a slut." He was stimulated by a movie where a virgin nun was raped, "a brutal act of domination, and that scares me."

He associated skiing (in the dream) to Aaron and their lobster dinners. Courting Madonna would be "different." He pondered raping the virgin nun versus Madonna the slut; "screwing a man in the ass is the same as violently raping a woman."

I interpreted that screwing a man in the ass was a displacement and discharge of his conflicted wish to violently rape a woman. He responded that the idea of loving sex with a woman was novel.

506.   Cory was throwing out old papers. Gustav now agreed Cory was straight because Cory had never touched Gustav's penis. Cory associated "asshole with violence."

Cory felt guilt because, in a way, he was happy Gustav was dying from AIDS, and that his mother was "stuck in her life." He was happy: "I'll never think of you again!" Suddenly, he felt "like crying."

He reported being "alone, like the umbilical cord is cut or the cord to a space suit." He was "not yet close to a woman" and fearful Mrs. Smith would destroy him.

Remembering his prior therapist, a Jewish psychologist, he felt guilty that "I was mean to him, cursed, yelled and made anti-Semitic remarks. When I've done that with you, it causes me too much pain."

Suddenly he reported pressure in his chest, tension, nausea, and sadness. He felt "like nitrous oxide at the dentist." He felt warm only to people he could pity, like his mother. He complained women were mushy, whereas men were hard. He was still looking at guys.

He wanted me to ask him what was wrong. He felt "like a child, when my mother didn't love me anymore." He wanted to fall in love "emotionally" with a woman. He said, "I'd like to be like you."

507.   Cory had done something "stupid." His mother called to wish him happy birthday and then hung up on him. He was so

upset, he walked to a gay bar, had four beers, and brought home a young black man whom he sodomized for a half hour, without orgasm. He then masturbated to orgasm, himself. The black man wanted to "rape" him, but Cory avoided being penetrated. However, Cory had not used a condom, and clearly had risked his life.

Cory knew this, interpreting that he was trying to punish himself because of rage toward his mother. I further interpreted that he generalized from his mother that all women would hurt him. The anger toward his mother was partly a defense against pain over loss and narcissistic injury. He concurred and added he is frightened of women's rejection. Therefore, he turned to men, ventilated his anger through sex, and rebelliously distanced himself from dependency or loving wishes toward women and toward me.

508.   Cory reported a dream: "My fraternity brothers [from college] are in it. I wanted to be like them. I had to go under water, and I was afraid and excited, like scuba diving."

Cory had sent out invitations for a graduation party. He had said to a woman he knows, "I'm from a poor family," and felt embarrassed.

The "black boy" he had picked up had returned, and he let the man "dry hump" him, but not penetrate him. With this man, he felt "half envy and one percent sexual arousal." Cory despaired at finding a wife. Maybe a woman would not rule him, nor would he rule her. Again he thought of being attracted to a man.

I questioned why he would have a party at his house. He said he wanted his parents to interact normally. His gay friends and Sandy, who were coming, were really not friends. I clarified that this was more of a "farewell party" than a graduation party.

He feared any woman he met would "be able to tell my defectiveness." He remembered being "a sissy on the playground and a prostitute in Copenhagen." He feared "coming up small," and doubted he could support a family. He might need a woman with money. He felt, "I'm kind of one of them. It's time for the men's room. I'm comfortable with women, except when they start comparing earrings. Men talk slow and have an urge to finish their sentences. It's unfamiliar territory."

I said Cory exaggerated differences between men and women. He responded that he was afraid he "won't pull it off" with women.

He thought of his college fraternity "pseudo" hazing, which he liked. In one activity, pledges "picked up an olive with their ass cheeks, and then walked and dropped it." They also chewed an egg with the shell on. He was told he was eating dog and vomited. Cigar smoke was blown in his face.

When Cory became a brother (authority), he said, "We would do things to fuck with the pledges. Take them down to the basement. I'd come behind them, and take a blindfold off and give them the bird."

509.   Cory thought he would be okay without me. He asked out a woman in a bookstore, but she turned him down. Upset, he wanted a guy to give him "blow jobs," which he associated with "anger at the girl for rejecting me. My murderous rage."

I interpreted he feared women here because he projected anger. He associated anger at Mrs. Smith and his landlord (male). He complained his mother did not pay attention to him.

I confronted his poor judgment in asking out an unknown woman in a public place. He agreed and felt "sad about my family." He wondered if he would outgrow me, and imagined I would "have breakfast with the family and then send your son to school, then go have patients and teach." He caught himself ridiculing me, realized he was envious, and said, "I'm continually recreating myself."

510.   We established his final appointment date in June. He reported seeing Gustav and getting blow jobs from him. Gustav now lived with another gay law student. Cory then dreamt:

> I'm in a pickup truck. I'm in the middle. My old girl friend, Sandy, is on one side. I yell out to a black guy on the street, something bad. She jumped out behind him and imitated the way he was walking. He backed in. The black guy was running at me. He reached in with a knife, like a spatula, or a rug knife, and he sliced my face. I felt it. There was cloth on it. Then I was being taken to the hospital, but I didn't want to. There was an ER surgeon and one other patient. I insisted on having a plastic surgeon see me. But this guy refused to see anyone since he didn't know anybody. I got out the yellow pages, and I got mad, and I went to throw it at him, but I didn't. I sat down. He said, "Are you in control of yourself? You were going to throw it!" I was afraid they would inject a sedative into me. I wasn't able to think as clearly, but I wanted someone to sew up my face.

Then I was at a graduation party, and my father was trying to
get friends to work in the garden.

In the first dream, he didn't care about the woman, he just
wanted his face fixed, since it had been cut through "to the skull."
He went to a gay bar, but was "tired of jerking off."

I interpreted that the dream might be a reaction to my confrontation of his effeminate gait, which apparently embarrassed him,
and perhaps about ending treatment. He associated wanting plastic
surgery with wanting more psychoanalysis. We discussed the possibility that he might want further treatment in L.A. He could afford
it better, and without loans. Impishly, he said, "I want to make
more money than you do, and be more famous."

511.   Cory felt guilty about his hostility toward a brother. He
thought he invited abuse from Sandy and from Gustav, "spurned
lovers." Gustav was not coming to the graduation.

Cory had met a "nice girl." Then he went to the beach and
looked at women. After a while, he began looking at men, and
eventually "wanted a blow job."

I interpreted that the shift in his thoughts to homosexuality
occurred after he was attracted to women. He said Mrs. Smith, his
father, and his male landlord had no integrity. Cory wanted to "fuck
the world," but felt guilty about it.

Looking in a mirror, he thought, "I'm good looking enough to
get a girl." To get a man, he had a "big dick, and that's all it
takes." He recognized an "urge to annihilate athletic guys." In the
past, he had tied up and played at raping one girl friend and Gustav.

512.   Cory had "sex," that is, blow jobs, five times between his
appointment yesterday and today. "The male trunk" [torso] got
him excited, but not sexually—he did not enjoy the sex, but liked
orgasm for tension relief.

Cory said his "obsession" with men now was not sexual. He
ogled couples, and imagined a male lifeguard with a woman.

513.   "I'm a lawyer! I've been happy for hours since I graduated.
I was with my family and Sandy last night and we went berserk.
They said, 'You're still my little brother.' My father cried and

hugged me and said, 'You did it' I was sad. I have to get away from them. I have guilt over wanting to say, 'Fuck you!' ''

Sandy called his family "vicious." Cory felt guilty because his father was proud. He described his mother and girl friend as "castrating," and he felt awful. He got drunk, went out and got a blow job.

I interpreted that he used an old method of destroying himself to relieve guilt. He responded, "To show myself how damaging my family really is. I feel like I'm being a coward, weak. I'm afraid Sandy will ridicule me. She's pretty and sexy. My family thinks I'm screwing her, and I'm afraid she'll deny it if they ask her. I had told her to pretend she's my girl friend. She is seductive, but then she brings up her boyfriend. When we were riding together after graduation, she told me she didn't want to be my girl friend, and I got angry.''

I further interpreted his turning passive to active by getting damaged, and turning anger on himself. He responded, "Forever. I've been afraid people were trying to castrate me and I wanted to prove that I still have my sword. The more the merrier. They beat me into submission, then I bounce back. It's my fault Sandy isn't married and my parents are sad. I'm as happy as a pig in shit! But the shit is not in me! I'm cleansed!''

514.   Cory reported a dream:

> I'm having dinner with a friend, cocktails and dinner. The price is $200, then $800, then $1,500. Then, I'm with my brother, and we're going on a trip. The luggage is packed on skateboards. We're going, then back on the main road. They wanted to return to get marijuana. I went along alone. I was tired from pushing uphill. A girl in my class, who is an attractive bitch, is there. Then, my mother is driving in my father's old red pickup truck. She picks us up. Then my sister is there. I'm glad she's there. It's the street where I grew up.

Cory thought of a past disturbed girl friend while on the way to my office. He then saw a "cute guy." He didn't like sexual thoughts toward his muscular older brother, who was into S&M. He wanted to get rid of homosexual thoughts because "they're troublesome." Cory said he worried that with time, he would drift back toward homosexuality.

Thinking that his dream might reflect feelings about my fee, I asked Cory if he had any associations about me. He responded, "Something about mass murderers of young boys, like a person's desperation before they're killed. I love to see that in someone's face. I have a lot of shit in me. I want to fuck boys and kill them. That's from all those young boys who trampled me when I was young. Now I do look at fewer boys."

515.   He got his "exorbitant" apartment set up in L.A. But he got drunk last night. He almost made a "sexual move" on his brother but fell asleep instead. Cory wanted "manliness, love, and to destroy him and make him into a woman."

No one had been attractive to him. He had not masturbated in four days. Today, he "jerked off" once. He was feeling "more normal." On trains, he used to have fantasies of fifty people having sex with him. He said, "I'm getting nostalgic for my pathology. I'm leaving friends, gayness, you." He could still go to gay places, "like home." He missed going to the park, "that whole fabricated way of dealing with things." He was experiencing diminution in tension and anxiety, although he still felt some guilt.

He wanted to buy his little sister something. He felt guilty that "I've left them behind, and they stay in their pits. Her husband is a plumber, and she watches *The Price is Right*." He remembered when she was 12, she babysat for the fellow she married at 19. Now she, her husband, and son were happy. He felt she was brighter and could have done better. However, her husband was nice and she worked.

He felt guilty because "I once tried to have sex with her, when we were very young. I was 10 and she was 12, and I got on top of her. I contributed to her problems and I should have known better. She went to the guy's house when she was 12!

"When she was 15, I tried to talk her into getting educated but she didn't. I'm feeling better about my job. There's potential. I feel like people who survive a plane crash or their buddies get maimed. I feel like it should be me."

Cory said it was hard to say goodbye, easier to say, "'Till we meet again." He felt there was a "slim possibility" that he might run into me and my family.

I clarified that he seemed nervous about how he was going to manage loneliness and tension in the future. He then thought about what had led to his drinking: "The desire to be one of the boys with my brothers. The whole gay network, day or night, sneaking off to Boston, prostitution. If I'm not careful, I'll get a woman pregnant. I think I need a couple of straight friends in L.A."

He plaintively asked me why I thought he had been gay. I reviewed some of the fantasies he had about obtaining gratification through the penis, especially the wishes to gain love and (ego) strength.

516.   Cory walked in and took my PDR off the shelf to look for an answer to his question about whether the erythromycin he was taking for strep throat might also treat oral gonorrhea. He was worried because of recent sexual contacts.

He asked why I gave him a strange look when he took the PDR. I responded that he had taken it without my permission, breaking a social code. He understood immediately and thought of other situations where he broke understood boundaries. He had done this as a waiter previously by making sexual comments to male customers, which then led them to bring in other people for sexual activity.

517.   Cory wondered whether he wasn't wasting his time coming to sessions, since he felt better, and thought perhaps he shouldn't bother "going to the doctor."

He listed the various ways he felt better: better ego strength, better control mechanisms, and stability of identity. Cory realized he was describing his progress in a businesslike way. He felt guilty about "hatred" toward me. I interpreted that feeling he didn't need to come, in part, rejected me before I rejected him. He responded that although he was not "tangled" with me, he worried that when he left, I would put "hooks" in him, like his mother did. I further interpreted that he hated his mother (me), (1) out of frustration; (2) to effect separation; and (3) to defend against fond feelings toward me which he equated with "entanglement." He concurred and associated to his future roommate, a homosexual attorney "friend," who is so passive and overworked that Cory predicted no anxiety about entanglement.

518.   Cory at first discussed his financial problems with me. He reported a dream:

> I am in a house, it looks like either my sister's house, the house I grew up in, or here. I am in the kitchen, and I see all these rats. They look like they are getting ready to bite. They are in the walls and floor. My sister says something about $200.
>
> There is a picture of me nude from childhood, and you must have it, you keep it, and you don't pay for it.
>
> There is a young black girl, a teenager, and she wants me to have intercourse with her. I start to, and then I realize she is a virgin, and I decide I shouldn't. Then the scene changes, and I am like in this school bus, and there is a black female school bus driver, maybe your wife. She is driving around and around, and I feel like I am never going to get out.

Cory associated that I was like his mother, and would extract money from him under the guise of being "magnanimous." He recalculated the amount of the loan he borrowed for treatment, and he has extra. He wanted me to feel free to use any material from his analysis in professional settings, if it would help others. I thanked him for the release, and also pointed out it might include a reaction formation against anger that I did not pay for the "picture" of him, and he had to pay me. He laughed, said he could "screw your wife to get back at you for depriving me." He again associated to his father's stinginess with love.

519.   Cory felt conflicted over fondness toward me. He wondered what I thought of him when I first met him. He imagined I saw him as a younger brother or a son, and wanted to help him out. I interpreted these transference wishes toward me relieved the deprivation from his father and brothers.

He still occasionally looked at and envied men on the beach. He concluded he should continue building up his own body to feel more confident about his own masculinity, physically.

Cory felt more comfortable with his 5-year-old nephew. He pondered how to meet a woman in L.A., what type of woman he wanted: his intellectual needs and his need for "kindness," which he now emphasized.

He expressed gratefulness to me for my help through the years.

At the end of the session, as we stood up, he realized he was taller than I am; he had imagined that I was taller, since he envisioned me as a father or as an older brother.

520.   Cory reviewed his associations of sadness with femininity and gruffness with masculinity, which made it hard for him to say goodbye to me. He felt grateful to me and friendly with me.

He was embarrassed about speaking in his "low voice." He still had some difficulty doing this, but forced himself in spite of anxiety that as a man, he might not be able to express affection for me. On the other hand, he wanted to feel individuated. He discussed his future optimistically.

521.   In this penultimate session, Cory analyzed that he had avoided heterosexual relationships because of guilt over outdoing his father. When he talked with his mother or older sister, he tried to steel himself, but wound up wanting to give a blow job or get one. He knew these were responses to anger, feelings of entanglement, and loss of identity with his mother and sister. Nevertheless, he aspired to have mutual empathy with a competent woman.

Cory had begun the session by complaining about his back. At the end of the session, when he got up from the couch, he again complained of his back. I interpreted that perhaps if his back hurt enough, he wouldn't be able to get off the couch. He laughed and said he was already off the couch—our session tomorrow will be sitting up.

522.   As I had long ago recommended, Cory sat up for his final session. He commented on his reaction to sitting up that it was nice "to see me." He ran through some of the changes that had occurred during his analysis, and some of his preparations for L.A.

He expressed sadness at leaving and some apprehension about being able to handle situations in the future. I concurred with him that his analysis might not be sufficient at this point, and although he had a good start at a new life, he could monitor his functioning and would have a wide choice of analysts in L.A. should he need further work.

CHAPTER 3

Paul Schreber's Sexual Desires and Imaginings: Cause or Consequence of His Psychosis?

ZVI LOTHANE, M.D.

Preamble: A Question of Method

A psychiatric or psychoanalytic case study should reflect the following aspects of method: (1) *descriptive*, consisting of a detailed, and accurate presentation of the historical facts and events in health and disease and a careful observation of the person, including his or her moral character and conscience; (2) *diagnostic*, derived from a longitudinal and cross-sectional view of the history; (3) *dynamic*, following from an understanding of both external and internal moral conflicts, not only as a clash of opposing forces but as the patient's moral character and conscience, in addition to his or her identifications, dreams, and fantasies; (4) *dyadic*, the conception of symptoms of mental disorder as relational, as a discourse, consisting of gestures and speeches for the purpose of communication of interpersonal meanings; (5) *doctor–patient dialogue*, which is the principal arena where symptoms and ethical issues are played out, both as reality and as transference discourse; (6) *deontological/axiological*, to be applied to the foregoing aspects, to ensure an accurate description, diagnosis, and dynamic formulation, derived from, not imposed on data, in order to meet the needs of the patient and the needs of society. (7) *Dialectical*, the debate that ensues as a result of conflicts between the person and others in his social orbit, and among the various commentators on the case, stemming from different theoretical or ideological positions. These aspects are traditionally pursued by clinicians striving to arrive at a comprehensive assessment of the person in a situation and a rational treatment plan assuring therapeutic success and quality of life. This means that the patient's story, his feelings, and his interpretations have to be believed, and accepted explicitly and implicitly before any other valid judgment can be reached. This ethical stance is possible in a good psychiatric or analytic situation, or among true friends. It is not always possible on a psychiatric ward, in a police or prison setting, or in a political system based on despotism. Given this ethical principle, the only reliable source about Schreber is his own story as told by him in his *Denkwürdigkeiten eines Nervenkranken*, mistranslated in English as *Memoirs of My Nervous Illness* (Schreber, 1903). The word *memoirs* now means memories or diaries, whereas in Schreber's time it meant: reflections of a nervous patient. In addition, a person's moral profile and ethical conflicts play an intrinsic role in the construction of symptoms of mental disorder (Lothane, 1998c, 1999).

Freud (1911a) made psychoanalytic and intellectual history with his interpretive paradigm when he used *selected* portions of Paul Schreber's immortal book (1903; henceforth abbreviated as *Memoirs*) to illustrate the etiological dynamic formula: homosexuality causes paranoia. Two sets of questions instantly leap to mind, one general and one particular: (1) Are homosexuality and paranoia clearly defined concepts or syndromes? The answer is no: there are many homosexualities and many paranoias (Schifferdecker and Peters, 1995). (2) Did Schreber himself disclose any homosexual desires and suffer from paranoia? The answer is also no: Schreber's illness was a mood disorder and, on Freud's own showing, he "had, by all accounts, shown no signs of homosexuality in the ordinary sense of the word" (1911a, p. 60). Another question arises: Were Schreber's sexual imaginings the cause of his psychosis or the consequence of it? Freud only considered them as cause; however, these also need to be considered as an effect of his psychosis. Whereas Freud's formulaic interpretation does not explain fully either Schreber's second illness or the content of the *Memoirs*, it is thanks to him that Schreber became immortal.

The other influential paradigm for explaining Schreber's illness was Niederland's (1974): the father's sadism toward the son in childhood caused the son's illness is adulthood, and it inspired a prodigious secondary literature. Here was a real traumatic cause for the son's adult paranoia, not merely "endopsychic perceptions of the processes whose existence [Freud has] assumed" (1911a, p. 79). As a devout Freudian, Niederland did not offer much about Schreber's sexuality other than a gesture of obeisance to "Freud's work [as] a classic analytic study of the first order" (1974, p. 26). Niederland's central idea linking Schreber's hallucinations and delusions to the traumatic father–son interaction during Paul Schreber's childhood was also an inference, not a finding, distilled from Moritz Schreber's (1858) book on child rearing and its later revised and renamed version by another physician (1891); it is discussed in detail elsewhere (Lothane, 1989a,b, 1992a). Niederland sought to reconcile his view of a father who practiced "studiously applied terror" by positing "compensatory periods of seductive benevolence" (p. 70). To account for the alleged homosexuality, Niederland posited that Paul Schreber was a victim of his father's "seductive manipulations performed on the child's body" (p. 60), resulting in "intense overstimulation, . . . interference with libidinal needs in general, and the . . . homosexual libido in particular" (p. 73), a rather un-Freudian view of the matter in contrast to Freud's assumption of spontaneous homoerotic desires. Niederland did not explain what caused such memories to surface in the distorted form of hallucinations or delusions at the time they did, or how they were related to current conflicts with his wife, to his deep-seated masochism, or life in the asylum. Whereas Freud's (1911a) explanatory theory was monadic, that is, intrapsychic, derived from endopsychic perceptions contained within one person, Niederland's model of pathogenesis was interpersonal, more in the manner of Ferenczi than Freud. However, any formulation of Schreber along developmental lines and conflicts must be viewed as conjectural, for the required historical–biographical data about his childhood and adolescence, the relationship with both his parents, with his siblings, and others have not survived. Schur's (1972) caveat against the pitfalls of the genetic fallacy is still valid: "It was probably especially difficult for Freud to realize that occasionally *the emphasis on infantile material can be used successfully as a defense against recent conflicts*" (p. 167; emphasis in the original).

These two heuristically pregnant paradigms can fairly be qualified as reductionist; neither Freud nor Niederland read the *Memoirs* with full attention to detail, nor did they listen to Paul Schreber on his own terms. Building on the work of my predecessors (Devreese, 1981; Schreber, 1987; Israëls, 1989; Busse, 1991), I have argued for a third paradigm of interpreting Schreber that corrects and amplifies the two previous ones: not just Schreber, a case, but Schreber, a life, speaking to us in his own voice (Lothane, 1989a,b, 1991, 1992a,b, 1993a,b,c, 1995, 1996a,b, 1997a,b, 1998a,b, 2000).

Who Was This Daniel Paul Schreber?

Here are the bare bones of Paul Schreber's (1842–1911) life. He was the third of five children born to Pauline Haase (1815–1907) and Moritz Schreber (1808–1861). Moritz Schreber earned his place in history as the forerunner of modern physiotherapy and rehabilitation medicine, of physical education in the school, and of parent–teacher associations, and only posthumously, as the spiritual father of the Schreber garden movement. Paul, the last bearer of the name Schreber, was preceded by the first-born Gustav (1839–1877) and Anna Jung (1840–1944), the mother of all past and present descendants. Paul's brilliant legal career was crowned with his appointment as presiding judge of the Third *Civilsenat* of the Dresden High Court of Appeals of the Kingdom of Saxony in the summer of 1893, which caused him to worry. He had married his wife Sabine in 1878, a year following the suicide by gunshot of his elder brother Gustav, who had suffered from tertiary syphilis and an unspecified psychosis. At that time Schreber experienced a mild bout of hypochondria. The marriage remained childless after six miscarriages and stillbirths, the last, a boy, in 1892.

Paul Schreber was hospitalized three times for depressive illness. The first illness, a moderate depression without psychotic features, occurred following his defeat at the polls, in his bid to be elected to the *Reidstag* as a National-Liberal candidate from Chemnitz. The illness lasted from the fall of 1884 to the end of 1885, and was treated at spas before and after the six months spent at the Psychiatric Hospital of Leipzig University run by Paul Flechsig (1847–1929), brain anatomist turned organic psychiatrist. The second illness began as a prodrome in the summer of 1893, in the wake of a crisis in the marriage and worries concerning his new assignment. Exactly six weeks after the assumption of his duties in Dresden the illness erupted explosively with intractable sleeplessness, agitation, and suicide attempts. On November 21, 1893, he was readmitted as a voluntary patient to Flechsig's Hospital, expressing depressive, nihilistic, and hypochondriacal delusions. Flechsig's diagnosis was "sleeplessness." By mid-March 1894, the agitated–depressive phase switched to an exalted state of hallucinations and delusions of sexual abuse, miraculous divine influences and ideas of a fantastic cosmology, a phase Schreber called his *soul murder*. Following Flechsig's referral, and after a two-week stay in Pierson's asylum, he was transferred, on June 29, 1894, to the public Sonnenstein Asylum run by organicist psychiatrist and forensic expert Guido Weber (1837–1914). In November 1894, Schreber's legal status was changed from voluntary to involuntary. Weber's initial diagnosis, acute hallucinatory psychosis, was later changed to paranoia, then regarded as a chronic and incurable disorder of systematized delusions caused by brain disease.

The agitated depression and the soul murder phase gradually abated in 1895. By 1896, Schreber regained his lucidity, and by 1897 he felt well enough to be discharged. In this he was opposed by Weber's diagnosis, his incompetency status, and his wife's reluctance to take him home. Over the next five years, while mentally and socially recompensated but continuing to display attacks of rage in the form of "bellowing miracles" and to entertain residual fantasies of transformation into a woman to redeem the world, he was able to write his *Memoirs*, win in the court where he had worked years earlier, and have his incompetency rescinded, and to return to his wife. From 1902 to 1907 Schreber functioned normally, built a new house in Dresden, and adopted the girl Fridoline, who was 13 years old in 1903, as his daughter. He left poems from that period that show no trace of thought disorder. The third and terminal episode, which started in 1907 following the death of his mother and his wife's stroke, led to his admission to the Leipzig-Dösen Asylum. This bout was also marked by psychotic depressive pathology, increasing mental and physical deterioration, and death due to heart and lung failure.

Schreber's Diagnoses and Beyond

Schreber's self-diagnosis was affective illness, melancholia, and it is borne out by his self-descriptions in the *Memoirs* and the hospital chart. Freud confused the issue by both copying Weber's diagnosis of paranoia, a delusional disorder in an otherwise intact personality, and combining it with "dementia paranoides" (or paranoid schizophrenia), from Kraepelin's term *dementia praecox*, introduced in 1896. But Schreber did not show any of Bleuler's fundamental signs and his persecutory ideas were almost entirely centered on Flechsig as soul murderer, or persecutor. Schreber did not show paranoid behavior or traits prior to becoming depressed, nor did his paranoid behavior crescendo to culminate in what Cameron (1959) called a paranoid pseudocommunity. Nor were his ideas of persecution gathered into a system: Schreber conceived a fantastic cosmology and a related theory of cosmic justice, but it was enlivened by a keen sense of ethics. In the Sonnenstein chart Flechsig was only mentioned once, while in the *Memoirs* the idea of being persecuted by Flechsig disappeared spontaneously by 1897, at a time when, as Freud noted, quoting from Schreber's (1901) writ of appeal, Schreber became "aware that the persons I see about me are not 'cursorily improvised men' but real and that I must therefore behave towards them as a reasonable man is used to behave towards his fellows . . . (409 [numbers in parentheses are page numbers in the original 1903 edition of *Memoirs*])" (1911a, p. 21). Weber's misdiagnosis and the dire prognosis of incurability, presented in court papers, needlessly prolonged Schreber's Sonnenstein stay for two more years. Schreber's reactions to this ongoing stress are reflected in the contents of his symptoms, according to dyadic dynamics of symptom formation as an adaptive reaction to environmental trauma (Freeman, Cameron, and McGhie, 1958, p. 70; Lothane, 1997b).

Had Freud listened to Schreber himself, he might not have misread as paranoid Schreber's bitter complaints against Flechsig, but would have seen the "kernel of truth" in them. Moreover, had Schreber been consistently paranoid, would he not have counted asylum superintendent Weber among his persecutors? After a nod to Kraepelin, Freud concludes: "However, it is not on the whole of very great importance what names we give to clinical pictures.

What seems to me more essential is that paranoia should be maintained as an independent clinical type, however frequently the picture it offers may be complicated by the presence of schizophrenic features'' (1911a, pp. 75–76). But there were no such features here, and what mattered to Freud was the syndromal, not the essentialist, approach to psychopathology: a delineation of a character constellation and its relation to psychodynamics of desire, dream, and defense. Early on, describing the clinical picture. Freud duly noted that "the second illness set in at the end of October 1893 with a torturing bout of sleeplessness" (p. 13), a cardinal manifestation of depression. Had Freud given equal attention to Schreber's mood, or the dynamics of repressed aggression, he might have come out with a different assessment of the total picture. Whither Freud's awareness of Schreber's suicidal dysthymia? Or the differential diagnosis of Schreber's stupor?

The Missing Link: Schreber's Depressive and Angry Emotions

Down the decades Schreber's words were mostly read for ideas, especially false ideas, or delusions, at the expense of emotions, true to a convention in German organic psychiatry of viewing psychosis as a disorder of perception, such that emotions of unpleasure, such as anxiety and depression, were seen merely as accompanying signs of ideas. Accordingly, hallucinations were viewed as quasi-neurological disorders of perception, or perceptions without an object, rather than as *sui generis* waking dreams (Lothane, 1982), with all the included emotions and conflicts, as formulated in Freud's dream psychology (1900) and in defense neuropsychoses (1894, 1896). His early interest in depression as emotion and syndrome took years to mature (Freud, 1917).

   While Freud's 1911 essay was being written, Freud focused on aggression and hate in Schreber in a letter to Ferenczi of October 6, 1910 (Brabant, Falzeder, and Giampieri-Deutsch, 1993), in which the following passage was suppressed by Jones (1955, pp. 83–84): "What would you say to Dr. S[chreber] senior performing 'miracles' as a physician? But who was otherwise a despot in his household who bellowed [i.e., yelled and scolded] at his son and understood him as little as the 'lower God' understood our paranoiac'' (Lothane, 1989b, p. 215). Earlier, in the case history of Little

Hans (Freud, 1909, p. 140), Freud acknowledged Adler's (1908) views on the role of aggression in pathogenesis only to dismiss them; Adler turned out to be right after all. But in 1911, Freud also knew that "[t]he intensity of the emotion is projected in the shape of external power, while its quality is changed into the opposite. The person who is now hated and feared for being a persecutor was at one time loved and honoured. The main purpose of the persecution asserted by the patient's delusion is to justify the change in his emotional attitude" (p. 41), which then led to the famous syllogism of "*loving a man*":

> "*I* (a man) *love him* (a man)' is contradicted by: (a) Delusions of *persecution*; for they loudly assert: "I do not *love* him—I *hate* him."
>
> This contradiction, which must have run thus in the unconscious (or in the "basic language" as Schreber would say), cannot, however, become conscious to a paranoic in this form. The mechanism of symptom-formation in paranoia requires that internal perceptions—feelings—shall be replaced by external perceptions. Consequently the proposition "I hate him" becomes transformed by *projection* into another one: "*He hates* (persecutes) *me*, which will justify me in hating him." And thus the impelling unconscious feeling makes its appearance as though it were the consequence of an external perception: "I do not *love* him—I *hate* him because HE PERSECUTES ME."
>
> Observation leaves room for no doubt that the persecutor is some one who was once loved [1911a, p. 63; emphasis Freud's].

Freud quest was a formula "to attribute to homosexual wishful phantasies an intimate (perhaps an invariable) relation to this particular form of disease" (1911a, p. 59), but its universality can no longer be maintained. Moreover, these "external perceptions" were strictly as-if "perceptions," projected fantasies: had Freud remained true to his own insight, he would have abandoned the erroneous view of paranoia as a disorder of perception in favor of it being a disorder of imagination; an emotional and defensive disorder of frustrated love and self-love and rage. As projection, the wish "I love him" should only have been transformed into another projection: "I do not love him, it is he who loves me." But like Columbus, who set out in search of a passage to India, Freud discovered instead the America of repressed aggression—hatred and rage, and the defense against them—but did not recognize aggression for what it was because of his then overriding interest in libido. In his delusions of persecution, Schreber neither loudly nor quietly asserted he hated either Flechsig or God, but that Flechsig had been his enemy, which in some sense he was, and that God turned against him, too. But he expressed no persecutory ideas toward Weber, even though the latter was even more inimical toward him, or his wife, who refused to take him home, or the other doctors or attendants who had variously angered or disappointed him. He expressed his own anger in the attacks of rage he called "bellowing miracles," for which he blamed God but not himself, his way of saying his anger was unconscious and for which he was not responsible. He may have, as a child, raged against his mother and father, but we do not know this for a fact, except for a number of occasions when unconscious aggressive feelings toward his mother, father, and father-in-law are hinted at in the *Memoirs*.

The aggressive valence of anger as rebellion was clearly invoked by Freud in the context of "Schreber's God and his relations to Him . . . [showing] the strangest mixture of blasphemous criticism . . . mutinous insubordination . . . and reverent devotion" (p. 51). For Freud this was still a " 'transference,' by means of which an emotional cathexis became transposed . . . on to the doctor who was in reality indifferent to him" (p. 47); that is, a transference repetition of oedipal rebellion. But Flechsig was far from indifferent and no blank screen, and Freud was quite aware that "after his [first] recovery [Schreber] had cordial feelings towards his doctor. . . . 'I was finally cured . . . and . . [felt] the liveliest gratitude towards Professor Flechsig. I gave a marked expression to this feeling both in a personal visit . . . and in what I deemed to be an appropriate honorarium' (35–36)" (p. 41). Not only did Flechsig have an overriding nonerotic significance for Schreber, as a real person in whom he and his wife had put their trust, but as a psychiatrist in whom considerable powers were vested by law. Therefore, whereas Freud believed that God had been a representation of Moritz Schreber, "a most eminent physician, and one who was no doubt highly respected by his patients" (p. 52), toward whom the boy Schreber would have evinced as a child "a mixture of reverent submission and mutinous insubordination" (p. 52), it is more important to realize that these feelings, when directed at Flechsig, were not just transference but also reality. It is for Flechsig, not his father, that Schreber intended "the bitter scorn . . . shown for such a physician . . . by declaring that he understands nothing about living men and only knows how to deal with corpses" (Freud, 1911a, p. 52), as one who "was incapable of learning anything by experience" (p. 51). Moritz Schreber had little to do with corpses, except when he studied anatomy in medical school, while Flechsig kept brains pickled in formaldehyde in the brain museum next to his office in his hospital and built up a system of organic psychiatry based on brain pathology and brain mythology. Schreber's alleged paranoia toward Flechsig, actually his rage at Flechsig, occurred *after* Schreber began having dealings with him as his patient, not *before*, in the summer of 1893. The scorn Schreber heaped on Flechsig stemmed from the latter's failure to cure Schreber's sleeplessness with the promising new drugs and the banishment to Sonnenstein. Neither did Freud consider Schreber's opposition and rage toward his wife, both as a target of a dependent maternal transference and as a responsive partner in the marriage.

The emotions of anger, especially suppressed and impotent ones, lay at the heart of Schreber's psychological makeup from early on. On the other hand, he was articulate almost to the point of obscenity, by Weber's standards, in discussing his sexual emotions, and such matters as defecation and urination; yet he could not avow his anger directly but only indirectly, in "basic language," that is, as caused by divine miracles, remaining utterly mystified by his "bellowing miracles." He was equally overwhelmed and inarticulate about his other complex emotions, such as grief and sadness, contempt, and irony. However, his many encoded utterances should be read, as Freud said a dream should be read, for the included emotions generated by frustrations in the actual relationship with his wife and his doctors. Thus, Schreber did not say in his *Memoirs* that his candidacy ended in a crushing defeat, that this was a painful loss, and that he became depressed as a result. The depression is, however, clearly documented in the chart and in the *Memoirs* (Lothane, 1992a).

At the level of ideas alone, what criteria would decide in favor of reading the fantasy of turning into a woman as a castration fantasy rather than a procreation fantasy? However, at the level of emotions of depression following loss, real and symbolic alike, becoming a woman would count as a compensatory wish to cure his depression, itself a derivative of conflicts about masculine identity and assertive aggressiveness on the new job as befits a man. The paradox of promotion as a symbolic loss and trauma, acknowledged by Freud (1916), could be explained as the loss of the security of closeness to Schreber's native Leipzig and to his mother who still lived there surrounded by her daughters and grandchildren. It would also awaken the envy of woman's accepted social dependence on a man and envy of her procreative powers. It could also revive memories of the failed ambitions of his father, his depressions, and his sudden death when Schreber was only 19. And if depression was there, could rage be far behind?

Freud was preceded in the psychoanalytic exploration of melancholia by his Swiss adherent (Maeder, 1910) and by Abraham (1911), but ignored both. Like Schreber, Maeder's analysand fell ill at age 42 with symptoms reminiscent of Schreber's: a mixture of neurasthenia, anginalike pains in the chest, disturbances of sleep, disturbing dreams toward morning, and a pervasive feeling of failure. As with Schreber, there was a history of depression in the mother. As a young man he was tyrannized by his father and older brother. The man was married and had children. He was hospitalized, and the depressed affect and self-blame were more pronounced than in Schreber; he had great concerns about losing money and property. His gender identity was somewhat ambiguous, although he was never overtly homosexual. He suffered from a degree of impotence, felt hatred toward his wife, in his behavior he showed feminine identifications, and in his wet dreams men were more frequent than women. Maeder noted the insufficiency of the infantile material and that the analysis was successful.

Abraham (1911) cited Maeder's paper and two others, one by Brill and another by Jones:

> Even in [his] first analysis of a depressive psychosis he was immediately struck by its structural similarity to an obsessional neurosis . . . [because] two different tendencies—hatred and love—are always interfering with each other. The tendency such a person has to adopt a hostile attitude towards the external world is so great that his capacity for love is reduced to a minimum. At the same time he is weakened and deprived of his energy through the repression of his hatred or, to be more correct, through repression of the overstrong sadistic component of his libido. There is a similar uncertainty

in his choice of object as regards its sex. His inability to establish his libido in a definite position causes him to have a general feeling of uncertainty and leads to doubting mania. He is neither able to form a resolution nor to make a clear judgement; in every situation he suffers from feelings of inadequacy and stands helpless before the problems of life [p. 139].

This characterization fits Schreber. Abraham also pointed out the tendency of the depressive, like the obsessional, to autoerotically "isolate himself from the world" (p. 142); "sexual inadequacy" (p. 143); for the "outbreak of the real illness [to occur] when the patient had to make a final decision about his attitude towards the external world and the future application of his libido" (p. 142); "an uncertainty as to his sexual role . . . a conflict of this kind between a male and female attitude" (p. 144). The difference was that in "depressive psychoses . . . repression is followed by a process of 'projection' . . . [here] a different conflict lies concealed . . . hatred predominates. This attitude is first directed against the patient's nearest relatives and becomes generalized later on . . . [according to] the following formula: 'I cannot love people; I have to hate them' " (pp. 144–145). Obsessional features were very prominent in Schreber, and there is evidence to suggest that he had potency problems with his wife who may have had corresponding frigidity. Moreover, the *Memoirs* were not written in an emotional vacuum: Schreber was angry about his transfer to Sonnenstein, the declaration of incompetency for life, the anxiety during the legal fight to regain his freedom, all this causing him "to bellow like a wild animal . . . particularly at night, when other defensive measures like talking aloud, playing the piano, etc. are hardly practicable . . . bellowing has the advantage of drowning with its noise everything the voices speak into my head. . . . This allows me to go to sleep again" (Schreber, 1903, p. 314). The foregoing shows the capacity of rage to hurt and to heal. After his release, Schreber's rage ceased and he lived in peace with his wife and adopted daughter until the last recurrence in 1907 of the agitated depression after his mother's death and his wife's stroke. It lasted unabated until his dying day in 1911.

Freud's Views on Paranoia and Homosexuality

It is an oft repeated misconception that Freud's understanding of paranoia started with Schreber. Actually, he began thinking about paranoid dynamics of defense in the letters to Fliess, in Draft K. that followed Draft I on melancholia (Freud, 1892–1899). In the early 1890s, Meynert, Freud's Viennese psychiatry professor, described a syndrome of acute paranoia, in the original Hippocratic meaning of paranoia as an acute state of delirium and hallucinatory confusion, now renamed Meynert's amentia (Freud, 1911a, p. 75), in distinction from the other forms of paranoia defined as a chronic organic and incurable mental disorder. Freud extended Meynert's dynamic idea into a psychodynamic conception of paranoia as a neuropsychosis of defense, structured like traumatic hysteria, that is, as an adaptive response to traumatic reality in which "the ego has fended off the incompatible idea through a flight into psychosis" (Freud, 1894, p. 59), such that hallucinations were not just an organic manifestation but an activity of ego defense. There were no ideas about the causal role of sexuality in these early formulations.

In 1896, Freud pursued these clinical and dynamic formulations about paranoia when he reconfirmed and extended the definition of a "psychosis of defense: it proceeds from the repression of distressing memories and that its symptoms are determined in their form by the content of what has been repressed" (1896, pp. 174–175). The difference lay in the kind of defense employed: not just repression, as in hysteria, but projection (the first appearance of the term in Freud) of the reproaches of conscience, hence the persecutory hallucinated voices. Comparing obsessions and paranoia, he stated that while in the former self-distrust was a conscious defense, in the latter self-distrust is projected as "*distrust of other people*': In this way the subject withdraws his acknowledgment of the self-reproach . . . he is deprived of the protection of the self-reproaches which return in delusional ideas," in the "mnemic hallucinations of paranoia, . . . in the form of thoughts spoken aloud," and in the form of "*interpretive delusions* which end in an *alteration of the ego*" (1896, pp. 184–185; emphasis Freud's). Here, projection was not viewed as an external perception, but as a fantasy of a perception, an as-if perception; for example, an *imagining* that the hallucinated voices are voices of real people talking out there (Lothane, 1982). A few years later, discussing paranoid ideas of reference, Freud (1901) recognized that "*There is in fact some truth in them*" (p. 256; emphasis Freud's), an idea to which he would return in 1937. The kernel of truth in the delusion was like the day

residue embedded in the manifest content of the dream: the paranoiac was testifying to something that was historically true but that,
due to censorship (i.e., defense), took the shape of manifest interpretive delusions and the *complex emotion* of distrust.

The received story is that Freud discovered the homosexuality–paranoia formula in Schreber's *Memoirs*. This is incorrect:
Freud had that causal theory in place by 1908, prior to his learning
about Schreber's book from Jung in 1910 (Lothane, 1997a) as he
declares himself: "I can . . . call a friend and fellow-specialist to
witness that I had developed my theory of paranoia before I became
acquainted with Schreber's book" (Freud, 1911a, p. 79). The fellow
specialist in question was none other than his beloved pupil Ferenczi
who was first, in 1910, to write a clinical study, "On the Role
of Homosexuality in the Pathogenesis of Paranoia," which was
published the same year as Freud's essay (Ferenczi, 1911), and
misdated as 1913 in the *Bausteine zur Psychoanalyze*, in 1927.

Ferenzi described how the hysteric is protected from his unwel-
come emotions toward the other by amnesia and the various mechanisms of displacement, whereas with the paranoiac the desire and
'interest [in others] becomes so unacceptable that it becomes ob-
jectified (with affect reversal, i.e., with "a negative sign"), cast out
of the ego . . . and returns as a perception . . . the feeling of love is
turned into a sensation of its opposite" (1911, p. 73). In a footnote
Ferenczi proposed the term *ambisexuality,* the psychical capacity
of the child to attach his primary, objectless eroticism to the male
or female sex [presumably the parents, Z. L.], to develop a fixation
to one or both sexes" (Ferenczi, 1911, p. 91; author's translation).

Why did Freud choose to illustrate his ideas via Schreber rather
than write up a case of his own, even though he did "see plenty of
cases of paranoia and of dementia praecox"? He gave two reasons:
first he did not see these cases long enough "to lead to any analytic
conclusions," and second, he found that Schreber shared with other
paranoiacs "the peculiarity of betraying (in a distorted form, it is
true) precisely those things which other neurotics keep hidden as a
secret" with the added advantage that in these cases "a written
report or a printed case history can take the place of a personal
acquaintance with the patient . . . suffering from paranoia (or, more
precisely, from dementia paranoides) whom I have never seen but
who has written his own case history and brought it before the

public in print" (1911a, p. 9). In private, he confessed to Jung: "Since the man is still alive, I was thinking of asking him for certain information (e.g. when he got married) and for permission to work on his story. But perhaps that would be risky: What do you think?" (McGuire, 1974, p. 358). But what was that risk? It might have been too late anyway, for Schreber was deteriorating and only six months away from his death. Had Freud traveled to Saxony, he would have found that highly coveted, expurgated third chapter of the *Memoirs* that was part of the patient's chart in Dresden, or interviewed his colleague Flechsig, from the neuroanatomy days, in Leipzig. It is a pity this never happened.

Freud's Method in Interpreting Schreber's Text

Freely commingling description, diagnosis, and dynamic interpretation, Freud did not rely primarily on Schreber's own words and chronology but gave equal if not greater authority to paraphrases of those in the reports by Weber, and mixed elements from various periods, to fashion an interpretation that was more formulaic than historical, and in the absence of the patient's associations to the material, an exercise in applied, not clinical analysis. In contrast to Jewish Biblical exegesis, according to which the text is treated as sacred and unalterable, Freud altered and rearranged details to suit his theoretical premises. But Schreber's text is the original and authentic text and primary to all others. Moreover, from an ethical viewpoint, Schreber is remarkably truthful and should be believed on his own terms.

Contrary to Freud's claim, Schreber wrote no autobiographical account of a case of paranoia. Freud followed the two basic definitions of paranoia current in German psychiatry: the broad one, as a term for any fantastic, bizarre, or baroque mental content, and the narrow, as ideas of reference and persecution without a cause (i.e., a figment of the patient's imagination). Freud viewed Schreber's paranoid delusions as an ideational and emotional complex, thus, as a syndromal, dynamic constellation and not an essentialist psychiatric disorder. Above all, he viewed paranoia "as an especially intense work of delusion-formation [*Wahnbildungsarbeit*], . . . [i.e.] paranoia on the model of a far more familiar mental phenomenon—the dream" (1911a, p. 38), based on the homology of dream work (*Traumarbeit*), and the transformation of reality perceptions into a hallucinatory (endopsychic) wish-fulfilling image. He combined the above with the dynamics of dream and desire: the conception of the symptom as a compromise formation of the libidinal impulse and the defense against it, handled by projection and coupled with a regression to developmental fixation points, or the return of the repressed. The question remains: What was repressed and what returned?

Schreber's Sexual Imaginings

Schreber's various sexual imaginings differ from such imaginings in Freud and may be grouped as follows: (1) mystical–religious ideas concerning the nature of God; (2) transformation into a woman as a gender identity issue; (3) soul murder; (4) fantasies of sensual pleasure; (5) fantasies of procreation.

As Freud duly noted, in the prodromal period of the second illness, Schreber "dreamt two or three times that his old nervous disorder came back" and "once, in the early hours of the morning . . . in a state between sleeping and waking, the idea occurred to him 'that after all it really must be very nice to be a woman submitting to the act of copulation' (36)" (Freud, 1911a, p. 13). The hypnopompic dream would become, as Freud quotes, Schreber's ultimate "delusional system: he believed . . . [that] he had a mission to redeem the world and to restore it to its lost state of bliss. This, however, he could only bring about if he were first transformed into a woman (475)" (p. 16).

Schreber had a dual redeemer identification, with Jesus Christ, the innocent sufferer crucified, and with a woman miraculously fertilized by God to bear a new race: they go hand in hand. Thus, in his footnote 103, Schreber's dating is explicit: "one of the first visions I ever had [was] (about the beginning of March 1894); as far as I can remember, in the *very first* vision in which God, if I may express it so, revealed Himself to me. . . . I do remember that I told Professor Flechsig on the following morning something about the content of these visions and that I had a conversation with him on this topic" (Schreber, 1903, p. 257); he does not tell us what the professor told him in reply. This dating is confirmed by the hospital chart: "*March 1* [1894]. Believes he is a young girl, fears indecent assaults'' (Lothane, 1992a). On the other hand, already in footnote 1 Schreber says that ''twice at different times (while I was still in Flechsig's Asylum) I had a female genital organ, although a poorly developed one, and in my body felt a quickening like the first signs of life of a human embryo; by a divine miracle God's nerves corresponding to male seed were thrown into my body; in other words fertilization had occurred'' (Schreber, 1903, p. 4). That this description of a male pregnancy plays out on a number of symbolic levels does not contradict its also being a vehicle for nihilistic persecutory abuse fantasies that often typify the aggression–ridden (un)consciousness and the guilt ridden-conscience of the melancholic.

Now emasculation usually means removal of the reproductive organs precluding procreation. Contrary to Freud's definition of the term, to mean, predominantly, the boy's fear of the paternal threat of genital mutilation, Schreber speaks of unmanning in the context of punishment for unbridled sexual excesses and redemption through renewal of the race by means of a sex change. He also describes that such a transformation was not achieved by anything being cut but by a reversal of a normal embryogeny in a process of a biological regression.

[Following] world catastrophes which necessitate the destruction of mankind . . . when . . . moral decay (''voluptuous excesses'') or perhaps nervousness has seized mankind to such an extent that . . . in order to maintain the species, one single human being—perhaps the relatively most moral—was spared . . . [i.e.,] the ''Eternal Jew'' . . . [meant in] a somewhat different sense from the legend of the same name of the Jew Ahasver [but related] to the legends of Noah, Deucalion and Pyrrha, etc. The Eternal Jew had to be *unmanned* (transformed into a woman) *to be able to bear children* . . . this process of unmanning consisted in the (external) male genitals (scrotum and penis) being retracted into the body and the internal sexual organs being at the same time transformed into the corresponding female sexual organs. . . . A regression occurred therefore, or a reversal of that developmental process by which occurs in the human embryo in the fourth or fifth month of pregnancy, according to whether nature intends the future child to be of male or female sex. It is well known that in the first months of pregnancy the rudiments of both sexes are laid down and the characteristics of the sex which is not developed remain as rudimentary organs at a lower stage of development, like the nipples of the male [Schreber, 1903, pp. 52–55; last emphasis added].

Schreber's "*Ewige Jude*" is different from the medieval anti-Semitic legend of the Wandering Jew who spurned Jesus and was cursed. Here it is a fantasy of a righteous man, who like the God of Jakob Böhme, has the attribute of self-begetting (*Urzeugung*, or spontaneous generation; Schreber, 1903, p. 251). Moreover, with his usual precision, Schreber defines unmanning as a transformation into a woman for the purpose of bearing a new human race, thus an ancient idea of messianic renewal of mankind, not a homosexual wish (Lothane, 1998a). He is also conversant with the embryological fact that both genders develop from a common bisexual prestage prior to subsequent sexual differentiation. No less illuminating is that Schreber also hints at a psychological dedifferentiation: from a fixed male gender identity to gender identity diffusion and a feeling that one is both genders at the same time. While the latter is of importance for understanding Schreber's sexual imaginings as consequences, rather than cause, of the psychotic process, it is also essential to underscore that Schreber's dual view of unmanning as harmful, as an ignominious *emasculation* and part of soul murder, and unmanning as *healing*, as a mystical and cosmic ethical principle.

The primacy given to homosexuality and castration as the main pathogenic cause of the delusion of persecution led Freud (1911a) to contradictions in assessing Schreber's major preoccupation, "his alleged transformation into a woman" (p. 32). Interpreting Schreber's original hypnopompic reverie about what a woman feels in the act of copulation, which "phantasy appeared during the incubation of his illness" (p. 20), as an "emasculation phantasy" rather than a transformation fantasy, even as he quoted Weber's assessment that "The idea of being transformed into a woman was the salient feature and the earliest germ of his delusional system" (p. 21), made Freud vacillate regarding the dynamics of the final fantasy of turning into a woman as one that completed the arc of Schreber's profound identification with woman: mother, sister, and wife. What remains obscure for lack of biographical data, is what was the repressed and what were its origins that returned with such force in Schreber's hypnopompic reverie in the summer of 1893. Schreber also called it the "cultivation of femaleness," indeed, as Freud himself said, "a realization of the content of that [incubation] dream" (p. 33). But as such it was a fantasy that had developed in its own right and independent of castration or the horrific visions of sexual abuse. This identification with woman gave Schreber the means to pursue "the cultivation of voluptuousness" not solely, as Freud thought, in order to become "God's wife" (p. 32), but also in order to overcome his "sexual asceticism" and thereby gain moral permission to enjoy sensuality for its own sake and thus to achieve "spiritual voluptuousness" as a cure for his sleeplessness.

The feminine identification and imaginings were Schreber's way to overcome his long-standing conflicts caused by conflicts of conscience concerning sexual emotions as such. It is here, as I have argued (Lothane, 1989a), that the son was pitted against his father's admonitions against undue sexual enjoyment prescribed as a health regimen in his *Medical Indoor Gymnastic* (the only work quoted by the son in the *Memoirs*) and reflecting a deep pietistic and puritanical streak in the father. This is how Paul Schreber alludes to such conflicts:

> This behavior [i.e., feeling and acting like a woman, Z. L.] has been forced on me . . . [which] may sound paradoxical. . . . On the other hand God demands *constant enjoyment*, as the normal existence of souls within the Order of the World. . . . If I can get a little sensuous pleasure in this process, I feel I am entitled to it as a small compensation for the excess of suffering and privation that has been mine for many years [Schreber, 1903, p. 283; emphasis Schreber's].

Freud (1911a, p. 34) was impressed enough to quote this passage and endorse the self-healing role of these and other fantasies as "a struggle between repression and an attempt at recovery by bringing the libido back again to its objects" (1911a, p. 77). "Before his illness . . . Schreber had been a man of strict morals. . . . After the severe spiritual struggle, of which the phenomena of his illness were the outward signs, . . . [h]e had come to see that the cultivation of voluptuousness was incumbent upon him as a duty, . . . that [it] had become 'God-fearing' " (1911a, p. 31). However, instead of understanding the resolution of conflict as within the context of heterosexual eroticism and the dynamics of feminine identification and crossdressing, Freud undid his deeper insight by insisting to the very end that Schreber was enabled "to reconcile himself to his homosexual phantasy . . . in something approximating to a recovery" (1911a, p. 78), for understanding such conflicts in the context of gender identity and experimenting with crossing of gender boundaries was yet to come (Lothane, 1993b).

The further evolution of this idea led Schreber down the path of splitting his gender identity into playing man and woman in fantasy, more a consequence of the psychotic process than a cause of it, a product of disintegration, or disinhibition, as Hughlings Jackson put it, or of regression, as Freud rephrased it. This process occurred in the depressive phase of his mood disorder and later followed by the redeemer fantasy. The regression showed an undoing of developmental sublimations and perhaps a return to earlier fixation points of the shifting identifications of childhood. And, again, it was also a way of overcoming his conflicts about sex as recreation versus the traditional religious view of sex as a means to procreation. Listen to Schreber himself philosophizing on the affinity between voluptuousness and everlasting Blessedness.

In this light Schiller's "Ode to Joy" is almost visionary and reminiscent of divine inspiration: "Voluptuousness is given even to the worm but it's the Cherub who stands before God." Nevertheless there is an essential difference. Voluptuous enjoyment is granted . . . to *human beings* and other living creatures *solely as a means for the preservation of the species.* Herein lie the moral limitations of voluptuousness for human beings. An excess of voluptuousness would render man unfit to fulfill his other obligations; it would even prevent him from ever rising to the higher mental and moral perfection; indeed experience teaches that not only single individuals but also whole nations have perished through voluptuous excesses. *For me such moral limits to voluptuousness no longer exist, indeed in a certain sense the reverse applies.* In order not to be misunderstood, I must point out that when I speak of my duty to cultivate voluptuousness, *I never mean any sexual desire towards other human beings (females), least of all sexual intercourse,* but that I have *to imagine myself as a man and a woman in one person having intercourse with myself,* or somehow have to achieve with myself a certain excitement etc.—which perhaps under certain circumstances might be considered immoral—but which has nothing whatever to do with any idea of masturbation or anything like it [Schreber, 1903, pp. 281–282; last emphasis added].

Schreber can fairly be said to anticipate Freud's pleasure principle and the motto, where id was there shall ego be. In his regressive fantasy, Schreber is enacting man and woman in one person, a kind of psychic hermaphroditism grafted upon a biological one, a compensatory daydream in a man not only bereft of children but attempting to cope with the chronic sexual deprivation, as happens in prisons. That fantasy also served Schreber to imagine an act of spontaneous generation, another way of assuring himself of progeny, in addition to being fertilized by God in a metaphorical sense to produce a new mankind issuing from the spirit of Schreber, fertilized by his ideas, as might be said to have materialized in all those delving into the subject of Schreber.

The cultivation of the androgyne in literature, film, and the pop culture is by now a commonplace. This idea of the androgynous being has been expressed in myths of many nations, in Plato's *Symposium* and in the Hebrew Mishna: God created man androgynous and is himself androgynous. In Greek mythology, the relevant story was about Tiresias, the only person ever who had lived both as man and as woman. Later, in the medieval cabalistic tract, the *Zohar, The Book of Splendor*, that is, light, the mystery of the *Shekhinah*, the divine immanence, consists in her gender ambiguity. Like a Gnostic female aeon, she is considered female as a Bride of God, and the mother of the sons of Israel, and a symbol of eternal womanhood. When sent down upon earth as a liberating angel, she assumes the form of a male when dispensing benedictions or a female when dispensing judgment. Other manifestations of the Shekhinah, as the Matrona and Metatron, may show gender fluctuations back and forth (Lothane, 1998b). Also in the *Zohar*, Moses is described as the " 'husband of the Shekhimah,' implying that he has mythical intercourse with this divine manifestation" (Idel, 1988, p. 228).

Such motifs may have been known to the well-read Schreber and they have bearings on his imagining himself a redeemer, which Weber branded as paranoia: "crystallized out so to speak into . . . a more or less elaborate delusional system . . . not amenable to correction by objective evidence . . . [as shown by] some of his writings" (Schreber, 1903, pp. 385–386). It was beyond a man like Weber to grasp the difference, intuited by Schreber, between the male, oedipal Jehovah, the clearly male and oedipal Apollanoan imago of Moritz

Schreber, and the Dionysian, mystical, feminine-to-androgynous Jesus—his son Paul.

Freud, however, did not remain oblivious to the fact that the fantasy of turning into a woman:

> [P]roved to be the one part . . . that was able to retain a place in his behaviour in real life after he had recovered . . . [when he would] "sometimes . . . be found standing before the mirror or elsewhere, with the upper portion of [his] body bared, and wearing sundry feminine adornments" (429). The Herr Senatspräsident confesses to this frivolity . . . [but he] never took any steps towards inducing people to recognize his mission as Redeemer, beyond the publication of his *Denkwürdigkeiten* [1911a, p. 21].

And Freud notes further that "The patient's sense of reality . . . had in the meantime become stronger . . . [and he was] compelled . . . to postpone the solution from the present to the remote future, and content himself with what might be described as an asymptotic wish-fulfilment" (1911a, p. 48), that is, playful fantasies, not incurable delusions, as Weber had maintained. Had Freud pursued further his insight that "the feminist attitude . . . would also be designed to offer him an escape from his childlessness" (p. 58) and focused more clearly on feminine identification as a wish to become mother and bear children—a wish that he was keenly aware of in the case of Little Hans—he would have taken away from Macalpine and Hunter (1953) their claim that they had introduced a new paradigm for interpreting Schreber. However, Freud did not write about transvestitism.

Doctors and judges do not like to see their opinions overturned. Thus, in the 1920s, Freud remains fixated on his patricentric formulation that like Schreber, the monk Haizmann fell ill due to the "boy's feminine attitude to his father and the phantasy of pregnancy that arises from it," stemming from "the unresolved conflict between a masculine and a feminine attitude (fear of castration and desire for castration)," and "masochistic phantasies which were wholly derived from a wish to accept castration" (Freud, 1923, pp. 91–92). Freud includes a reproduction of "the second appearance of the Devil to Christoph Haizmann" in which the Devil is portrayed with oversize feminine breasts. As Freud explains:

It is only since Senatspräsident Daniel Paul Schreber . . . that we can discuss the subject of [the boy's feminine attitude and pregnancy fantasy] and [we can] learn from [Schreber's] invaluable book that, . . . God—who incidentally, exhibited distinct traits of his father, the worthy physician Dr. Schreber—had decided to emasculate him, to use him as a woman, and to beget from him "a new race born from the spirit of Schreber." . . . The gifted author of his own case history could not have guessed that in it he had uncovered a typical pathogenic factor [Freud, 1923, p. 91].

While the above sheds light on the feminine oedipal attitude of the boy to his father, it still misses the boy's important positive identification with the mother, seeing that the Devil's oversize breasts could be a reverse portrayal of the big-breasted phallic mother, where the breasts are the primary symbol upon which are superimposed the masculine attributes of power and control, as they appear to the little boy in his shifting identifications between mother and father.

In a letter of 1926 to Marie Bonaparte, Freud freely admitted that he had known that "[A]fter being discharged [Schreber] lived contentedly for a number of years until his wife fell ill of severe apoplexy. After that he felt insecure and again entered the hospital. There is no later information, but it may be guessed that the motive for his illness was the turning away from his wife and the dissatisfaction over not bearing any children. With the apoplexy feelings of guilt and of temptation returned" (Quoted in Jones, 1957, p. 447). Does "the motive of illness" refer to his second or third illness? Freud did not mention issues of guilt and temptation in 1911, but I think it is a stretch that in 1907 Schreber had guilt over homosexual temptation.

The fantastic–delusional myth spun here is Schreber's attempt to portray himself, in grand and heroic terms, as redeeming a sinful mankind in the manner of Noah. That this grandiose fantasy might be viewed as a psychotic compensation for guilt, shame, and low self-esteem, or express envy of his mother's and sister's ability to have progeny while his wife has had repeated miscarriages and stillbirths—the last of them a boy, in 1892—does not diminish the sublimity of the moral vision itself, or that Schreber's unmanning was only of importance in the context of sexual abuse as a component of the famed soul murder.

Schreber's Soul Murder

Freud introduces the theme of soul murder by quoting Schreber:

> In this way a conspiracy against me was brought to a head (in about March or April, 1984). Its object was to contrive that, when once my nervous complaint had been recognized as incurable or assumed to be so, I should be handed over to a certain person in a particular manner: my soul was to be delivered up to him, but my body—owing to a misapprehension of what I have described above as the purpose underlying the Order of Things—was to be transformed into a female body, and as such surrendered to the person in question with a view to sexual abuse, and was then simply to be "left on one side"—that is to say, no doubt given over to corruption [in the Macalpine translation: 'Being forsaken' in other words left to rot] (56).
>
> It was, moreover, perfectly natural that . . . I should regard Professor Flechsig or his soul as my only true enemy . . . and that I should look upon God Almighty as my natural ally. . . . It was not until much later that the idea forced itself upon my mind that God Himself had played the part of accomplice, if not instigator, in the plot whereby my soul was to be murdered and my body used like a strumpet. I may say, in fact, that this idea has in part become clearly conscious to me only in the course of writing the present work [Freud, 1911a, p. 19].

Freud's apodictic conclusion from this passage, was that " 'the person in question' who was to practice this abuse was none other than Flechsig" (1911a, p. 19, note 1), although Schreber never said that, and that the abuse was exclusively sexual. But Schreber refers to a triple soul murder: to declare him incurable, to destroy his soul, and to leave his sexually abused body to rot. This is either decided by God himself, or by God swayed by Flechsig, who, like Satan in the Book of Job and Goethe's Faust, "had succeeded in making his way up to heaven . . . and in becoming a 'leader of rays' . . . (56)" (Freud, 1911a, p. 39); that is, seduced God to persecute Schreber. This is Schreber's poetical recreation of the events of 1894 that led to his banishment from Flechsig's University Hospital to a public insane asylum, in 1897, when he was drafting the *Memoirs* in preparation for his suit for rescinding of the incompetency and for release

from Sonnenstein. Freud clearly referred to these matters, fully described in the *Memoirs* (Lothane, 1992a), stating in the *Gesammelte
Werke* that the patient took appropriate steps to rescind his *Kuratel*
(Freud, 1911b, p. 246), the legal term in Austria referring to incompetency and guardianship, which Strachey inadequately renders as
"regaining control over his own affairs" (1911a, p. 15). Freud was
full of admiration for the "acumen and the cogency of his logic"
and Schreber's "*Triumph*" (1911b, p. 248), more emphatic than
Strachey's "success" (1911a, p. 16), following lifting of his "*ver-
hängte Entmündigung*" (= fateful incompetency; Freud, 1911b, p.
248), which Strachey translates as: "Dr. Schreber's civil rights were
restored" (p. 16). However, it did not occur to Freud to consider
the involuntary stay at Sonnenstein as a real life privation, about
which Schreber raged bitterly in his attacks of bellowing right up
until the writing of the 1903 "Open Letter to Professor Flechsig"
in which he accuses Flechsig of having committed "malpractice
[also] called 'soul murder', the souls, for lack of a better term, using
a term already in current usage and because of their innate tendency
to express themselves hyperbolically" (Schreber, 1903, pp. viii–ix),
thus, no schizophrenic neologism, as commonly asserted, but an
obsolete term meaning psychological or moral abuse and defined
in old German dictionaries and other sources as spiritual murder
(Lothane, 1992b, 1993a). This concept was later applied by the
German judge Feuerbach to fashion a legal concept, "Verbrechen
am Seelenleben des Menschen," a crime against a person's psychological life (Devreese, 1996). Nor did it occur to Freud to consider
Schreber's real and transference relationship with Weber, or connect these matters with soul murder (Lothane, 1992a).

There was an unnamed coconspirator in the malpractice plot
called *soul murder,* unknown to Freud, Carl Edmund Werner,
Schreber's boss at the Dresden Court of Appeals. When a money
dispute erupted between Paul and Sabine Schreber in May of 1894
and, in a fit of anger, Schreber refused to sign papers against which
his wife could cash in his salary, Werner, with a wink from Flechsig,
recommended that Sabine make an application to declare her spouse
incompetent and gain control of the assets, which she did (Lothane,
1992a, 1992b). When at the end of the statutory six months at
Flechsig's Schreber was transferred to Sonnenstein, his fate became
doubly sealed by Weber's diagnosis of incurable paranoia and the

incompetency status. In this manner, Schreber's soul murder was completed and he was left to rot. A double victim of psychiatric expertise and the legal system, a mighty judge lost his civil liberties to become like a 7-year-old child in the eyes of the law, indefinitely warehoused in the asylum, without any treatment or plans for rehabilitation, abandoned by his family, wife, and friends, his soul murdered and his body abused by rough attendants. Referring to soul murder for the second time, Freud reaffirms that "It is unnecessary to remark that no other individual is ever named who could be put in Flechsig's place" while in the next sentence we read: "Towards the end of Schreber's stay in the clinic at Leipzig, a fear occurred to his mind that he 'was to be thrown to the attendants' for the purpose of sexual abuse (98)" (1911a, p. 44). However, Schreber gave utterance to this fear not only toward the end but already at the very beginning:

> About the fourth or fifth night after my admission to the Asylum, I was pulled out of bed by two attendants in the middle of the night . . . because I had no idea what one intended to do with me and therefore thought I had to resist, a fight started between myself clad only in a shirt, and the two attendants, . . . was eventually overpowered and removed to [an isolation]. . . . I must mention that during a later conversation Professor Flechsig denied the whole occurrence . . . and tried to make out that it was only a figment of my imagination—this by the way was one of the circumstances which from then on made me somewhat distrustful of Professor Flechsig [Schreber, 1903, p. 41].

Freud did not consider that the behavior of the attendants or Flechsig's handling of the situation could have in any way caused Schreber's symptoms. But it did in two ways: it exposed Schreber to their brutality and possibly to unwanted sexual stimulation at a time of mounting psychotic vulnerability. Their incomprehensible action seemed to suggest that not only was Flechsig behind it, but, more gallingly, that he sided with attendants against the patient and had the chutzpah to insinuate that the whole scene was but a figment of Schreber's morbid imagination. This was a deplorable and unprofessional lack of empathy, not uncommon not only in those times, that added insult to injury. No wonder Schreber lost trust, no wonder he accused Flechsig of an attempt to murder his soul, or to plain drive him crazy. But the worst was yet to come: the ultimate betrayal in the breaking off of the doctor–patient relationship by Flechsig.

Freud disregarded Schreber's dating of the onset of soul murder—a trauma within a trauma, or a drama within a drama—in March or April of 1894, that is, four or five months into the hospitalization at Flechsig's, and his defining soul murder first and foremost as a spiritual murder related to the declaration of incurability and the banishment to Sonnenstein, a blow to his pride and an end to his legal career. To put it succinctly, Freud invented a scenario instead of reproducing the historical one, based on his sexual imaginings about Schreber.

Freud's Sexual Imaginings about Schreber

Of the various paranoias and homosexualities, Freud chose to ''limit [his] assertion to a single type of paranoia'' (1911a, p. 63), passive male homosexual wishes resulting in delusions of persecution, a syndrome whose universality has been questioned by various analysts (e.g., Rosenfeld [1949], quoted in Lothane [1989a]). In thus explaining Schreber's *entire* second illness, Freud dismissed Schreber's own stated reasons for falling ill, his fearful anticipation of the new job, even though he noted Schreber's worries that ''His family line threatened to die out'' (p. 58), duly acknowledging the chief frustration in Schreber's life, '' 'the oft-repeated disappointment of our hope that we might be blessed with children' '' (p. 13), or his awareness that ''libido becomes collaterally reinforced owing to some disappointment over a woman, or is directly dammed up owing to a mishap in social relations with other men—both of these being instances of 'frustration' '' (1911a, p. 62), or ''some privation in real life'' (p. 57). Nor was Freud blind to the possibility that ''we must not omit to draw attention to a somatic factor which may very well have been relevant. At the time of the illness Schreber was fifty-one years old, and he had therefore reached an age which is of critical importance in sexual life: . . . for men as well as women are subject to 'climacteric' and to the susceptibilities to disease which go along with it''(1911a, p. 46). Was he thinking that the somatic factor could also be psychic and related either to problems with potency or of frigidity in the wife? However that may be, all these factors were reduced to one: Schreber's alleged pathogenic homosexual desires that Freud believed to have been reconstructed according to the following libidinal–dynamic progression.

Step 1. The fantasy about a woman's feeling in intercourse, occurring in the summer of 1893, the prodrome of the second illness, was read as a prima facie homosexual manifestation.

Step 2. That fantasy, experienced by Schreber in the summer of 1893, prior to any renewed, actual contact with Flechsig in November of 1893, was equated with "the appearance of a feminine (that is, passive homosexual) wishful fantasy, which took as its object the figure of his doctor [i.e., Flechsig]" (1911a, p. 47). Freud could "well imagine what a dubious hypothesis it must appear to be that a man's friendly feeling towards his doctor can suddenly break out in an intensified form after a lapse of eight years and become the occasion of such a severe mental disorder" (p. 46). However, he was satisfied that he had been able to infer that Schreber's "second and severe illness [started] during the incubation period . . . that is between June 1893, when he was appointed to his new post, and the following October, when he took up his duties" (p. 42), and was caused by none other than "an outburst of homosexual libido . . . and his struggles against the libidinal impulse produced the conflict which gave rise to the symptoms" (p. 43), so that "the basis of Schreber's illness was the outburst of a homosexual impulse" (p. 45). Freud further argued that this breakthrough of homosexual desire was prompted by the "feeling of affectionate dependence upon his doctor, which by now, for some unknown reason, became *intensified to the pitch of an erotic desire*" (p. 42; emphasis added), that is, a fully conscious desire with full affect, that "had its root in a longing, intensified to an erotic pitch, for his father and brother" (p. 50). Such equations and inferences remain biographically unproved, no less than the assumption that a feminine fantasy is a universal proof of homosexual desire, or that it suggests unmanning in the sense of castration: the above scenario is purely Freud's invention. Uneasily, Freud claimed it was Schreber "himself [who] has given us the right to occupy ourselves with his phantasy, and in translating it into the technical terminology of medicine we have not made the slightest addition to its content" (1911a, p. 43). But have we?

Step 3. Freud further argued that Schreber's sexual desire for Flechsig in the prodromal period was repeated and mirrored in soul murder, "a sexual delusion of persecution" (1911a, p. 18), since he, Freud, was able to "divine the fact that the patient was in fear of sexual abuse at the hands of his doctor himself" (p. 43), based on the assumption that a fear equals a wish. However, Schreber only spoke ambiguously of "the person in question" and his associations to that statement are not available. But we saw that Freud was well aware that Schreber's fears of sexual abuse included being " 'thrown to attendants' for the purpose of sexual abuse (98)" (p. 44), so that Flechsig was *not* the only possible "seducer," or that in Pierson's asylum "the Flechsig soul was joined by the soul of the chief attendant" (p. 39). Did Schreber also have desires for these attendants before he ever met them?

Step 4. To bolster this hypothesis, Freud further argued that: This hypothesis harmonizes "with . . . the patient [having] had a fresh 'nervous collapse', which exercised a decisive effect on the course of his illness, at a time when his wife was taking a short holiday on account of her own health. . . . 'What especially determined my mental break-down was a particular night, during which I had a quite extraordinary number of emissions—quite half a dozen, all in that one night (44)' " (1911a, p. 45). Freud assumed that: "It is easy to understand that the mere presence of his wife must have acted as a protection against the attractive power of the men about him; and if we are prepared to admit that an emission cannot occur in an adult without some mental concomitant," and instantly converts his premise into an unfounded inference: "we shall be able to supplement the patient's emissions that night by assuming that they were accompanied by homosexual phantasies which remained unconscious" (p. 45). Freud also overlooked the fact that the emissions occurred not after the wife's departure but *after* she returned, thus a reaction to something else has happened, disregarding Schreber's statement on that same page that the wife went to Berlin to visit her father, clearly to confer with her father about what to do next with her sick spouse, thus causing Schreber to feel threatened after Sabine's return. Not only was Schreber enraged at his wife, and refused to see her, but also at his father-in-law as well (Lothane, 1992a).

Step 5. Freud went on to draw two equations: God equals Flechsig, and God equals father, and to bridge the two, in order to show that "persecutor Flechsig was originally a person whom

Schreber loved . . . this other person must have been his father (p. 50) . . . by no means unsuitable for transformation into a God in the affectionate memory of the son from whom he had been so early separated by death" (p. 51). The death of the father occurred when Schreber was 19, while the transformation into God Freud considered as an oedipal achievement. The point of these equations was to show once again that Schreber harbored nothing but erotic wishes or needs toward Flechsig, a transference from father, transformed into a delusion of persecution by means of the defense of projection. Freud missed Schreber's thinly veiled mockery in speaking of Flechsig as Godlike. Nor did Freud allow that Schreber's God was not only a father substitute but, as he expressly said, an embodiment of divine providence, and thus accused by Schreber clamoring *de profundis*, not unlike Job or the survivors of the Holocaust, as having abandoned a suffering human being. Moreover, Freud did not allow that Schreber was entitled to realistic need satisfactions from Flechsig as his doctor. For Freud these equations are probative: "Any remaining doubts that we have upon the nature of the part originally attributed to the doctor are dispelled when, in the later stages of his delusion, we find Schreber outspokenly admitting his feminine attitude towards God. The other accusation against Flechsig echoes over-loudly through the book. Flechsig, he says, tried to commit soul-murder on him" (1911a, p. 44), invoking soul murder for the third time in its exclusively sexual sense of a fear betokening Schreber's erotic wish.

Step 6. As the culmination of his sexualization of Schreber, Freud postulated that Schreber's other famous delusion, that "Schreber became convinced of the imminence of a great catastrophe, of the end of the world: . . . [that] he himself was 'the only man left alive', and the few human shapes that he still saw—the doctor, the attendants, the other patients—[were] 'miracled-up cursorily improvised men' " (p. 68), was nothing but "the consequence of the conflict which had broken out between him and Flechsig" (1911a, p. 69). A conflict there was, but not any sexual conflict to explain "the detachment of the libido from the figure of Flechsig" (1911a, p. 173); and even if it were true, it could not account for the magnitude of the depressive ramifications of the end-of-the-world mood because his despair was far greater than that caused by his disappointment in Flechsig. Even psychiatrists, for example,

Jaspers, have agreed that such fantasies abound in depressive states. But Freud's hypothesis crumbles under the weight of his own reasoning, presaging, as it does, the birth of ego psychology: "that a secondary or induced disturbance of the libidinal processes may result from an abnormal change in the ego. Indeed, it is possible that processes of this kind constitute the distinctive characteristic of the psychoses" (1911a, p. 75).

Freud's exclusive focus on the "characteristically paranoic . . . warding off a homosexual wishful phantasy" (p. 59) prevented him from seeing, as Schreber saw, that "*there may have been a profound internal change*" (Schreber, 1903, pp. 84–85), that "the end of the world was . . . the inevitable result of his illness" (p. 69); i.e., his depressive illness—resulting in Schreber's detachment of love and affection not only from Flechsig but from the world entire, due to despair and giving up. "It is certain," Freud presciently adds to his sexual interpretation, "that in normal mental life (not only in periods of mourning) we are constantly detaching our libido in this way from people or from other objects without falling ill . . . there must be some special characteristic which distinguishes a paranoic detachment of libido from other kinds . . . in paranoia the liberated libido becomes attached to the ego and is used for the aggrandizement of the ego" (p. 72). The back flow of libido, not of sexual libido only but of ego libido as well, may be either concrete or metaphorical, but an aggrandizement of the ego does indeed occur in the manic phase of the cycle that followed the mourning caused by the loss of attachments to the world. Moreover, it is not libido economy alone that causes megalomania, as Arlow and Brenner (1964, 1969) have argued, but its connection to loss of self-esteem and the ensuing need to compensate for it, as in melancholia.

Not only is the aforementioned sexual scenario implausible, but so is the very attribution of conscious homosexual desires to Schreber, for, as Freud noted, "So long as he was healthy, Dr. Schreber . . . had, by all accounts, shown no signs of homosexuality in the ordinary sense of the word" (p. 60). But Schreber showed no sign of homosexuality in the ordinary sense throughout the entire stay in the asylums either. In fact, in the *Memoirs* he described himself as busy with searching for pictures of female nudes in illustrated magazines, with drawing such pictures, and with daydreams about female shapes; such behavior is also described in the hospital chart (Lothane, 1992a). All this begs a basic methodological question: besides having meanings other than the exclusive one Freud read into it, the feminine fantasy and the fantasies of sexual abuse, rather than being only the *cause* of the illness, are rather a *result* of the illness and the conditions of hospital life. Thus the psychotic process results in an undoing of repression of dependent and feminine identifications and promotes a return of the repressed; that is, the repressed feminine side and conflicts about dependent and sensual pleasure. The homosexual hypothesis prevented Freud from acknowledging the role of aggression and gender identity issues.

What If Schreber Were Freud's Patient?

I have not conducted a survey to see how often analysts actually apply Freud's homosexual–paranoid formula to patients in treatment. Dr. Socarides, for one, does not use Freud's formula in his analytic work (personal communication). Would Freud have done so himself? A probable answer is provided by the case of a psychotic man Freud did treat (Lynn, 1993): in that case Freud did not use his dynamic formula. For all its prominence, Freud did not mention the Schreber case in his two papers on the history of psychoanalysis (1914a,b), or in his *Autobiographical Study* (1925), except for his aforementioned essay on Haizmann and a passing reference in the Wolf Man case. There were some noteworthy contemporary contributions on the dynamics and treatment of psychotic patients, for example, by Bjerre (1911) and Spielrein (1911), that centered on interpersonal and nonsexual dynamics.

A pivotal criticism has been that Freud staked everything on the assumption of Schreber's sexual wishes, confusing issues of homosexual dread and homosexual desire, a clinical and dynamic concept of fundamental importance, as formulated by Dr. Socarides (2001) and his numerous publications on the subject of homosexuality. It is thus significant that in the light of his vast experience with people with homosexual conflicts, Dr. Socarides agrees with me that Schreber's was not a problem with homosexual desire but homosexual dread. This is borne out by Schreber's initial reaction to his "idea that it really must be rather pleasant to be a woman succumbing to intercourse. This idea was so foreign to my whole nature that I may say I would have rejected it with indignation if fully awake," and not having the concepts of the unconscious and the return of the repressed, Schreber "could not exclude the possibility that some external influences were at work to implant this idea in me" (Schreber, 1903, pp. 36–38). This idea later evolved into the horrific dread of being unmanned contrary to the Order of the World and transformed into a woman to serve as an object of sexual and other forms of abuse. The formulation offered by Socarides could fairly apply to Schreber: his negative sexual fantasies "are experienced as a threat of the loss of self-representation and sexual identity, together with the further loss of narcissistic supplies and the loss of heterosexual love object" and so does his invoking of a case of Rosenfeld's (1949). I cannot say it better than applying the formulations of Socarides to Schreber: "it is Schreber's fear of a narcissistic sought-after love object's denial of him, as well as his fear and hatred of the mother," and father, "together with his failure to attain such an object in a love relationship," in addition to childlessness, "which catapulted him into such terror" and he felt obligated to use his various sexual imaginings as "internalized soothing structures."

Concluding Remarks

Freud overplayed his interpretive hand and did not heed his own caveat: "the psychoanalyst needs no small amount of tact and restraint (p. 36) . . . He has every reason . . . to guard against the risk that an increased display of acumen on his part may be accompanied by a diminution in the certainty and trustworthiness of his results . . . [given the choices of] caution . . . and boldness, [i]t will not be possible to define the proper limits of justifiable interpretation until many experiments have been made and until the subject has become more familiar" (1911a, p. 37).

I heeded Freud's caution in approaching the story of Paul Schreber as a clinical, historically grounded psychoanalytically and ethically informed longitudinal case study. This approach has resulted in reappraisal and reintegration of descriptive, diagnostic, dynamic, and therapeutic aspects of the case and offers corrections and amplifications to previous paradigms. When considering *all* the available historical and clinical data; that is, Paul Schreber's adult social and family context and career conflicts, and his own statements about his body, character, and mind, coupled with a reanalysis of causes, differential diagnosis, and other possible dynamic and theoretical explanations, a different picture emerges. It suggests a diagnosis of major psychotic depressive illness with hypomanic and paranoid admixtures. There is no evidence for homosexuality but there is prominence of cross-dressing and gender conflicts both phenomenologically and dynamically. Combining Freud's original conception of the neuropsychoses of defense with the concept of psychological conflict (Schreber's passivity, dependency, self-esteem problems, and compensatory feminine identification) makes possible an adaptive explanation of such famed symptoms as soul murder and the end-of-the-world fantasy, as a reaction to a traumatic reality residue, or the kernel of truth in the delusion. In addition to psychological conflicts, the trauma in the relationship with Flechsig and the transfer to Sonnenstein, over and above its transference aspects, was seen as a precipitant of the acute delusional phase, a traumatic neuropsychosis of defense framed by the psychotic depression, in which frustration and rage played a preponderant role. Thus, the psychotic process results in a regressive destabilization and dedifferentiation of established identifications and representations, transformed into the kinds of fantasies and imaginings so vividly portrayed in Paul Schreber's *Memoirs*.

References

Abraham, K. (1911), Notes on manic-depressive insanity. In: *Selected Papers of Karl Abraham, M.D.*, tr. B. Douglas & A. Strachey. London: Hogarth Press, 1949.

Adler, A. (1908), Der Aggressionstrieb im Leben und in der Neuroses. *Fortschritte der Medizin*, 19:577–584.

Arlow, J. A., & Brenner, C. (1964), *Psychoanalytic Concepts and the Structural Theory*. New York: International Universities Press.

———— ———— (1969), The psychopathology of the psychoses: A proposed revision. *Internat. J. Psycho-Anal.*, 50:5–14.

Bjerre, P. (1911), Zur Radikalbehandlung der chronischen Paranoia. *Jarbuch für Psychoanalytische und psychopathologische Furschungen*, 3:795–847.

Brabant, F., Falzeder, C., & Giampieri-Deutsch, P., Eds. (1993), *The Correspondence of Sigmund Freud and Sandor Ferenczi*, Vol. 1. Cambridge, MA: Harvard/Belknap Press.

Busse, G. (1991), *Schreber, Freud und die Suche nach dem Vater.* Frankfurt am Main: Lang.

Cameron, N. (1959), Paranoid conditions and paranoia. In: *American Textbook of Psychiatry,* ed. S. Arieti. New York: Basic Books, pp. 508–539.

Devreese, D. (1981), De "personalakte" van Daniel Paul Schreber bij het "Königliche Justizministerium" te Dresden. *Psycho-analytische Perspektieven,* 1:17–97.

———— (1996), Anatomy of soul murder: Family romance and structure of delusion in the memoirs of D. P. Schreber. *Psychoanal. Rev.,* 83:709–735, 913–927.

Ferenczi, S. (1911), Über die Rolle der Homosexualität in der Pathogenese der Paranoia. In: *Bausteine zur Psychoanalyse,* Vol. 1. Vienna: Internationaler Psychoanalytischer Verlag, 1927, pp. 120–144.

Freeman, T., Cameron, J. L., & McGhie, A. (1958), *Chronic Schizophrenia.* New York: International Universities Press.

Freud, S. (1892–1899), Extracts from the Fliess papers. *Standard Edition,* 1:173–280. London: Hogarth Press, 1966.

———— (1894), The neuro-psychoses of defence. *Standard Edition,* 3:41–71. London: Hogarth Press, 1962.

———— (1896), Further remarks on the neuro-psychoses of defence. *Standard Edition,* 3:157–185. London: Hogarth Press, 1962.

———— (1900), The Interpretation of Dreams. *Standard Edition,* 4&5. London: Hogarth Press, 1953.

———— (1901), The Psychopathology of Everyday Life. *Standard Edition,* 6. London: Hogarth Press, 1960.

———— (1909), Analysis of a phobia in a five-year-old boy. *Standard Edition,* 10:1–147. London: Hogarth Press, 1955.

———— (1911a), Psycho-analytic notes on an autobiographical account of a case of paranoia (dementia paranoides). *Standard Edition,* 12:1–82. London: Hogarth Press, 1958.

———— (1911b), Psychoanalytische Bemerkungen über einen autobiographisch beschrebenen Fall von Paranoia (Dementia paranoides). *Gesammelte Werke,* 8:239–320.

———— (1914a), On the history of the psycho-analytic movement. *Standard Edition,* 14:1–66. London: Hogarth Press, 1957.

———— (1914b), On narcissism: An introduction. *Standard Edition,* 14:67–102. London: Hogarth Press, 1957.

———— (1916), Some character types met in psycho-analytic work. *Standard Edition,* 14:309–333. London: Hogarth Press, 1957.

———— (1917), Mourning and melancholia. *Standard Edition,* 14:237–258. London: Hogarth Press, 1957.

————— (1923), A seventeenth-century demonological neurosis. *Standard Edition*, 19:67–105. London: Hogarth Press, 1961.

————— (1924), Neurosis and psychosis. *Standard Edition*, 19:147–153. London: Hogarth Press, 1961.

————— (1925), An Autobiographical Study. *Standard Edition*, 20:1–74. London: Hogarth Press, 1959.

————— (1937), Constructions in analysis. *Standard Edition*, 23:255–269. London: Hogarth Press, 1964.

Idel, M. (1988), *Kabbalah: New Perspectives*. New Haven, CT: Yale University Press.

Israëls, H. (1989), *Schreber Father and Son*. New York: International Universities Press.

Jones, E. (1955), *The Life and Work of Sigmund Freud*, Vol. 1. New York: Basic Books.

————— (1957), *The Life and Work of Sigmund Freud*, Vol. 3. New York: Basic Books.

Lothane, Z. (1982), The psychopathology of hallucinations: A methodological analysis. *Brit. J. Med. Psychol.*, 55:335–348.

————— (1989a), Schreber, Freud, Flechsig and Weber revised: An inquiry into methods of interpretation. *Psychoanal. Rev.*, 79:203–262.

————— (1989b), Vindicating Schreber's father: Neither sadist nor child abuser. *J. Psychohist.*, 16:263–285.

————— (1991), Review of *Schreber Father and Son* by H. Israels. *Psychoanal. Books*, 2:466–481.

————— (1992a), *In Defense of Schreber: Soul Murder and Psychiatry*. Hillsdale, NJ: Analytic Press.

————— (1992b), The missing link: Schreber and his doctors. *Hist. Psychiatry*, 3:339–350.

————— (1993a), Daniel Paul Schreber: A case of psychiatric persecution. In: *Proceedings 1st European Congress on the History of Psychiatry and Mental Health Care*, ed. L. Goei & J. Vijselaar. Rotterdam, Netherlands: Erasmus, pp. 96–103.

————— (1993b), Schreber's feminine identification: Paranoid illness or profound insight? *Internat. Forum Psychoanal.*, 2:131–138.

————— (1993c), Freud's Schreber: A reappraisal. Poster paper presented at the 38th International Psychoanalytical Congress, Amsterdam, Netherlands.

————— (1995), El caso Schreber: una revision. *Revista Española d Neuropsiquiatria*, 15:255–273.

————— (1996a), Le meurtre d'âme: Un cas de Persécution psychiatrique. In: *Schreber et la Paranoia*, ed. P. de Oliveira. Paris: L'Harmattan, pp. 221–235, 317–319.

——— (1996b), Die Verknüpfung von Sohn und Vater Schreber mit Hitler: Ein Fall von historischen Rufmord. *Werkblatt,* 36:108–127.

——— (1997a), The schism between Freud and Jung over Schreber: Its implications for method and doctrine. *Internat. Forum Psychoanal.,* 6:103–115.

——— (1997b), Freud and the interpersonal. *Internat. Forum Psychoanal.,* 6:175–184.

——— (1998a), Pour la défense de Schreber: meutre d'âme et psychiatrie: postscriptum 1993. In: *Schreber Revisité/Colloque de Cerisy.* Louvain, Belgium: Presses Universities de Louvain, pp. 11–29.

——— (1998b), Goethe, Schreber, Freud: Themes in metamorphosis. In: *Il Divano 'l'immaginazio La Cura.* Bolzano: Richerche-Imago-Forschung, pp. 67–86.

——— (1998c), Ethics in morals, psychiatry and psychoanalysis. *Dynamische Psychiatrie/Dynamic Psychiatry,* 31:186–215.

——— (1999), Ethics in psychiatry and psychoanalysis. *Psychopathol.,* 32(3):141–151.

——— (2000), Zur Verteidigung Paul Schrebers: Selbs biographie und Seelenbehandlung. *Psychosozial,* 23(80):105–116.

Lynn, D. (1993), Freud's analysis of A. B., a psychotic man, 1925–1930. *J. Amer. Acad. Psychoanal.,* 21:63–78.

Macalpine, I., & Hunter, R. A. (1953), Translators' analysis of the case. In: *Memoirs of My Nervous Illness.* Cambridge, MA: Harvard University Press, 1988, pp. 369–411.

Maeder, A. (1910), Psychoanalyse bei einer melancholischen Depression. *Zentralblatt. für Nervenheilkunde und Psychiatrie,* 33(21):50–58.

McGuire, W., Ed. (1974), *Freud–Jung Letters.* Princeton, NJ: Princeton University Press.

Niederland, W. G. (1974), *The Schreber Case/Psychoanalytic Profile of a Paranoid Personality.* New York: NY Times/Quadrangle.

Rosenfeld, H. (1949), Remarks on the relation of male homosexuality to paranoia, paranoid anxiety and narcissism. In: *Psychotic States,* ed. H. Rosenfeld. New York: International Universities Press.

Schifferdecker, M., & Peters, U. H. (1995), The origin of the concept of paranoia. *Psychiatr. Clin. N. Amer.,* 18:231–249.

Schreber, D. G. (1858), *Kallipädie oder Erziehung zur Schönheit durch naturgetrene und gleidmässige Förderzung hormaler Körperbildung, lebenstüchtger gesundheit und geistiger Veredelung und insbegondere durch möglichiste Benutzung specieller Erziehungshüttel: für Aeltera, Erzieher, und Lehrer.* Leipzig: Fleischer.

——— (1891), *Das Buch der Erziebung an Leib und Seele: Für Eltern, Erzieher and Lehrer. Dritte stark vermehrte auflage. Durchgearbeitet und mit Rücksicht auf die Erfahrung der neuren Kinderheil Kunde erweitert von Dr. Carl Hennig.* Leipzig: Fries.

Schreber, D. P. (1901), Grounds of appeal. In: *Memoirs of My Nervous Illness,* ed. & tr. I. Macalpine & R. A. Hunter. Cambridge, MA: Harvard University Press, 1988.

——— (1903), *Memoirs of My Nervous Illness,* ed. & tr. I. Macalpine & R. A. Hunter. Cambridge, MA: Harvard University Press, 1988.

Schreber, E. (1987), *Schreber und der Zeitgeist.* Berlin: Matzker.

Schur, M. (1972), *Freud: Living and Dying.* New York: International Universities Press.

Socarides, C. (2001), On homosexual dread and homosexual desire. In: *Mankind's Oedipal Destiny: Libidinal and Aggressive Aspects of Sexuality,* ed. P. Hartocollis. Madison, CT: International Universities Press, pp. 139–170.

Spielrein, S. (1911), Über den psychologischen Inhalt eines Falles von schizophrenie (Dementia praecox). *Jahrbuch für Psychoanalytische und Psychopathologische Forschungen,* 3:329–340.

PART II

Female Homosexuality

CHAPTER 4

The Female Homosexual: Causative Process and Clinical Picture

CHARLES W. SOCARIDES, M.D.

Introduction

In this paper I present my findings from forty years of experience as regards some theoretical and clinical aspects of female homosexuality. These views are contemporary ones in that they represent major breakthroughs, which have led me to the conclusion that oedipal phase conflict in obligatory female homosexual patients is always superimposed on a deeper basic preoedipal nuclear conflict.

In these cases of homosexuality, object-relations conflicts contribute more to the development of homosexuality than the vicissitudes of the drives. In other words, the central conflict of the female homosexual, as well as the male homosexual, is an object-related one rather than a structural one. Object-relations conflicts consist of anxiety and guilt associated with the failure of development in the phase of self-object differentiation (Dorpat, 1976).

These views apply to relatively pronounced cases in which the perverse development is clear and definite. In these patients nonengagement of perverse acts induces anxiety. Because the deviant acts are usually the only avenue for the attainment of sexual gratification and are obligatory for the alleviation of anxieties, and because the intensity of the need for gratification is relatively pronounced, these cases may be termed *well-structured* sexual deviation.

I preface my views by noting that psychoanalytical clinical data gathered through psychoanalysis of adult female cases have acquired theoretical underpinnings in the work of Mahler and her associates among others who have delineated symbiotic and separation–individuation phases of human development. The combination of infant observational studies and developmental theories derived from adult female homosexuals helps to explain that the fixation of the homosexual lies in all probability in the later phases of the separation and individuation process, producing a disturbance in self-identity, as well as in gender identity, a persistence of primary feminine identification with the malevolent mother (in the case of a female, perceived as malevolent and hateful), separation anxiety, fears of engulfment (restoring the mother–child unity), and disturbance in object relations and associated ego functions. By combining data and theory, major advances into the question of causation have been made. Furthermore it is quite likely that the significant number of homosexuals in the general population is due to the necessity for all human beings to traverse the separation–individuation phase of early childhood, which is decisive for gender-defined self-identity. A substantial number of children fail to successfully complete this developmental phase and are therefore unable to form a healthy sexual identity (the core disturbance of all homosexuals) in accordance with their anatomical and biological capacities.

Most recently, new problems are being conceptualized and solutions suggested by advances in our knowledge of the pathology of internal object relations, developmental psychology (including self psychology) and new concepts of narcissism. Clinical forms of homosexuality I have divided into oedipal, preoedipal Types I and II (dependent upon the degree of pathology of the object relations) and schizohomosexuality (the coexistence of homosexuality and schizophrenia).

The female homosexual has no choice with regard to her sexual behavior. The condition is unconsciously determined, and should be differentiated from the behavior of the person who deliberately engages in female–female sexual contact due to situational factors, a desire for variational experiences, and on some occasions due to severe disappointments with regression to a mother–child relationship. The latter constitute nonclinical forms of *homosexual behavior*. The nuclear core of true homosexuality is never a conscious choice, an act of will. Rather, it is determined from the earliest period of childhood (in terms of its origins, of course, not its practice). The presence of external conflicts will complicate the lives of female homosexuals but should not be allowed to obfuscate the valid clinical data secured through in-depth psychoanalytic studies for this would misinform psychiatrists, psychologists and the patient.

Etiological Considerations

The nuclear conflicts of female homosexuals originate in the earliest periods of life, as they do in male homosexuals, forcing them into choosing partners of the same sex for ego survival. The obligatory female homosexual has been unable to pass successfully through the later stages of the separation–individuation phases of early childhood, the rapprochement subphase, as well as earlier phases, practicing and differentiating. Severe ego deficits and insufficient self–object differentiation are a consequence of this maturational (psychological) developmental failure. Homosexuality serves the repression of a pivotal fixation in which there is a desire for and dread of merging with the hateful/hated mother in order to reinstate the primitive mother–child unity.

Fast's (1984) exhaustive study of the vicissitudes in the development of female gender identity appears to corroborate my position as to etiological factors.

> To boys a recognition of their gender difference from their mothers may seem another and powerful dimension of difference to be added to those required of them in separation–individuation processes. Now any regressive wishes to merge with the mother stimulate a new anxiety: to merge with the mother means the loss of masculinity. Such fears appear to be represented in perversions. . . . For girls the problem is different. Merging with the mother does not threaten their femininity. It does, however, threaten their *independent* femininity. Girls, like boys, develop their gender-defined relationship to their mother in the context of [the] earlier separation–individuation process. . . . In the separation–individuation processes girls have normally made major progress in establishing themselves as individuals distinct from their mothers. Now they must perceive themselves as both like their mothers in gender and distinct from them as individuals. They must establish secondary identifications with their mothers

as feminine, in which attributes, previously shared with their mothers in a two-person unity now become depersonified aspects of their individual feminine selves distinct from but related to the mother whose way of being feminine is her own. Each of the secondary identifications represents a separation. The developmental danger is of a regressive return to the more primitive identification and relationship of a two-person feminine unity with the mother. One reaction, to avoid the dangers of both fusion with the mother and separation from her, is the repudiation of the mother and turning to the father [pp. 105–106].

In the mother–child unity one can discern: (1) a wish for and dread of incorporation; (2) the threatened loss of personal identity and personal dissolution; (3) guilt feelings because of a desire to invade the body of the mother; (4) an intense desire to cling to the mother which later develops, in the oedipal period, into a wish for and fear of incestuous relations with her; and (5) an intense aggression of a primitive nature toward her.

On a conscious level, the patient attempts to compensate for her primary nuclear conflict by certain activities designed to enclose, ward off, and encyst the isolated affective state of the mother–child unity. She does not approach any man sexually, as this will activate fears of narcissistic rebuff, oedipal fears, preoedipal fears of castration, separation, or fragmentation anxiety. She is tied to the mother and does not attempt to leave her, both because of her primary feminine identification with the hateful object and her fears of provoking engulfing, incorporative tendencies by the mother. Any attempt to separate from the mother produces an exacerbation of her unconscious ties. All sexual satisfactions are carried out through substitution, displacement, and other defense mechanisms. Her secondary identification as a male leaves her prone to invent a fictive penis with which she attempts to approach other women (the good mother) and simultaneously find her lost femininity. Another alternative to her primary feminine identification (a hateful one) is to restore strength and reaffirm her sense of self through a transitory feminine identification with the (good) female partner. In so doing she unconsciously enjoys *sexual closeness with the good mother and avoids oedipal rebuff by the father.*

The female homosexual is prone to regression to earlier stages of development. She experiences a threat of loss of her (constructed) self representation, loss of the object (separation anxiety related to the mother). In sexual union with a man, an event to be avoided at all costs, she fears narcissistic mortification in her lack of a penis. The female homosexual's life and development are designed to forestall and prevent the realization of this powerful affective state. Homosexual behavior is a solution to the anxiety connected with the pull to return to this earlier, less differentiated phase of ego development, when she attempted to disturb the optimal distance/ closeness to the mother by separating from her during the course of attempting heterosexual relations. The homosexual object choice, achieved through the Sachs's mechanism, is crucial to the repression of the basic conflict: the fear and dread of the mother–child unity.

From her analysis of a number of homosexual women, McDougall (1970) arrives at conclusions that are similar to my own as regards the meaning of female homosexuality, although she does not conceptualize her findings in terms of separation–individuation theory. She states:

> When a woman builds her life around homosexual object relations she is unconsciously seeking to maintain an intimate relation with a paternal imago but symbolically possessed through identification. At the same time she achieves an apparent detachment from the maternal imago represented in the unconscious as dangerous, invading and all-forbidding. The idealized aspects of the maternal imago are now sought in the female partner. . . . With the creation of a pathological identification with the father the young girl need no longer fear a return to the fusional relation with the mother which spells psychic death [in my terms, the fear of engulfment, fear of fusion with the engulfing mother].
>
> We might sum up the psychic economy of female homosexuality as follows: an attempt to maintain a narcissistic equilibrium in the face of a constant need to escape the dangerous symbiotic relationship claimed by the mother-imago [an attempt to find her unique, individual identity separate from the primary feminine identification with the mother] . . . through conserving an unconscious identification with the father, [this being] an essential element in a fragile structure. Costly though it may be, this identification helps to protect the individual from depression or from psychotic states of dissociation, and thus contributes to maintaining the cohesion of the ego. . . . [One may conclude that she] can now believe that she still contains all that is essential to *complete* her mother. Unconsciously she assumes the role of the mother's phallus—but it is a phallus with an

anal quality which only the mother may control or manipulate. A devouring love for the mother and a phobic clinging to her in child-hood is paralleled by unconscious wishes for her death in order to acquire the right to separate from her. In that decisive moment, when the girl decides to leave her mother for the woman who will become her lover, she symbolically castrates the mother of her phallus-child. It is a moment of intense triumph. It is to the other woman that she will now offer herself as the incarnation of all that she has symboli-cally taken away and what she believes is needed to complete or repair her partner . . . [pp. 209–212].

One may conclude that in female homosexuals there is an at-tempt to regain "essential femininity with an idealized female part-ner" while in male homosexuality there is a need to find (idealized) masculinity in an identification with a male partner and his penis.

Contrasting Features to Male Homosexuality

It is useful to compare some dynamic features found in the female homosexual with those in the male homosexual. In the study of family patterns of female homosexuals, one uncovers a fear and dread of the mother and a fixation to her similar to that found in the male. The female, however, directs a more intense aggression toward the mother. In their early histories one commonly finds a dread of being hurt, devoured, or destroyed by a mother perceived in her unconscious to be malevolent. This dread is aggravated by the girl's secret wish to be loved exclusively by the father—a wish which she renounces almost completely because of her conviction that her father not only refuses to love her but also rejects and hates her—especially for a phallic deficiency. If, in late childhood, the father does offer care and affection, she turns away "in revulsion," seeking the company, admiration and love of other females. With the onset of homosexual behavior, she displays to the mother her guiltlessness regarding unconscious sexual wishes toward her father. Through this apparent lack of interest in the male organ, she thereby hopes to insure maternal love and care. Her negative oedipal com-plex has been realized.

As regards oral–sadistic feelings, as in the male, the potentially homosexual female always presents a history of oral deprivation and intense sadistic feelings toward her mother. Such patients, some breast-fed, complain that they did not receive enough milk, lost weight, and screamed continuously as infants. They fear that the mother wished them dead, often had fantasies of poisoning, and fears that the mother would punish them to the point of killing them. Analysis reveals that these semidelusional convictions are usually projections of the little girl's sadism toward her mother.

Primitive psychical mechanisms in female homosexuality are even more pronounced than in the male. They often take the form of outright denial of the anatomical differences between the sexes. For example, the girl often hallucinates the fictive penis, identifies her entire body with the male organ, or may substitute some characterological features, such as intellectuality, for the penis. She may then continue to a protracted age to deny feelings of having been castrated, and to cling to the idea of somehow acquiring a penis of her own.

She engages in wholesale projection of her own fear and hatred onto the mother, who, she is convinced, has denied her the male organ as a punishment, often for masturbatory practices in early childhood. The mother, and subsequently all women, are unconsciously perceived as malevolent or potentially malevolent beings who must be placated through a show of affectionate behavior. They thereby become good, safe, and loving. If this belief collapses as a result of personal slight or threat of infidelity, the homosexual woman may develop temporary or permanent delusional fears of being poisoned or future mistreatment, at least from her homosexual partner. With the patching up of differences what may remain is a chronic distress and suspicion of the partner.

Psychodynamic Features

The homosexual woman is in flight from men. The source of this flight is her childhood feelings of rage, hate, and guilt toward the mother and a fear of merging with her. Accompanying this primary conflict are deep anxieties and aggression secondary to disappointments and rejections, both real and imagined, at the hands of the male (father). Any expectations of the father fulfilling her infantile sexual wishes poses further masochistic dangers at an oedipal level. On the other hand, her conscious and unconscious conviction that her father would refuse her love, acceptance, and comfort produces a state of constant impending narcissistic injury and mortification. This refusal she bases on her lack of a penis and a sense of narcissistic defeat. Such narcissistic injuries commonly occur at the birth of a brother at a specifically vulnerable phase (i.e., that of rapprochement). Some homosexual women complain that this event was the most fateful and harmful day of their lives, especially if it involved the mother's almost complete turning from the daughter to the little boy, producing threats of object loss, which is experienced as preoedipal castration anxiety (Roiphe and Galenson, 1981) and a subsequent intensification of penis envy.

The conviction that one is not appreciated, admired, and loved by the father leads the female child to turn to the earliest love object, the mother, with increasing ardor despite her fear of her. What prevents a complete regression to this primitive unity is an unconscious fear of merging with and being engulfed by the mother. In this connection, Deutsch (1932) noted that the advantage of this attachment to the homosexual partner (a substitute for the mother) decreases guilt feelings and protects against threats of her loss.

The genital pressures of adolescence in the female are less distinctly expressed than in the boy. At adolescence, the girl is forced to make a change of genitals which the boy never has to make. The girl feels at the same time that she must shift from clitoris to vagina, feels a lack of interest from her father and hostility from the mother, and is likely to repudiate vaginal erotism and attempt to create a male role for herself. If she believes that nobody wants her in this "castrated, mutilated state"—not even her father—a prolonged and pathological extension of tomboy behavior into middle adolescence ensues. Such a renunciation of feminine strivings may create a temporary equilibrium. During this period she may engage in mutual masturbation or sexual investigation with girl friends, but this is accompanied by considerable anxiety and guilt and is soon relinquished. The shift between ego, id, and superego drives instituted by physiological sexual pressures does not usually produce in the female a multiplicity of overt sexual practices or disturbances, although some masochistic, masturbatory, heterosexual, or homosexual fantasies may be entertained for brief periods. It is only upon reaching late adolescence and early adulthood, when she is confronted with society's and her own demands for appropriate role-fulfillment, and is forced to consider sexual intercourse, marriage, and children, that her previous conflict, apparently laid to rest in early adolescence, is reactivated in all its intensity.

Preodipal fears of being poisoned and devoured by the mother lead to giving up in utter failure when confronted by the later conflicts of the oedipal period (Klein, 1954). The homosexual woman resorts to flight to the mother in an attempt to gain her love and protection, to alleviate fears of murderous aggression toward her, and to protect herself against the assumed murderous impulses of the mother. These fears of poisoning and being devoured relate to the earliest anxiety of the infant Therefore, this type of homosexual patient, beset by primitive anxieties, demands the utmost effort and concentrated attention on the part of the analyst.

In homosexual women there are intense desires for revenge and uncontrollable aggressive feelings. The impulse to attack is associated with revenge ideas for betrayal by the father, especially, as noted above, in instances where another sibling has been born, replacing the patient during the preoedipal years. Strong penis envy components are mixed with intense oral wishes. The oedipal revenge ideas may exist in nonhomosexual women whose behavior stops short of the complete avoidance of men. These women get along fairly easily with less virile, presumably impotent men. This is due not simply to these men being less dangerous; they offer less temptation to the woman's sadism. Although oedipal revenge ideas may exist in nonhomosexual women, these revenge impulses reinforce violation anxiety, and the two together produce a strong tendency to complete detachment from the father. It is a truism, however, that hate as well as love can bind, and the homosexual can find herself neurotically bound to the father, his life, and his activities.

All homosexual women markedly identify with the father, since they must renounce any approach to femininity. A striking feature of these identifications was suggested by Jones (1927), when he termed them *maimed*. The ego is always a castrated father or a barren, shattered mother, and the ego's conduct in life is correspondingly crippled. This nevertheless provides an economic advantage as it protects the homosexual woman from the dangers of gratification of her intense sadism, although at great expense to her ego.

Some prepubescent or adolescent girls may identify with the sexuality of an older female who they know participates in sexual intercourse with men. I have referred to this form of identification, following de Saussure's (1929) suggestion, as "resonance identification" (Socarides, 1968). In so doing, they attempt to bolster up a burgeoning femininity. By sharing the guilt in sexual encounters with these females, they increase their own capacity for erotic feelings.

Those women who openly identify with males are, in effect, saying to the mother that she has nothing to fear from their sexual wishes toward the father, that they themselves wish only to be male (negative oedipal position). In such instances, the oedipal conflict is superimposed upon a deeper preoedipal nuclear conflict, that is, the fear of engulfment and merging with the preodipal hateful mother. They thereby escape the fantasied retaliatory aggression of the mother toward them.

Other homosexual women, after identifying themselves with the father, choose young adolescent girls as love objects who are representatives of themselves (narcissistic object choice). They then love these girls as they wish their father had loved them. In those homosexuals who assume a very masculine manner toward men, there is an open wish to acquire traits of virility of their own. They believe they can be loved by the father only if they have a penis, convinced that the father once denigrated and demeaned them for this lack. In extreme cases of such male identification, homosexual women may adopt transvestism as an ancillary perversion.

Certain women manifest their homosexuality only after marriage. There are common features in their reaction to marriage in that they suffer from excessive guilt due not only to the incest and oedipal meaning that intercourse has for them, but even more from the rude awakening of their sexual sadism when engaged in the sexual act. Violation-revenge impulses are frequently found. These patients are demanding revenge for childhood injuries but they often express disappointment if they are not hurt enough in heterosexual relations. This apparent contradiction is resolved when one realizes that actual sexual intercourse satisfies neither their primal scene expectations nor their need for punishment. Continuing to feel guilt-ridden, their superego threatens them with severe bodily punishment after marriage. The husband may symbolize the safe and tender father without sexuality and therefore without sexual satisfaction or danger (Brierley, 1932). Deutsch (1932) described a similar type of homosexual woman, in whom sexual sensation depends entirely upon the fulfillment of masochistic conditions. These women are accordingly faced with the necessity of choosing between finding happiness in pain or respite in renunciation.

Being married provokes already-present masculine trends: penis envy takes the form of rivalry with the husband. The unconscious conviction that the penis ought to have been the wife's, based on the fantasy that the mother had deliberately given the infant's breast/penis to the father, is further augmented. The failure of the marriage transforms unconscious (latent) homosexual attitudes into overt homosexuality.

Homosexual women are exceedingly sensitive to being financially dependent because they regard this as a mark of inferiority. Beneath this resentment are deep feelings of guilt for their inordinate wishes to be completely sustained by the husband. These demands derive from their insatiable need for oral supplies from the mother. Prior to marriage they may "enjoy all the advantages of a man's life plus certain prerequisites belonging to womanhood without the disadvantages of either" (Brierley, 1932, p. 444). If such women are obliged to give up a career for marriage, this loss of outlet may play an important part in precipitating severe neurotic symptoms with or without overt homosexuality.

Meaning of the Homosexual Symptom

The female homosexual usually does not seek psychoanalytic treatment in order to change her homosexuality. She may enter therapy because of family pressure, or due to a depression secondary to the loss of a love partner, or accompanying symptoms more often neurotic than psychotic. It is usually feelings of loss, loneliness, and severe anxiety arising out of rejection by another woman that impels her to seek help.

Although many overt homosexuals experience little conscious guilt over their deviant sexual practices, many suffer intensely from a deep sense of inferiority, often masked by the outward appearance of self-confidence and superiority. Indeed, inferiority feelings have been largely responsible for their covert homosexual activities, enabling them to lead double lives among their peers and associates. Some homosexual women engage only in a companionate relationship, having little orgastic desire, while others intensely seek orgastic and erotic pleasure. Homosexual women may suffer from vaginismus or vaginal anesthesia. Recently it has been noted that many homosexual women do not feel that they have a vagina (do not, in effect, possess a genital) but have an "empty hole" at a position where the vagina would be (E. Siegel, 1988). In some, orgastic desire for persons of the same sex may be so strongly repressed that there may be complete or almost total unawareness of homosexual desires and wishes.

The homosexual libidinal relationship is basically masochistic: it temporarily wards off severe anxiety and hostility, only to give way at times to florid neurotic symptoms. The mother-substitute (homosexual partner) temporarily neutralizes infantile grievances by providing sexual satisfaction. Many overtly homosexual women acknowledge the mother–child relationship implicit in their choice of love object. Sexual satisfaction is usually obtained by a close embrace; mutual sucking of the nipples and genitals; anal practices; mutual cunnilingus; and vaginal penetration by the use of artificial devices. There is quadruple role-casting for both partners: one now playing the male and the other the female; one the mother and the other the child. Female homosexuals are particularly engrossed in and satisfied by the sameness of their sexual responses.

In analysis it readily becomes apparent that in sexual experiences occurring between homosexual females, the homosexual is able to transform the hate of the mother into love. At the same time, she is being given the mother's (partner's) breast, and thus obtains what she once felt deprived and frightened of as a child. Invariably present is an intense conflict over masturbation which began in early childhood. In the homosexual act, "mother" sanctions masturbation through sharing the guilt mechanism.

Many homosexual women suffer from a double disappointment: that they are in a primary feminine identification with a hateful, malevolent, and hated mother whom they believe wishes to destroy them, and a feeling of rebuff and lack of acceptance of their femininity by the father. They are attempting, therefore, to find their lost femininity (compared to men who are attempting to find their lost masculinity) in the body and personality of their female partner. The object relationship, therefore, is a narcissistic one, similar to that described by Freud (1914).

If she can overcome her reticence to confide in a man, the female homosexual may display intense envy of the penis and hostility toward a male analyst from the very beginning of therapy. Often she suffers from suicidal ideas and murderous fantasies toward her mother (and partner), both arising from preoedipal unconscious wishes and dreads. The aggressive, murderous hatred occurs simultaneously with the desire to merge with the mother and fears of such merging. As in the male, this is the nuclear conflict.

Sexual excitement in most homosexual women is bound up with maternal prohibition. On a conscious level, there are extremely intense aggressive impulses toward the mother. These aggressive impulses are resisted and, in reaction to them, unconscious guilt toward the mother is generated. Hate impulses are then transformed into a masochistic libidinal attitude that disguises these feelings, diminishes guilt, and punishes through suffering. By punishing the mother, these patients are unconsciously dramatizing their self-defeat and reproaches against the mother.

Deprived of their love object, homosexual women very often become suicidal. They interpret this loss as a threat to survival and a total abandonment: they fear total extinction, that is, aphanisis (Jones, 1927). Similarly, the male homosexual has a marked proclivity to become suicidal whenever he is rejected by a man who represents his ideal narcissistic image.

Phenomenological View of Homosexual Women

The clinician treating homosexual women encounters varied and at times even bewildering forms of this disorder. The behavior and appearance of the patient depend on the strength of repression, the capacity for sublimation, the defensive techniques of the ego and superego, the ego-adaptive capacity of the individual, and a complex series of multiple identifications. Thus, homosexual women show great variation regarding their external appearance, general behavior, and their choice of an attitude toward their sexual partner. The following groupings are useful in illustrating this complexity by describing the content and degree of their identifications.

Group I

The women in this group have an intense identification with the father. Their aim is to procure acknowledgment of this "masculinity" from their female partners. They have exchanged their gender identity but retain their first love object, the mother.

Group II

In the second group, some femininity is retained, but external object relationships to other women are very imperfect; they merely represent the patient's own femininity through identification. Women in this group wish to enjoy vicariously gratification at the hand of the unseen man (the father incorporated in themselves). An identification with the father is present in all forms of female homosexuality but is more intense in the first group (according to Jones [1927]). This identification with the father serves the function of keeping feminine wishes in repression and constitutes a complete denial of harboring guilty feminine wishes, for it asserts that one could not possibly desire a man's penis for gratification since she possesses one of her own.

Group III

These women are reared in an environment in which their fathers' disapproval of their femininity engenders a strong sense of guilt, self-condemnation, and inferiority. In response, they create a masculine identification superimposed upon their maimed feminine one, and may equate their bodies with a phallus and often fantasy a fictive penis on their own body.

Group IV

This type derives from a "warped bisexuality" (Jones, 1927) conditioned by the ideas of castration and penis envy. In these cases, homosexual fixations correspond to the patients' projections. A woman may therefore project and thereby relinquish her femininity to the mother and displace it into other women who continue to represent the mother. She then sees herself mirrored in other women who must have a high degree of feminine narcissism.

Group V

This group identifies with the active mother and plays out a mother–child relationship in the conscious and unconscious context of excluding the intruding father.

Group VI

The younger member of this group plays a passive role with an older, maternal, protective partner. The clitoris is their executive organ of pleasure and they abhor the presence of a penis or a penislike substitute.

Group VII

This group has a double identification: with the primary active mother who cares for the child, and with the father. In these women the double identification is superimposed one upon the other, with clitoral fantasies. They wear masculine clothing and many find it extremely difficult to admit to any passive wishes to be caressed, fondled, genitally stimulated, or penetrated.

Group VIII

This group cannot appreciate any love object that lacks a phallus. Although basically homosexual in their search for a loving female (the mother), they seek the father as their love object. Psychoanalysis reveals that unconsciously they cling tenaciously to the idea that they possess a phallus that they can put on or take off at will. Although they may engage in heterosexual relationships, these are extremely ambivalent, and their greatest pleasure is to be admired and sought after by women with whom actual sexual relations are infrequent and transitory. They are the most difficult of all homosexual women to treat psychoanalytically as they have established what they consider to be fulfilling adjustments to both sexes.

Group IX

In this group there is the appearance of extreme femininity, due to the special configuration of the castration complex: having identified herself with the father, she then chooses young girls as love objects to serve as ideal representatives of her own person. She thereby preserves her femininity. Feminine-appearing homosexual women then behave toward masculine-appearing homosexual women as they wish they had been treated by their fathers (Jones, 1927; Bonaparte, 1953; Socarides, 1963).

Classification of Female Homosexuals

In Socarides (1978), I presented three detailed, lengthy psychoanalytic studies of female homosexuals, placing them in my new classification system. The reader is referred to this material (pp. 349–401) for a complete illustration of preoedipal Type I, preoedipal Type II, and oedipal forms of homosexuality as they occur in the female. I shall cite here the major clinical findings reported and the rationale for the position of each patient in my classification system.

The Case of Anna (Preoedipal Type I Female Homosexual)

Anna, an aspiring 24-year-old actress, had been unable to successfully traverse the separation–individuation phase of development, the rapprochement subphase. In addition, she utterly lacked the support, reassurance, protection, and strength of her father. The mother, upon whom she depended for all gratification, denied and deprived her. This intensified her oral craving and produced a desire to be close and never separated from her mother. She experienced any attempt to move away from the dependency on her mother with grave anxiety because of a fear of retaliation and the fear of her own aggression toward the mother. She had a deep need to have substitute teachers, older girl friends, and other females for love and affection. Her father reacted to her during her childhood with severe aggression, kicking her in the head, deploring her femininity, openly wishing for a boy, becoming depressed and severely rejecting, and shaming her for her sexual interest in him during the early oedipal phase. She could only regress to the previous fixation to her mother, but her image of her mother was filled with malevolence, inadequacy, and martyrdom. As a result, she searched for other women (good mothers). She greeted all signs of femininity, including the wearing of feminine clothing, the development of breasts, and menstruation, with antagonism. She felt that these would lead to further devaluation and demeanment. While unconsciously desiring femininity, she equated it with worthlessness.

Anna was representative of those patients who suffer from preoedipal Type I homosexuality. The deep unconscious tie with the malevolent mother (revealed in the analysis) represented a wish for and dread of merging with the mother. She expressed this as a fear of loss of self, being swallowed, becoming a fecal mass, and so on. Her salvation lay in finding the good mother in the form of a loving and caring female in homosexual relations. Superimposed on her preoedipal conflict was an oedipal conflict of severe proportions that could be discerned only during the course of analytic therapy. Her denial of tender, affectionate, loving feelings for men arose from traumatic incidents suffered at the hands of a rejecting father whose love she urgently desired, attempted to acquire, and finally despaired of finding. Successful working through of the oedipal material was of paramount importance to the ultimate solution of her problem.

As in other preoedipal Type I cases, the degree of ego deficits was mild. A transference relationship was possible once she had worked through her feelings that she would be demeaned by the analyst for her lack of a penis. Her object relations were from object to self, and the self was equated with the good loving female sexual object.

The Case of Sarah (Preoedipal Type II Female Homosexual)

Sarah, a 35-year-old accountant, was representative of those cases of female homosexuality in which the basic disorder and fixation occur in the earliest period of infancy. Compared to milder preoedipal forms of homosexuality (Type I), in which the fixation is likely to have occurred in the rapprochement phase (just prior to the formation of object constancy), the fixation in this instance occurred in the practicing and differentiating subphases. Such fixation indicated a greater tendency to psychosis. Sarah's conflicts revolved around the most primitive, aggressive, destructive, and incorporative urges of the infant toward the mother, and defenses against them. Her defenses were those of projection and splitting, and the anxieties associated with them resembled those seen in borderline cases. This type of homosexuality is frequently seen in patients entering therapy for concomitant symptomatology (e.g., paranoid anxieties), rather than because of a desire for heterosexuality. Attempts to challenge or change their homosexual state should proceed with great caution, as there is marked possibility of severe decompensation to psychotic symptomatology. Sarah's fear of destruction by the female was clearly evident in her fear of being poisoned by her partner. The fear of merging was represented as a fear of contamination and death at the hands of a woman. Because of her projective sadism there was a compensatory death wish for the destruction of the homosexual love object.

Preoedipal Type II female homosexuality carries with it a guarded prognosis as to therapeutic reversal, because there is a severe degree of pathology of internalized object relations, object relations are severely impaired, sometimes bizarre and distorted. The preoedipal Type II female homosexual loves the partner in order to achieve narcissistic restoration. There is a failure in the development of sufficient self–object differentiation, and when regressive states appear, they may completely disrupt the analytic relationship. Projection, introjection, and splitting are common defense mechanisms, and impulses of aggression are poorly bound.

The Case of Joanna (Oedipal Female Homosexual)

Joanna was a 19-year-old, attractive college student whose college career was abruptly terminated by a dramatic, attention-getting suicide attempt when rejected by a potential female sexual partner. In Joanna's case, genital oedipal conflicts dominated the clinical picture with a renunciation of her oedipal love for her father and a turning toward a woman. She experienced a structural conflict (in contrast to the other two patients mentioned, who suffered from an object-relations class of conflict) between aggressive and libidinal wishes on the one hand, and her own inner prohibitions on the other. There was no fixation at a preoedipal level, but there was at times a partial regression to that earlier period. Her homosexuality represented a failure to resolve the Oedipus complex and castration fears leading to a *negative oedipal position*. This involved a sexual submission to a parent of the same sex. This form of homosexuality is the only type in which it can be accurately stated that the flight from the opposite sex partner is *the major etiological factor*. The tendency to regress was mild, although there was some regression as in neurotics. In these cases, although the homosexual symptom appeared to be ego syntonic, it was upon careful analysis revealed to be ego alien, that is, quite unacceptable.

Since the self was bound and cohesive and there was no impairment in ego boundaries, the orgasm in Joanna's case did not fulfill the unconscious purpose of buttressing a failing self representation, as in preoedipal female homosexuals. The patient could therefore much more easily terminate her homosexual activity when the underlying neurotic symptomatology was analyzed. Joanna, like other oedipal female homosexuals, developed analyzable transferences similar to those found in neurotics, which can be dealt with effectively. Reactivation and reenactment in the transference of oedipal wishes led to their resolution. Her object relations, as well as other ego functions, were unimpaired.

Concluding Comments

In this brief paper, I have stressed the importance of psychopathology antedating the negative oedipal phase in girls as it leads to obligatory female homosexuality. In so doing I hope I have cast light on the significance of the oedipal period and especially its negative oedipal component through which a girl afflicted with preoedipal pathology must pass. An understanding of the contribution of both phases, preoedipal and negative oedipal, are vital for our comprehension of this ineluctable disorder, its clinical manifestations, and its psychoanalytic therapy.

References

Bonaparte, M. (1953), *Female Sexuality*. New York: International Universities Press.
Brierley, M. (1932), Some problems of integration in women. *Internat. J. Psycho-Anal.*, 13:433–488.

Deutsch, H. (1932), On female homosexuality. *Psychoanal. Quart.*, 1:484–510.

Dorpat, T. (1976), Structural conflict and object relations confict. *J. Amer. Psychoanal. Assn.*, 24:856–875.

Fast, I. (1984), *Gender Identity: A Differentiation Model*. Hillsdale, NJ: Erlbaum.

Freud, S. (1914), On narcissism: An introduction. *Standard Edition*, 14:67–102. London: Hogarth Press, 1957.

Jones, E. (1927), Early development of female homosexuality. *Internat. J. Psycho-Anal.*, 8:459–472.

Klein, M. (1954), *The Psychoanalysis of Children*. London: Hogarth Press.

McDougall, J. (1970), Homosexuality in women. In: *Female Sexuality: New Perspectives*, ed. J. Chasseguet-Smirgel, E. Grunberger, J. McDougall, & C. David. Ann Arbor: University of Michigan Press, pp. 171–217.

Roiphe, M., & Galenson, E. (1981), *Infantile Origins of Sexual Identity*. New York: International Universities Press.

Saussure, R. de (1929), Homosexual fixations in neurotic women in homosexualty. In: *Homosexuality*, ed. C. W. Socarides. New York: Jason Aronson, 1978.

Siegel, E. (1988), *Female Homosexuality: Choice without Volition*. Hillsdale, NJ: Analytic Press.

Socarides, C. W. (1963), The historical development of theoretical and clinical concepts of overt female homosexuality. *J. Amer. Psychoanal. Assn.*, 13:386–414.

——— (1968), *The Overt Homosexual*. New York: Jason Aronson, 1974.

——— Ed. (1978), *Homosexuality*. New York: Jason Aronson.

——— (1988), *The Preoedipal Origin and Psychoanalytic Therapy of Sexual Perversions*. Madison, CT: International Universities Press.

CHAPTER 5

Multiple Functions of Object Choices That Are Compromise Formations to Unconscious Conflicts

ALBERTO MONTES, M.D.

Introduction

This paper is a detailed presentation of how psychoanalytic treatment helped a woman to understand the multiple unconscious conflicts that led her to repeatedly make unhappy homosexual and heterosexual object choices. I will focus on the multiple functions of these choices.

In the narrative of the analysis, I shall include the development of the analytic process, to include my technique in dealing with the patient's associations to allow the reader to make a clinical judgment as to its analytic validity. I will demonstrate that with the analysis of the *defensive* function of her envy of men, and the resolution of her preoedipal conflicts, the analysis led to the liberation of her femininity to struggle with the pleasures, guilt, and fears of her oedipal conflicts, the resolution of which liberated energies for more creative and nonconflictual endeavors in her present personal and professional life, as well as developing a greater freedom to choose in her future professional and personal life.

Acknowledgment. I wish to express my gratitude to Sylvia Brody, Ph.D., for her constructive comments and suggestions in earlier drafts of this paper.

Brief Review of the Literature on Female Homosexuality

Freud (1905) considered unconscious psychological conflicts as influential in the development of homosexuality. He reported a case of female homosexuality (1920) in which the object choice served the dual purpose of substituting for what the mother was lacking, and of defying the father. Abraham (1920) emphasized that the intensity of unconscious penis envy in women and the wish to castrate the man, could lead to homosexuality. Jones (1927) thought that female homosexuality was a defensive oedipal problem with strong oral–sadistic fixation on the mother Deutsch (1932) and Klein (1928) stressed the part played by strong feelings of anger and hatred toward the mother. Radó (1933) emphasized the fear of castration of the female illusory penis. Bak (1968) described the fantasy of the "phallic" woman ubiquitous to all perversions. Socarides (1963, 1988) highlighted the preoedipal origins of sexual perversions as a result of unsuccessful resolution of the separation–individuation conflict, which interfered seriously with the development of gender identity, which in turn affected the outcome of the oedipal conflict. Johnson and Szurek (1952) described homosexuals who act out the *unconscious* homosexual wishes of at least one parent.

McDougall (1970, 1980) considered female homosexuality to be a compromise formation, and likes Jones, Klein, and Deutsch, postulated a core trauma with the mother. She emphasized the parts played by profound castration anxiety, penis envy, and a wish to have a phallus in order to be able to repress feminine sexual desires. Siegel (1988) emphasized, among other factors, the inability of these patients to cathect their vaginas as an important and pleasurable part of their body-image, due to severe preoedipal problems with their mothers. Other authors have pointed out a variety of etiological conflicts contributing to female homosexuality, or have contributed significantly to related areas of research: de Saussure (1929), Stoller (1968), Kirkpatrick and Morgan (1980), Roiphe and Galenson (1981), Fast (1984), Mayer (1985), H. Blum (1989), Tyson and Tyson (1990), Schuker and Levinson (1991), Gilmore (1995), Olesker (1995), Person (1995), Frenkel (1996), and Chodorow (1996).

From the review of the pertinent literature, I infer that the specific unconscious conflicts may vary from patient to patient, depending on (1) the specific and repeated traumata (if any) experienced by the child; (2) how she subjectively interpreted the traumata; (3) the stage of development at which the trauma is experienced and whether the trauma continues to affect stages of further development or not; (4) the specific personalities of father and mother and the quality of interaction with the child through adolescence; (5) the intensity of ambivalent conflicts with parents that induce conflictual identification with either one or both; and (6) the degree to which parents unconsciously encourage the child to form a gender identity with the opposite sex.

But, how is it that these multiple conflicts end up in homosexuality as a compromise formation rather than in other clinical pictures? Coen (1981) has described sexualization as a defense (aside from drive consideration) and as a way of relating to the mother when she is insensitive to the child's emotional needs. As I said before, Johnson and Szurek (1952) described homosexuals who act out the *unconscious* homosexual wishes of at least one parent. I think this factor has not been emphasized enough in the literature except for H. Blum (1989). Considering the various relevant unconscious conflicts described in the literature, I think that the three critical variables described by Abraham, by Coen, and by Johnson and Szurek may "turn the tide" into a homosexual compromise formation.

The case report that follows corroborates most of the etiological factors enumerated above. In the conclusions, I shall focus primarily on the object choices as compromise formations to unconscious conflict, as well as on the multiple defensive functions (Waelder, 1930) of each object choice since these two aspects have not been discussed more systematically in the literature, with the possible exception of Olesker's contribution (1995).

Narrative of the Analysis

At the time Lokelani started psychoanalysis, she was a 35-year-old single woman who suffered from being a homosexual, excessive drinking, some depression, and an inability to write a thesis for an advanced degree. She wanted to overcome her homosexuality. Her first overt homosexual experience followed rejection by a man, Kimo, allegedly because of her refusal to engage in sex with him. She had dated Kimo for eleven years. Later she dated Kainoa, a married man almost twice her age. She had intercourse for the first time, but found it painful and unsatisfying. Kainoa also dropped her. Following this second rejection, she became exclusively homosexual, and at the time of the evaluation lived with her lover.

She was the second child in a family of twelve, born eleven months after her older brother, Kaimana. Her mother was devoutly religious, and her father worked on three neighboring Pacific islands, returning home for the weekends. She experienced mother as a beautiful but cold and fanatically religious woman who was insensitive to her children's emotional and physical needs.

Lokelani began analysis by complaining about her disappointing experiences of rejection by the two men she had dated, followed by complaints that this was a man's world since men "had it made" and exploited women. She had met a woman, Eloise, who told her she, Eloise,[1] had a "crush" on me. Lokelani decided to have an affair with her. I asked her if it was easier to talk about developing a relationship with Eloise than to express her feelings about me. "You are not going to do anything," she retorted contemptuously. About one year into the analysis, she had begun to wear pants to sessions, wrapped her long dark hair in a bun almost on top of her head, and spoke in a tough manner.

Because of comments I had made, Lokelani thought that I was talking like her mother, who was always telling her what she should or should not do as a good Christian girl. "The bitch drove me crazy. I wanted to kill her. If she and father knew I was a homosexual, it would have killed them. I did everything she forbade me to do. I drank. I swore. I had sex. I smoked." I wondered with her whether she was doing what she wanted to do, when she wanted to do it, where she wanted to do it, with little concern for consequences toward herself or others, all for the purpose of defying and hurting her mother. She said that pleasure came first. She never wanted to be a woman because she did not want to be like her mother. I listened empathically, asked for clarifications, but mostly listened. She became progressively more frustrated by my silence. She

---

[1]Eloise and I worked at a psychiatric department in a local institution.

wanted me to talk with her more, be kind and soothing, caress and kiss her, and comb her hair. I asked if she wanted me to be the way she wished her mother had been with her. "Of course, but you will not do anything," she would say. With increasing frustration, and over the next two years, she hurled "anal" epithets at me: "You are an asshole, a shit-head, a stupid ass." I asked her for what purpose she was calling me names. She said she wanted to provoke me to pay attention to her, to chase her angrily, and punish her. After a phone call I received which interrupted the session, she became very angry and said that she wanted to hit me with a black umbrella, and then "shove it up your ass and screw you." I inquired what came to mind about these thoughts. She remembered the repeated enemas mother had given her, when she would tell mother she had not moved her bowels in days. "We need to wonder," I said, "whether you wanted to do to me with the umbrella what your mother did to you with the enemas?" She concurred. Perhaps it would get her some attention from me, too, she added. With the help of clarification and interpretive questions, she was able to realize that since mother was fanatical about daily bowel movements, she derived some pleasure in mother's chasing her, since she was "forcing" mother to pay attention to her. With the analysis of these feelings, she gradually stopped calling me names, and some of the anger toward mother abated.

On a visit to her paternal home on another Pacific island, she started an affair with her older brother's girl friend, Dalia. The girl friend became her primary lover throughout the analysis, besides the lover she already lived with, and Eloise. Due to her increasing involvement with the three homosexual women, by the fourth year of analysis, Lokelani was not sure whether she wanted to become heterosexual. I pointed out that changing from homosexuality to heterosexuality need not be a goal of analysis. Rather, if psychoanalysis could help her resolve her unconscious conflicts, she might have more freedom to choose which way she wanted to go. She agreed.

As Dalia settled in with Lokelani in her home, she acted as the "husband" and Dalia was the "wife." The original lover eventually moved out, but Eloise remained in the picture. Lokelani observed that Dalia was very beautiful but cold, like mother. Lokelani became curious as to her own motivation for taking her older brother's girl friend away from him. In exploring her purpose for doing so, she came to realize that she wanted Dalia (as representing mother) to prefer her and not her older brother. I asked her what made her think that mother preferred Kaimana to her? She recalled that when she was about 3 years old she became painfully aware that she did not have a penis like her brother. She felt strongly that it was because mother had given him a penis. From then on, she wanted very much to grow a penis inside of her so that she could be a boy that mother would prefer. She remembered a desire to cut off his penis with a sickle and change him into a girl. She had entertained the fantasy that she had a hidden penis inside her vagina which was injured during menstruation. She also remembered that she and her older brother were always together. Her mother had told them once, "You are like husband and wife," and that she acted like the husband. We needed to find out, I said, whether she was trying to fulfill her childhood wish to reverse the sexes between her and her brother by acting like a man, with Dalia as representing both mother and brother, whom she had wanted to castrate. Thoughtfully, she said she had never had such an idea.

It struck me that the triangular relations of the patient, her brother, and Dalia displayed parallels with the triangular pattern of the patient, Eloise, and me. In the context of the above-mentioned interpretative work and her continued involvement with Eloise, I reminded her that she had decided to have an affair with Eloise *after* she learned Eloise had a "crush" on me. Was she trying, I asked, (1) to take Eloise away from me, so that Eloise would prefer her to me; (2) as she had wanted mother to prefer her to her brother; and (3) as she was later to take Dalia away from her brother? She thought that over, and later agreed. I asked her whether I may have represented her older brother and her envy of him. She again agreed, and with some hesitation, confessed that she had had a wish to cut off my penis, rendering me impotent and unable to analyze her. I remarked on how easily she could free associate and recover memories from her earliest years. She concurred. She wanted to be an "analytic athlete," as she had been in her youth when she won over boys. She wanted to "beat me at my own game," to prove that she did not need my help, and that she had "what it takes." Quite pensively, she expressed a fear of making a perversion out of this analysis as she had made of her sexual life.

She concluded that I was homosexual, and that I preferred men to women because I had not made sexual overtures to her. I suggested the possibility that she wished to believe that I was homosexual in order to protect herself from having sexual feelings for me. She agreed that she liked me and had felt uncomfortable at times, particularly when she experienced orgasmic vaginal contractions while on the couch. She had been reticent about telling me about them. Soon thereafter she reported a dream: "A man is chasing me. I run away and I turn into a man." This seemed to be a self-evident dream to her. I considered with her whether her wish to be a man might be intended, among other factors, to protect her against feelings for me that she felt were dangerous. Maybe, she said, because soon after starting analysis she had become involved with three women. Through the analysis of another dream ("I lose a tooth"), she became aware that if she lost a tooth she could not hurt me. I inquired which part of me she could not hurt. "Your penis," she said. She had a fantasy that she had little teeth or blades in her vagina, and that if she had sex with a man and was vaginally orgasmic, she could injure or cut off his penis and he would kill her. I asked, "Do you wish and at the same time fear cutting off my penis if you like me and have sexual fantasies about me?" "You would kill me," she replied.

She began to miss appointments more frequently, at times several weeks at a time. Attempts to analyze her behavior were difficult because she either refused to discuss it, or rationalized it away. This was one of the factors that contributed to the length of the analysis: ten years. Finally, she admitted that she had many sexual fantasies of intercourse with me which at times got so "hot" that she had to miss sessions to "cool off." She gradually began to wear skirts instead of pants and literally and symbolically, let her hair down and looked more attractive.

By the fifth year of analysis, she slowly shifted from being the "man" to being the woman in her relation with Dalia. She would imagine Dalia was me. With orgasm, she would have a severe headache. "What comes to mind about the headaches?" I asked her. She imagined that I was cutting off her imagined penis with mine, and that would hurt. The headaches gradually disappeared.

She had another dream: "I am having sex with a man. I am lying flat on my back, and the man is in a sitting position. He is very gentle and careful to guide his penis inside of me. I am surprised I did not experience pain and it fitted perfectly. I have a vaginal orgasm. I wake up and feel disturbed." Her thoughts led her away from the dream. I asked her whether the thoughts which led her away from the dream might be related to perceiving a danger if she discovered what was so disturbing about it. After some hesitation, she said that after complaining so much about men, she did not want to give them (me) the pleasure of knowing that she could enjoy sex with them. "It feels like surrendering . . . like a defeat . . . maybe my homosexuality is a defense against being heterosexual . . . the sitting position reminded me that you sit behind me . . . maybe it has to do with you and the special place you have in my life."

Gradually over the sixth year into analysis, she had more sexual dreams in which she wanted to have children by artificial insemination from unknown sources. Later, these included policemen, priests, professionals who worked with me, and later, me. These ideas slowly developed into a wish to be my mistress. She had a dream in which she was having sex with me, and my wife chased after her to kill her. The dream reminded her that she had been the mistress of Kainoa, the married man almost twice her age. She regretted now what she had done to his wife. She remembered that as a child she had thought that when mother died, she and father would take care of all the children. Later in life she thought her homosexuality was the punishment for having wished mother dead and for the desire to replace her. Thus, I wondered with her whether the punishment could have included robbing her of the capacity to be a wife and a mother? She agreed.

During the seventh year of analysis, and in the midst of angry recollections about mother, I announced my summer vacation. Shortly thereafter, she had a dream: "I am in a fort surrounded by water. I am in a panic because I do not know whether the ships are coming to attack us, or to bring supplies and replacements." Her associations led to the conflict between her wish to express anger toward her mother versus her need for mother's love. When I interpreted that she might be angry with me because of my impending vacation and reluctant to complain about it, for fear that I might get angry and never want to see her again, this left her in conflict about her need for my loving care. She responded that she wanted me to nurture her, and care for her. Yet I never did it! She told me defiantly that for as long as I did not give her what she wanted, she would continue to get it from women. This led to having more "oral sex" with Dalia. She had the following fantasy: "I am sucking at her breasts, and I want to take her breasts into my mouth, then her whole body into my mouth as if she would go inside of me, and fuse with me." I asked her whether she would like to do the same with me before I went on vacation so that she would not miss me as much, since I would be part of her? That made sense, she said. I also wondered whether she might have had similar feelings for mother very early in life that she might not be able to remember, perhaps at those times when mother was not available to her. She did not remember any of that, only that she had to share mother with eleven other siblings. This was followed by fantasies of wanting to suck my penis. I asked her whether this was a symbolic way of getting me to nurture her and give her my strength the way she had wanted it from mother. She agreed. This was followed by oral sexual fantasies with mother, which the patient found revolting. By this time she had become aware that she had to share mother mostly with father, rather than her siblings. I asked her whether her oral sexual fantasies with mother might have been for the purpose of taking mother away from father and gaining more attention from mother. She concurred. She remembered that when father was away during the weekdays, mother would be afraid to sleep alone, and would ask her daughters to rotate sleeping with her.

During her seventh year into analysis, she found it very difficult to work on the thesis. She remembered that when she did not do something she was supposed to do, mother would do it for her. I asked her if she wanted mother to write the thesis for her and, in mother's absence, whether she wanted me to do it for her, in conflict with the part of her that wanted to do it herself? She agreed. With increasing pressure to write the thesis or lose her job, she protested that I should *make her* write the thesis, and *force* her to give up drinking and homosexuality. I commented that perhaps she wanted me to give her a "'mental" enema that would "make" her "produce" the thesis. Angrily, she said I should; otherwise, I really did not care for her. She felt that her thesis was of no value. She feared that mother would compare her thesis with that of her brother's and find his better than hers. She felt that by not writing it, she made mother suffer, causing mother to feel that she had failed as a mother. I asked, "As if it were for her benefit if you wrote the thesis?" She reluctantly agreed that it was for her own benefit. She became aware that she did not want to write the thesis to make me feel like a failure. "As you wished your mother would feel if you did not write the thesis?" I asked. She agreed. Eventually, she wrote the thesis, received her advanced degree, and became entrusted with a position of great responsibility. She also began to enjoy cooking and housekeeping for herself and Dalia.

During the eighth year in analysis, my impending vacation brought forth many painful memories about father. After he would leave home for a business trip, she wondered whether she had driven him away by doing something wrong. She felt certain that mother annoyed him and she was a reason he worked away from home. Was he a homosexual who did not want to sleep with his wife? Did he have another family that he would see during the weekdays? She suspected I was homosexual because I did not have sex with her. "The way you suspected father?" I inquired. She feared she was such a difficult patient, that I went on vacation because I could not "stand" her. "The way you feared your father did?" I asked. She feared that mother was really crazy. For example, mother walked naked around her daughters, but with socks and shoes on. She also gave herself daily enemas.

Dalia had developed a steady friendship with a man, but insisted that it was only a platonic friendship. Lokelani did not believe her and became intensely jealous, to the point of physically attacking Dalia on several occasions to force her to give up her friend—to no avail. We need to ask, I suggested, whether the intensity of your feelings might be related to an earlier jealousy of having to share mother with father. "Yes!" she screamed.

She felt extremely envious of Dalia's physical beauty and her popularity with both men and women, and began to lose all hopes that she would be the primary love in Dalia's life. "She is like a Greek god," Lokelani said. "God?" I asked. "I meant goddess," she said. She associated the expression "Greek god" with her father who was strikingly handsome and popular and became painfully aware that Dalia reminded her of her father. Both were beautiful, popular with both sexes, self-centered, and exploitative of others. Dalia also was demeaning to her, as father was to mother. She realized that in her sexual relations with Dalia, she had gratified womanly desires for father that she had never dared contemplate before. Only through her feelings for Dalia and me did she get a glimpse of them.

She became aware that her wish to have a penis became more intense when she feared losing Dalia to her friend. "As you felt with mother in reference to your brother and your father?" I inquired. She agreed, angrily, wanting to chop off my thought, wanting to smack my penis, and cut if off. "As you wanted to do to your brother and father?" I asked. "Yes!" she screamed. As she calmed down, she remembered that father encouraged masculine behavior by teaching her competitive sports, for the purpose of encouraging her to compete and win against boys. He even told her locker-room jokes, treating her like "one of the boys." She found this very inappropriate, and got the impression that he was disappointed with his oldest son, wanting her to be the son Kaimana had not been. On the other hand, father seemed to prefer her, since he spent so much time playing golf with her to the exclusion of the rest of the family. In teaching golf, he would stand behind her and put his arms around her. That was too intimate and she found it seductive. She sobbed and expressed a lot of rage.

Gradually, and over a period of one year, during her ninth year of analysis, she lost interest in Dalia, as well as in other homosexual relations, and several months later they separated. She realized no homosexual relation would give her what she had wanted from mother, her brother, father, or me. She gave up homosexuality and gradually developed an interest in dating men. She was attracted to professional colleagues of mine. I asked her if they reminded her of me. Of course, she said, but she found out that they were not like me.

During her tenth year of analysis, she decided it was time to terminate analysis. She cried as she told me she loved me and that I had really helped her. She was very sad and guilty that she had taken Kainoa away from his wife. After all, he had represented her father, being married and older. She also felt guilty about having been so angry with mother and father. She wrote to them that she loved them, and called father to tell him for the first time how much she loved him. Eventually she stopped drinking and did not experience depression. She realized now that she had "dumped" on Dalia many of the problems she had with me; that mother was a very disturbed woman who had little time or emotional resources to care for twelve children and a home, while father was away most of the week.

In the last session she told me some of the things she had learned in analysis. She learned how to differentiate right from wrong, morally speaking. For example, she paid her bills and parking tickets on time, without waiting until creditors threatened legal action. She stopped using her workplace during working hours to have sex with one of her lovers. She also learned that one should not covet a neighbor's spouse. She learned to separate her fantasies from reality. She could now openly express love for her parents and siblings. She gave up homosexuality but did not know what the future would bring. She realized that her homosexuality was to hurt (and psychologically kill) her parents.

Unfortunately, I do not have any follow-up information. She left town after she earned another advanced degree in her field. She did not wish to stay in a town where she was known as a homosexual. She preferred to start a new life elsewhere.

Conclusions

The discussion of the multiple object choices and the multiple functions of each object choice will be artificially separated into two separate issues for the purpose of clarity of exposition, even though they are intertwined and occur simultaneously.

Object Choices

Freud (1914) stated: "A person may love: (1) According to the narcissistic type: (a) what he himself is (i.e., himself), (b) what he himself was, (c) what he himself would like to be, (d) someone who was once part of himself. (2) According to the anaclitic (attachment) type: (a) the woman who feeds him, (b) the man who protects him, and the succession of substitutes who take their place" (p. 90).

The words *anaclitic* and *narcissistic* are not to be construed as having derogatory connotations, otherwise confusion will surely ensue. For example, Eisnitz (1969) mentions that "Most often the term 'anaclitic' is used to describe object relations which are infantile and pregenital in their aims, characterized by passivity and the requirement that the object be need-fulfilling, relatively lacking in stable object constancy, and actually bearing a close relationship to descriptions of narcissistic object choice.'' A. Blum and Shadduck (1991) make the same point. Quoting Eisnitz (1969) as above, they ask, ''Is not this description of anaclitic object choice precisely what most writers refer to as narcissistic?'' I agree with Eisnitz (1969) who suggests that the use of the term *anaclitic* be restricted to the descriptive sense, and he thinks that most object relationships, and particularly those that are highly cathected, have both narcissistic and attachment elements. A. Blum and Shadduck (1991) think that in object choice there is an attempt to *repeat or rework conflictual aspects* of the original objects and the self. This comes closer to my own position. I will describe now the object choices as they were studied in the analysis.

Heterosexual: Kimo probably represented her older brother, from whom she could not separate, and with whom she had to maintain a sexual taboo; Kainoa represented the father that she wanted to take away from his wife (mother), and with whom she could not enjoy sex.

Homosexual: Eloise represented the first transferential object choice who represented the mother that the patient wanted to take away from her older brother (me).

Dalia represented a condensation of mother, father, and brother. Dalia also became the repository of transferential feelings toward me, allowing Lokelani to experience with Dalia what Lokelani felt was forbidden or dangerous to experience with me. Dalia represented, also, the preoedipal mother she could not share with anyone else. Dalia (mother) also represented a narcissistic and negative oedipal object choice as representing the beautiful mother whom she wanted to take away from father. Dalia also represented the father as an oedipal and narcissistic object choice. Dalia also represented her ego ideal; that is, what Lokelani herself would have liked to be: beautiful and popular with both sexes.

Multiple Functions of Her Object Choices

The concept of unconscious psychical condensation and simultaneity was described by Freud (1900) in dreams as a quality of the primary process of thinking. R. Waelder (1930) incorporated that idea into the structural theory (Freud, 1923) and the signal anxiety theory (Freud, 1926) as the economic principle of multiple functions. As Waelder states in that article, "According to this principle, no attempted solution of a problem is possible which is not of such a type that it does not at the same time, in some way or other, represent an attempted solution of other problems" (p. 49). Coen (1981) succinctly summarized Waelder's principle of multiple functions: "The model of psychic acts had eight perspectives, representing the intersection of eight vectors: the outer world, the repetition compulsion, the id, the superego, and the ego's active attempts to master each of these [four] by assimilation into its own organization" (p. 506).

I shall apply that principle by describing the multiple functions of her object choices by numerically stating the multiple ways in which her defensive sexual behavior communicated what she could not express verbally. This is followed by a statement, in parentheses, of the feelings she was expressing in her sexuality.

1. Heterosexual object choices (Kimo and Kainoa) protected her from early, and potentially traumatic, awareness of her homosexual feelings. ("I am not homosexual. I really like men."). 2. Homosexual object choices protected her from ever experiencing again the humiliating blow to her feminine self-esteem caused by the rejection she experienced from the two men she had dated. ("It will never happen again. I really like women, not men."). 3. Since she chose Eloise and Dalia *after* analysis had started (homosexual activity had increased to three women), homosexual object choices also protected her from transferential heterosexual and homosexual feelings toward the analyst. 4. She was enabled to express her contempt, scorn, and murderous rage for the mother ("I do not want to be a woman like you! I want to kill you. I hope that makes you suffer."), followed by the reaction formation ("I do not hate and want to kill you. I really love women."). 5. Homosexuality enabled her to receive from her homosexual partner, Dalia, the love and understanding that she felt she had not received from mother, father, Kimo, Kainoa, or the analyst. 6. Homosexuality expressed a wish to please (and concomitantly punish) mother by acting out her mother's own *unconscious* homosexual desires—the enemas, nudity, and sleeping with her when father was absent. ("Maybe mother would

love me more if I were homosexual. That will also make her suffer.'') The vicissitudes of the anal drives had a most powerful influence on the development of her homosexuality. 7. Homosexuality was experienced as a punishment to atone for the guilt experienced for wishing mother dead, and wanting to replace her with father. This atonement would result in denying herself the happiness of being a wife and a mother. 8. She was enabled to express her anger and disappointment with father, and the wish to make him suffer. (''I do not like men like you; I like women, and I hope you feel rejected!'') 9. She could protect herself from the seductive behavior of her father, as well as her own unconscious incestuous feelings for him. (''I really do not like men. I like women.'') 10. By choosing a female lover who reminded her of her father, she could, in a disguised and safe manner, have a vicarious sexual relationship with him (''I like women, but not men like father.''). 11. Homosexuality expressed an unconscious wish to both please and punish her father for wanting her to be the son he felt he did not have (''Maybe father would love and approve of me more if I acted and felt like a man. That will make him suffer, too.''). 12. She could express her envy and desire to identify with her father and her brother's masculinity. (''If I act like a man, mother will prefer me. Dalia already prefers me to my brother.'') 13. Homosexuality protected her from her fear that if she had intercourse with a man, his penis would damage or destroy her fantasied phallus (castration fear). 14. Homosexuality protected her from her fear that if she enjoyed sex with a man and were orgasmic, her powerful vaginal contractions could castrate him, which would lead him to retaliate by killing her (castrating wishes which would end in the threat of total extinction ([aphanisis?]; Jones, 1927). 15. Homosexuality helped her to deny or repress the love she had for her parents and brother, thus reducing the guilty anxiety for harboring murderous and castrating wishes for them.

Discussion

It seems to me that from a nosological point of view, it may be more useful to describe the homosexualities as a form of *heterophobia*, a term that is descriptive, neutral, and devoid of moralistic connotations. In my opinion, heterophobia is caused by many contributing factors leading to an unconscious fear of sexual attraction to the opposite sex, which leads to a conscious inability to be aroused by the opposite sex, thus the need to displace sexual arousal and needs to members of the same sex. Heterophobia shares the involuntary aspects of any symptom (compromise) formation: 1. It develops without the patient *willing* it to develop, or knowing how it developed. 2. The patient is unable to "shake it off" at will. 3. He or she fights it for the rest of his life, or lives with it as best he or she can. 4. The patient is unable to treat himself. 5. Heterophobia causes psychological suffering or inhibition of heterosexual functioning.

In reference to nonpsychoanalytic etiological considerations, I think that it is doubtful that Mother Nature made an exception in humans to the fundamental biological fact that all higher animal species (except the earliest ones like ameba and paramecia) exist as males and females that copulate and perpetuate the species. Friedman and Downey (1993) seemed to be puzzled by the apparent exception to that fact in the homosexualities. They say, "Only among humans does a significant population exist that is motivated to engage in sexual activity with members of the same sex, and not to seek sexual activity with members of the opposite sex. Moreover, *sexual behavior in humans is greatly influenced by gender identity, a form of behavior for which there is no animal model*" (p. 1174; emphasis added).

Disturbances in this uniquely human contribution, gender identity, follows a failure to identify with the parent of the same sex, for whatever reasons, and may begin to describe the psychological derailment of heterosexual development in heterophobia. Money and Ehrhardt (1972) have shown that in the case of hermaphrodites, gender identity is not determined by chromosomal or gonadal sex, but according to which sex the parents assigned to the child.

Problems of Technique and the "Biological Bedrock"

It seems to me that Freud's (1937) pessimism about the analysis of penis-envy in women, and men's passivity toward other men, rather than being unanalyzable because they are a "biological bedrock," may have been due to the limitations of his analytic technique because he included the element of suggestion. As Freud says:

At no point in one's analytic work does one suffer more from an oppressive feeling that all one's repeated efforts have been in vain, and from a suspicion that one has been "preaching to the winds," than when one is trying to persuade a woman to abandon her wish for a penis on the ground of its being unrealizable or when one is seeking to convince a man that a passive attitude to men does not always signify castration and that it is indispensable in many relationships in life [p. 252].

To try to reason, persuade, or convince an analysand that it is for his own good to give up those wishes or fears, may inevitably lead to the analyst's frustrating experience that he is "preaching to the winds," because such recommendations fail to analyze the multiple *defensive* functions of the wishes and fears. It does not mean that such fears and wishes are biologically determined, thus fixed and unanalyzable. Suggestions from the analyst may unwittingly foster the externalization of an intrapsychic conflict into a conflict between the analyst and the analysand: "He wants me to change, but I can't!" or, "I don't want to change! Who is he to tell me that I should want to change?" Such reactions to the analyst's suggestions may increase the patient's resistances to change for his own benefit, rather than for the analyst's benefit. The patient may turn it around into one more way to defeat the analyst's wish that the patient should change, for the *analyst's* own narcissistic benefit. With the fundamental contributions of A. Freud (1936), Searl (1936), and Gray (1994), and their emphasis on shifting the focus of attention from the analysis of the drives to the analysis of the defensive functions of those wishes and fears in both sexes, one may hope that successful analysis may liberate both men's and women's energies for more creative personal and professional aims.

I am raising this issue because it has been debated in the literature (Kolb and Johnson, 1955) whether a strongly suggestive analytic technique should be applied to patients who suffer from heterophobia, recommending that they should refrain from homosexual relations (because it is self-destructive) as a condition to continue analysis with the strong suggestion that heterophobic behavior *should* be changed, or else no treatment. The same applies to the other extreme view that strongly *suggests* that patients should *not* change their homosexual orientation and object choices. That is precisely what we should *not* do, since we should not *suggest* to the patient, what he should or should not do with the results of his analysis.

Results of Psychoanalytic Treatment

Macintosh (1994) summarizes the results of psychoanalytic treatment of the homosexualities, and the need for neutrality in their treatment in the following manner: "In response to a survey, 285 psychoanalysts reported having analyzed 1215 homosexual patients, resulting in 23% changing to heterosexuality, and 84% receiving significant therapeutic benefit . . . virtually all the respondents rejected the idea that a homosexual patient in analysis 'can and should' change to heterosexuality" (p. 1183).

Summary

One can reasonably conclude that the object choices (heterophobic and conflicted heterosexual) served multiple defensive functions that protected the patient from experiencing the severe anxiety and guilt aroused by her unconscious conflicts associated with her parents and brother, especially her murderous, incestuous, and castrating wishes. Thus, heterophobia and conflicted heterosexuality became compromise formations—a "final common path"[2]—an attempted but, nevertheless, unsuccessful solution to her problems.

Since this study pertains to only one case, no generalizations can be made from it. However, analysts are encouraged to report, in detail, *completed psychoanalyses* of female or male heterophobic patients to throw further light on the multiple unconscious functions of object choices as well as to further explore the probable *unconscious* psychological contributions of families to the development of heterophobia in their offspring.

References

Abraham, K. (1920), Manifestations of the female castration complex. In: *Selected Papers on Psychoanalysis.* New York: Brunner/Mazel, 1979, pp. 338–369.

[2]The "final common path" was an expression used originally by Lord Sherrington (1937) to describe the function of the lower motor neuron in the spinal cord as being the final common path of all tracts coming from the brain before passing them to the peripheral nerves.

Bak, R. C. (1968), The phallic woman, the ubiquitous fantasy in perversions. In: *The Psychoanalytic Study of the Child*, 23:15–36. New York: International Universities Press.

Blum, A., & Shadduck, C. B. (1991), Object choice revisited. *Psychoanal. Psychol.*, 8(1):59–68.

Blum, H. (1989), Shared fantasy and reciprocal identification, and their role in gender disorders. In: *Fantasy, Myth and Reality. Essays in Honor of Jacob Arlow*, ed. H. Blum, Y. Kramer, A. K. Richards, & A. D. Richards. Madison, CT: International Universities Press.

Chodorow, N. J. (1996), Theoretical gender and clinical gender. *J Amer. Psychoanal. Assn.* (Suppl.) 44:215–238.

Coen, S. (1981), Sexualization as a predominant mode of defense. *J. Amer. Psychoanal. Assn.*, 29:893–920.

Deutsch, H. (1932), On female homosexuality. *Psychoanal. Quart.*, 1:484–510.

Eisnitz, A. (1969), Narcissistic object choice, self-representation. *Internat. J. Psycho-Anal.*, 50:15–25.

Fast, I. (1984), *Gender Identity*. Hillsdale, NJ: Analytic Press.

Frenkel, R. S. (1996), A reconsideration of object choice in women: Phallus or fallacy. *J. Amer. Psychoanal. Assn.* (Suppl.) 44:133–156.

Friedman, R. C., & Downey, J. (1993), Psychoanalysis, psychobiology, and homosexuality. *J. Amer. Psychoanal Assn.*, 41:1159–1197.

Freud, A. (1936), *The Ego and the Mechanisms of Defense*. New York: International Universities Press.

Freud, S. (1900), The Interpretation of Dreams. *Standard Edition*, 4&5. London: Hogarth Press, 1953.

——— (1905), Three Essays on the Theory of Sexuality. *Standard Edition*, 7:123–243. London: Hogarth Press, 1953.

——— (1914), On Narcissism: An introduction. *Standard Edition*, 14:67–102. London: Hogarth Press, 1957.

——— (1920), Psychogenesis of a case of homosexuality in a woman. *Standard Edition*, 18:145–172. London: Hogarth Press, 1955.

——— (1923), The Ego and the Id. *Stanard Edition*, 19:1–59. London: Hogarth Press, 1961.

——— (1926), Inhibitions, Symptoms and Anxiety. *Standard Edition*, 20:75–172. London: Hogarth Press, 1959.

——— (1937), Analysis Terminable and Interminable. *Standard Edition*, 23:209–253. London: Hogarth Press, 1964.

Gilmore, K. (1995), Gender identity disorder in a girl: Insights from adoption. *J. Amer. Psychoanal. Assn.*, 43:39–61.

Gray, P. (1994), *The Ego and Analysis of Defense*. Northvale, NJ: Jason Aronson.

Johnson, A. M., & Szurek, S. A. (1952), The genesis of anti-social acting-out in children and adults. *Psychoanal. Quart.,* 21:323–342.

Jones, E. (1927), Early development of female homosexuality. *Internat. J. Psycho-Anal.,* 8:459–472.

Kirkpatrick, M., & Morgan, C. (1980), Psychodynamic psychotherapy of female homosexuality. In: *Homosexual Behavior,* ed. J. Marmor. New York: Basic Books, pp. 357–375.

Klein, M. (1928), Early stages of the Oedipus conflict and of superego formation. In: *The Psychoanalysis of Children.* London: Hogarth Press, 1954.

Kolb, L. C., & Johnson, A. M. (1955), Etiology and therapy of overt homosexuality. *Psychoanal. Quart.,* 24:506–515.

MacIntosh, H. (1994), Attitudes and experiences of psychoanalysts in analyzing homosexual patients. *J. Amer. Psychoanal. Assn.,* 42:1183–1207.

Mayer, E. D. (1985), "Everybody must be just like me": Observations on female castration anxiety. *Internat. J. Psycho-Anal.,* 66:331–347.

McDougall, J. (1970), Homosexuality in women. In: *Female Society: New Perspectives,* ed. J. Chasseguet-Smirgel, E. Grunberger, J. McDougall, & C. David. Ann Arbor: University of Michigan Press, pp. 171–212.

———— (1980), The homosexual dilemma: A study of female homosexuality. In: *Plea for a Measure of Abnormality.* New York: International Universities Press, pp. 87–139.

Money, J., & Ehrhardt, A. A. (1972), *Man and Woman, Boy and Girl.* Baltimore: Johns Hopkins University Press.

Olesker, W. (1995), Unconscious fantasy and compromise formation in a case of adolescent female homosexuality. *J. Clin. Psychoanal.,* 3:361–382.

Person, E. S. (1995), *By Force of Fantasy.* New York: Basic Books.

Radó, S. (1933), The fear of castration in women. *Psychoanal. Quart.,* 2:425–475.

Roiphe, H., & Galenson, E. (1981), *Infantile Origins of Sexual Identity.* New York: International Universities Press.

Saussure, R. de (1929), Homosexual fixations in neurotic women. In: *Homosexuality,* ed. C. W. Socarides. New York: Jason Aronson, 1978, pp. 547–601.

Schuker, E., & Levinson, N. A., Eds. (1981), *Female Psychology: An Annotated Bibliography.* Hillsdale, NJ: Analytic Press.

Searl, M. N. (1936), Some queries on principles of technique. *Internat. J. Psycho-Anal.,* 17:471–493.

Sherrington, C. (1937), *The Brain and Its Mechanism.* New York: Macmillan.

Siegel, E. (1988), *Female Homosexualty: Choice Without Volition.* Hillsdale, NJ: Analytic Press.

Socarides, C. W. (1963), The historical development of theoretical and clinical concepts of overt female homosexuality. *J. Amer. Psychoanal. Assn.,* 11:386–414.

——— (1988), *The Pre-Oedipal Origin and Psychoanalytic Therapy of Sexual Perversions.* Madison, CT: International Universities Press.

Solomon, B., Schuker, E., Levy, M. A., & Martinez, D. (1991), Gender identity disorders, paraphilias, and the ego-dystonic homosexualities in women. In: *Female Psychology: An Annotated Bibliography,* ed. E. Schuker & N. A. Levinson. Hillsdale, NJ: Analytic Press.

Stoller, R. J. (1968), *Sex and Gender,* Vol. 1. New York: Science House.

Tyson, P., & Tyson, R. (1990), *Psychoanalytic Theories of Development.* New Haven, CT: Yale University Press.

Waelder, R. (1930), The principle of multiple function. *Psychoanal. Quart.,* 5:45–61, 1936.

CHAPTER 6

On the Genesis and Conversion of Sexual Orientation: A Single Psychoanalytic Case Study

IAN DAVIDSON GRAHAM, M.D., F.R.C.P.(C)

Introduction

Recently, psychoanalytic treatment that involves the elective conversion of a sexual orientation by psychoanalytic means, has come under political as well as renewed scientific scrutiny. The ensuing polarization in the analytic scientific and corporate institutional community has challenged our very right to research the nature and modifiability of sexual object choice even when it is ego dystonic (Acosta, 1975). A supplement of the *Journal of the American Psychoanalytic Association* on the psychology of women included an article by Eleanor Schuker (1996) entitled, "Toward Further Analytic Understanding of Lesbian Patients." It is representative of the extensive expansion of perspective on the subject and challenges analysts that "the dynamics in lesbian patients should not be confused with pathology and that an object choice originally embedded in conflict can become secondarily autonomous or remain fluid" (p. 486). Stimulated by this and by the writings of Charles Socarides and Elaine Siegel, I was encouraged to review my notes on a case, one of several from my regular psychoanalytic practice, in which my technical stance was ostensibly that of classical psychoanalysis, namely, neutrality with regard to sex and sexual orientation as with all other aspects of the patient's life choices and behaviors. That treatment had been conducted in relative naiveté with regard to the recent burgeoning of theory on the analytic treatment of homosexuality. However, it is sufficiently revealing of many of the issues brought forth by Socarides and Siegel to serve, I hope, as a contribution to what Schuker recommends we do, namely, continue to study case material with more awareness of our own biases.

At the time that she came for treatment, the patient had been an active homosexual from ages 28 to 37. She had met and fallen in love with Martha, several years her senior, while studying in a distant city. She was attracted to Martha's intense personal interest and empathy, so lacking in the responses of men she had dated. While this relationship was initially gratifying and ego syntonic, the patient came to see it eventually as alien to her ultimate life goals (see Decker [1984] regarding the complication of dyadic fusion in same-sex couples). She returned home at 36 and went into treatment intending to change her sexual orientation and practice. As will be seen, this conscious "choice" was not feasible until a considerable amount of unconscious psychic conflict had been resolved psychoanalytically, in addition to the considerable success in her previous psychotherapy which had permitted her to reach this determination.

Case Study

The patient, when referred, was single, 40 years old, and a professional. She had been in a stormy but productive preliminary psychotherapy with an analytic colleague three times a week for four years (ages 36 to 40) in an attempt to wean herself from the long-term relationship with Martha. It was characterized by what felt like an encumbering merger quality that gradually became dystonic and interfered with other goals for independent work and sexual behavior. Although she felt that she had been helped considerably with this tempestuous problem, she now felt that she needed psychoanalytic help in her problem with making a close attachment to a man. She was self-conscious about turning 40 and because of that, felt an increased need to "get my life in order." A serious athlete in her teens and twenties, she had become more sedentary in her thirties as a graduate student enthralled with her female sexual partner, who tended to indulge her passive needs. She resumed exercising actively and became more efficient at work and home, but she felt unable to deal with her chronic frustration in her relationships with men. She wondered if she was also afraid of getting married.

Shortly after discontinuing her regular visits with her previous therapist, the patient met a bright, young bisexual women Terry, who, like herself, was a professional from a very similar middle-class WASP background, whom she described as very attractive, intelligent, and sensitive. When that woman made sexual overtures to her, she at first denied them and then, although she had been upset at the idea of getting involved with a woman again, she submitted. It was a familiar feeling to feel alive ''again'' after a recent six-month period in an unrewarding and unprogressive relationship with a new man, George, whom she dropped immediately.

She blamed this recurring problem with men on her tendency to equate them unconsciously with her father's problem with self-esteem. Her latest heterosexual relationship, like a number of long-term serious efforts at forming a permanent relationship with a man, frustrated her in that she felt unable to connect with George in a mutually exciting and permanent way, something she could achieve relatively easily with another woman. She thought that if George had been more sensitive to her feelings she would not have been involved again with another woman. She thought that this new relationship with Terry had ''snuck up on me from behind'' because she couldn't separate from her feelings toward her previous therapist whom she had regarded as motherly, and maintain her focus on a new orientation.

She thought that her problem with her father was that he was a nice, intelligent, but underachieving, dependent professional man. She comes from a long line of overbearing women, specifically her mother, a maternal aunt, and a maternal grandmother. Not surprisingly, the men the patient became involved with, who were sensitive, tended to be dependent and carry a lot of baggage and she did not want to be a ''social worker'' to them. She was recurringly discouraged about men, none of whom seemed to want to be permanently and closely involved with her, and her repeated efforts to engage them felt like flipping television channels. She mourned the verbal intimacy and self-reflection that she could have with her previous therapist, and her current girl friend in some ways was able to provide this kind of experience. She felt her main achievement with the previous therapist had been in breaking away from the issue of exclusivity with the previous woman. The therapist, encouraging other relationships, especially with men, had helped her to disentangle herself from and mourn her merger relationship with Martha.

During the assessment, we concluded that her confusion about her sexual orientation and behavior, at least on the surface, was linked with her residual attachment to her father and her tendency to choose men like him, only to be recurrently disappointed by them. Her current sexual relationship with Terry reflected a long-standing compromise solution. She realized that she had also become dependent on a therapist for making life decisions, and that habit was scaring her. Her previous therapy, while it was valuable, convinced her that therapy was inadequate compared to psychoanalysis, and she was afraid that without it, a commitment to a single heterosexual relationship threatened her with developing the qualities of her parents' fixed, rigid, incomplete, middle-class lifestyle.

Her parents still lived in the same small middle-class home, an isolated and close family that was socially weak. Her father, 68, was described as a small-town professional who, while moderately successful financially, had remained a timid person, dependent on his wife. He was also gradually becoming senile. Her mother, 65, was an unempathic, controlling, isolated woman. The patient's sister, Tammy, several years her junior, lived and was married in the parents' conservative fashion, to a successful professional who preferred to live in a small town. She had two children and lived a stable middle-class lifestyle, primarily defining herself through her husband's achievements, and her family.

The patient's relationship to her father was disappointing. Though tender, it was ineffectual on a practical level in achieving her developmental goals. She described her relationship to her mother as conflicted: they lived in two different worlds, that of a compliantly conventional mother and a rebellious, lesbian daughter. In her relationship to her sister, she had felt second in a competitive sense to Tammy's more petite and feminine attractiveness and life-focus on a successful marriage and child rearing. She had felt unsuccessfully competitive with her, and it was not until the patient was well into treatment with me and felt more personally accomplished, that they became pleasantly close and mutually supportive.

The emotional environment in which she was raised was described as basically adequate and child centered, but rigid and unempathic, especially regarding needs in the area of separation, independence, and aggressive competition. The patient felt that she was second to her sister in her parents' favor, in that she had failed to be married and have children.

Her early memories were significantly barren of early attachment features with the mother and she seemed relatively amnesic about the birth of and early relationship with the sister. She more frequently remembered playing games with her father and curling up with him in front of the television, especially after the birth of the sister, who was to be preferred by the mother.

When she entered grade school, she was preoccupied with getting her father's attention by performing socially, academically, and athletically. She found that she had good physical skills in competitive games and preferred these tomboyish activities to playing with dolls or other girls. These preferences seemed to outline her strong masculine identifications and interfere with developing a clearer sense of her female body image.

Her menarche was unremarkable, in that she felt well prepared for it and was ready to become a young woman. However, she lacked confidence and was shy and awkward, particularly because her growth was rapid—she quickly became taller than her peers. In order to help her with these difficulties, the father encouraged and supported her in becoming a competitive athlete in sports that emphasized intense one-on-one encounters that seemed to have cemented and made characterological her excessive masculine identifications. However, he seriously disappointed her when she was becoming a ranked competitor by refusing to allow her to attend the provincial championships in another city.

The sporting skills did not help her social and dating abilities to any degree, in that she felt that boys were indifferent to her as a young woman. Her only heterosexual activity in high school was limited to some petting. She had her first heterosexual relationship only when she was in her early twenties. While she felt, on the surface, physically capable in sex with men, at this time she mentally focused on dreams of being discovered by someone who would recognize her latent talents and affirm her unique personality. Consistently, the married men she dated failed in this respect.

In the adult work world, in her chosen profession, she developed a local reputation for work that required good interpersonal skills. She ascribes the development of these skills to the facilitating membership in a unique group of which she was a part in college. This group consisted of six people who, though they were pursuing majors in different fields, formed a close bond as they regularly discussed their intense ambition and their needs and desires for achievement. Away from work, the patient preferred competitive and individual sports and socializing with woman friends who were similarly ambitious. Her masturbatory activity remained persistently about conventional sex with men, as did her dating efforts while she was in her early twenties.

In the interview, she presented as a tall, muscular, smilingly attractive, middle-aged white woman with a coy and guarded facade, which periodically loosened up to reveal more spontaneous affective behavior. Her perception was alert and active, and her fantasies were about her relationships with both men and women, especially the one with the analyst and her former therapist whom she saw as an idealized, accomplished marital couple. (She had learned of my training relationship with her therapist, who is also an analyst.) Her major attachments, besides the current lesbian one with Terry and the string of men with whom she was involved, included Ginger, a competitive, ambitious overachieving woman of the same age and in the same field as the patient, with whom she maintained a barely friendly competition over their identical ambitions. Early in the period in which I was working with her, my patient's envy of her friend became more intense and demoralizing when the latter made a successful marriage and very quickly had a child. Only with prolonged analytic work could she successfully compete with these challenges.

By comparison, the patient felt unable to resolve her developmental arrest in her libidinal life, feeling that men were mostly angry, superficial people whose loyalty was usually elsewhere than with her. She found women safer and more available to her. With Martha she had enjoyed a wealthy, talented, bright woman who was supportive, understanding, and empathic, as well as threateningly engulfing. With Terry, she found an attractive, intelligent, and compassionate partner, with whom she enjoyed a high level of comfort and intimacy. At the same time, she was concerned about Terry's relational instability. Again, the men that she had been able to date were like "second stringers," nice but not dynamic. She described the fact that she was not feminine like her mother, who supposedly had been the prettiest woman in the small city in which she grew up. The only consistent relationships with men were the ones that resembled a brother–sister relationship. The relationship with Terry, by contrast, was intense because of the delight in the mutual discovery of bodily pleasures with a feminine partner who was gentle, knowing, sensitive, and a safe person with whom to be passively receptive. At the time I did not challenge these descriptions of their intimacy, uninformed as I then was of Siegel's (1988) observations about the potentially defensive use of gay women's erotic pleasures.

At her job, the main difficulty the patient encountered was in her work with a small group of senior men whom she experienced as controlling and domineering. She said that she was intimidated by their "brains" and their aggressive use of authority. In fact, this theme came out in the early phase of the formation of the therapeutic alliance, in that it made her doubt my commitment, in spite of the fact that she had a very idealized picture of my confidence and reputation.

Treatment Process

Early complaints centered around a major difficulty in trusting in intimate relationships and the tendency to go back to operating out of a false self derived from her feeling that she always had to be in an "up" mood for her parents. In her previous therapy, it had taken a long time for her true feelings to come out and there was a lot of stormy negativity and chronic anxiety. She felt that she had developed a separate, real, respectable self-image and an ability to appreciate what others had to give. Now, it was her intention to find the right man and make it work. She knew that she would have to overcome her concern about the difference between men's and women's brains. It was only when she enjoyed brotherlike relationships with athletic men that she could feel self-confident. She was looking to our partnership with a view to a sharp-minded figure in the analyst, and immediately she began comparing the relationship with me with the one with Terry. The patient reported that Terry was feeling concerned and threatened about the newly proposed analytic relationship with me and tended to see it as interfering with the development of an ongoing relationship with her.

The opening phase of the analytic process demonstrated the need for a remarkable range of functions for the analyst and the analytical alliance. He needed to be attentive and tolerant as an antidote to the critical father, envious friend, Ginger, and challenging three-month lesbian relationship with Terry. This needed, feared, and understanding father-analyst was required to provide an analytical sexual neutrality to counter her former therapist's heterosexual bias. The resulting increased sense of safety in the analytic space reduced her explosive transference anger, intensely increasing wishes for a relationship with a man to counter her girl friend's "disturbing" obsession with "reality." When she was agitated by an intense relationship with a man, she felt soothed by the analytic conversation and was able to relax and sleep at night. These qualities facilitated the search for "confrontations" with available men. In facing her fear of men as menacing and competitive, she needed a mythic, feminized analytic doctor to provide protective parental mirroring (search for the idealized mother [Siegel, 1988]).

Reinforced by the developing alliance, the patient was able to reflect on her mixed heritage of a supportive maternal grandfather and a passive, ambivalent, and competitive father. The early dominating, idealized maternal transferences were displaced onto the lesbian girl friend, Terry, highlighting the nearly twenty-year estrangement that the patient felt from her family, with its model of the depressed mother and the passive but consoling father. This estrangement grew out of her adolescent disillusionment with the limitations of her father's support and the constrictions implicit in her mother's rigid attitudes about the proper role for a woman. This had left her with a developmental sense of emptiness against which she had defended by activities that were variously altruistic, intellectualized, or distracted, as in the lesbian relationship. Her sense of the empathic analytic holding seemed to increase her capacity for independent behavior, as she began to try to deal with her envy of more successful women by trying to become a successful female executive, instead of finding this accomplishment vicariously with her lesbian partner Martha. This materialized in reality as the patient received several excellent new job offers, one of which she accepted. In response to her improving mood and self-esteem, she was able to help her mother with her father's emerging dementia and elicit more gratifying reactions from men.

Early signs of inner shifts in her sexual feelings as well, were reflected in dreams of active, vigorous sex with men and women in which each of the partners expressed a mutual sexual self-confidence. Slowly, she shifted from her envy of her sister's financially successful marriage and Ginger's marriage and pregnancy by generating her own new job in which she no longer felt second class but rather more complete and proud of herself. This success, however, was still contingent on the presence of the analyst. For example, in a conflict between the visit of the former lover Martha and her current one Terry, she felt temporarily paralyzed until I returned from a brief absence. At that time, she was able to resolve the conflict and continue with her program of dressing and presenting herself in a more pleasing way, losing some excess weight, and saving money.

This new optimism and confidence permitted the emergence of more intense erotic feelings about men. In a dream, the analyst shut the door on a dangerous (because?) accomplished man who wanted her. At that point, I apparently represented a possessive father who was not ready to let her find a fulfilling relationship with a complete man. In reality, she found an inspiring colleague who was a model of the attractive, confident female professional, and focused more on emulating this woman (displaced idealized maternal transference).

As she developed a stronger sense of the analyst's commitment, she imagined that he, with her former female therapist, formed a united couple whose presence remoralized her and improved her reality attunement. She felt more detached from her real mother and ready to confront the feared male phallus with me present. However, she felt shattered and abandoned when I went on vacation. Nevertheless, while I was away, she was able to overcome her envy of her friend Ginger and earn her gratitude by doing a good job helping her organize her wedding.

We then went through a summertime depressive period involving her persistent denial of the need for and recreation of the mother–child dyad in the further development of her self-image (Siegel, 1988). The resolution of this occurred in conjunction with a dream of an empathic analytic stepmother who helped her to feel more empowered with men and with a female oedipal rival at work, Suzanne. The depression was also related to her persisting feeling that there were two parallel worlds in her life, one with women and the other with men. However, men could now be soothing and exciting, depending on her own level of self-acceptance. If it were high, she felt more attractive and more differentiated in her relationship with her parents. On one such occasion, she was able to participate in an appropriate way in the celebration of her father's retirement. She felt a new determination about herself that was expressed as a renewed identification with the heterosexual women in her family, her sister and her mother. From this vantage point, she could see that the indifference and indecisiveness of her parents had developmentally blunted her capacity for heterosexual desire and ambition.

The second year of the analysis began with a continuing instability in her mind, both regarding her family and her own attitude toward financial independence and entitlement for recognition and a healthy sexual life. This came partly from the family and partly from her own lack of self-confidence. In her dreams, the analyst was represented as a protective, effective good man and this feature seemed to facilitate her resolution to become more independent and assertive. A better feeling about her family support was represented in a dream with a spaceship with equipment and a welcome from a heterosexual couple. As Christmas approached, she was confidently able to confront her mother about mutually agreeable Christmas plans instead of submitting to the mother's controlling behavior. It was when dealing with this aspect of her family life that the patient came to appreciate how her relationship with Terry and the latter's seductive theories about freedom and independence had replaced something missing from her family: maternal empathy and generative facilitation (Schafer, 1959).

My own faltering attunement was ill-timed at this point when she very much needed me to understand her father's role in the family in which he seemed to be both favoring her sister and infantilizing the patient about money. She had a dream in which her sister gets to take away the patient's new state-of-the-art sports equipment and she is enraged. Mother is narcissistically preoccupied and her father, while capable, is uninvolved.

The patient was now confronted with a surprising response from her parents who provided the money she needed for her investments and a new maternal interest that she had not known before. It was difficult for me to comprehend this shift in her parents' attitude toward her, but it was significant and sustained, and not undermined by father's gradual senescence. Afterwards, I reflected that it was perhaps as a result of inner shifts in the patient involving maternal images becoming more loving and accepting, which was in turn reflected in more optimistic and less hostile approaches to her parents. I noted that this resulted in an increasing amount of positive oedipal material in her dreams and associations. There was, for example, a dream in which an ideal self played the role of a majorette leading a family parade. Reality supported this increasing inner confidence because she was now financially out of debt and had been prompted to work in a high-powered independent working group. She was able to make a brief visit to her long-standing lover Martha and found that she no longer idealized her and her advice and no longer felt drawn into her potential for a seductive merger. She was amazed at the new internally generated energy and self-confidence that she had developed over the past year.

In her relationship with Terry, the latter's absence on vacation left the patient free to work on her inhibitions, self-respect, and work responsibilities. However, she was mourning the loss of the exclusive access to her lover's body, and as the latter went away there were erotic dreams replete with elements of competition, seduction, and performance. Some of these themes connected with her own family, such as early memories of competing with her sister for her mother's body. As she worried about what would befall Terry, she took pride in her relationship with her analyst, seeking to move closer to me by supporting some medical–political activities that were going on at the time. This situation reminded her of how difficult it had been to bring her feelings to, and collaborate with, her detached childhood father, as well as mother.

There seemed to be a particularly distinct repetition of past experience as she began to be aware of the ability to talk realistically with men and not just be their buddy. A negative version of this issue in the transference occurred when, in a brief failure in my attunement, a challenging and competitive piece of behavior on her sister's part reminded her of a period in her childhood when the mother, who could not deal with her energy, had turned her over to the care of the maternal grandmother, while on summer vacation. The latter was painfully unresponsive, apparently preferring the sister's and the mother's low-key feminine style to the patient's boyish hyperactivity. However, as I have seen many times in this treatment relationship, the activation and analysis of earlier memories anticipated reality shifts. This time, she was more popular with her golfer parents, who were taking up her favorite sport, in spite of father's slowly progressive forgetfulness and confusion. "If only they had been this way before, I wouldn't have needed two female relationships." She was afraid that I wouldn't treat this issue and its associated grief seriously enough, although I reviewed this with her as a residual, disappointing oedipal maternal transference.

Further adolescent memories were revived, particularly around the helpful sports-providing father and a fearful dream of his loss through death. This was mirrored in feelings of attachment and separation in the disappointing, limited paternal transference, which she now handled in a more informed, realistic, and competent fashion.

Understandably, she now, at this point, found a gratifying date, Peter, who looked like the man in a dream in which someone was telling her that her father was dead! She now felt that she was doing better, competing with Ginger with her new male attachment, her organized life, and her good relationship with her parents. However, this now made her feel still vulnerable to her boyfriend's phone calls. Fortunately, Peter turned out to be sensitive to this, and consistent in his attentions.

As the third year began, the patient was finding that her closer relationship with her boyfriend was exacerbating her ambivalence abut men in new ways. A dream warned her that they can become evil, and this fear led her to tend the react to her boyfriend's European prejudices rather than exploring them. Would he behave like a momma's boy like the rest of them? Would he leave her hurt and disappointed? To protect herself from this, she worked extra hard in trying to become self-sufficient at work. She then accused the analyst of treating her like a "cog in the system." However, her mood was softened and gratified both by a male friend's apology for recent insensitivity and a good date with her more engaged boyfriend. Increasingly, she thought about ending the lesbian relationship with Terry.

Now, both real and fantasy relationships with the mother became surprisingly improved. In an apparent indication of the new "analyst introject phase" (Siegel, 1988), the mother was seen as responsive and more separate. She had a dream of a rapprochement with a stern, maternallike critical woman. She visited an old lover, C, who was now married to a man and supportive of her perceived sexual maturation. This discussion prompted her to realize that there was a "Henry and June" theme ("bisexual equivalence" of sexual orientation) to her life now as the relationship with her boyfriend became better and closer and demonstrated its potential for a long-term relationship. The strength in that area of her relationship permitted her to have a dream in which Ginger (her designated rival) was seen as the queen mother unsexing and disidentifying her as a female. This dream provided valuable representations of the previously mystifying destructive impact of her early relationship with her mother that seemed to have necessitated the gay solution.

Her competitive, aggressive, and assertive issues evolved as she strove to be a self-reliant, independent worker and manager, especially with an employee who behaved like a competitive sister. She remained equally vulnerable to my absence and to that of her boyfriend, but these feelings could be buffered by the first-class feeling she got from her job and its reinforcing effect on her ego identity. She met her former therapist and proudly told her about the "man in my life." These issues also were worked through in the relationship to the boyfriend Peter as she protected herself from being undervalued, and sensitized him to North American expectations for emotional sensitivity, her priority over his sisters, and the value of her advice regarding his problem managing his father's dementia. This successful resolution of some minor arguments about degrees of attachment led them to plan seriously to move in together.

There was now a phase in the analytic relationship involving her improved capacity to recognize separation emotions and enhanced sensitivity to failures of my attunement to her (further introjection and implementation of the analytic introject [Dorpat, 1990]). This empathic failure reminded her of the self-absorbed mother and she finally felt not alone about this issue after working it through with me. This enhanced sense of closeness in the transference and therapeutic alliance prompted her to increase the analytic frequency to five sessions per week and indulge herself in nostalgic feelings about the good things that her father did do for her. She decided not to vacation with Terry and she wondered where that relationship would be in two years.

Where it would be "in two years" gave way to the immediate present in what the patient describes as her "summer from Hell." Terry's mood instability required that the patient extend herself considerably in giving her support. This made her angry with T's selfishness and she felt strung out by it. She was glad that her mother was now in the wings, prepared to be supportive. That improved her mood and enabled her in the analysis to focus on her core feelings of helplessness as a child.

As the fourth year of the treatment began, the patient was continuing to reflect on her difficulty in separating from Terry. During this time, she was especially sensitive to my lack of attunement and impending vacation.

My long-seeming absence ushered in a negative father transference displaced into the family of origin and into a parallel process at her work. Both situations were resolved by the patient's increasing capacity for clear, open communication, particularly around sibling issues with her sister. She continued to be prone to dream about the former friend, Martha, and reflected on the recurring theme of female losses in her life. It seemed as though this analytic space permitted her both to work on these issues but at the same time to maintain an optimistic future dream about a heterosexual romance that would be permanent.

The failure of a concurrent date with her friend Peter evoked associations blaming her problem with men on her intrusive, controlling, unsexing mother. Her mood fell. She felt fat and unglamorous, but was able to use her free associations to reflect on the pattern of her rebellious, self-isolating self-sufficiency. Most of the time, as an alternative to object-connected conventional relationships with men and women, she felt depressed in a disconnected "cocoon." This had come about as a result of what she took to be her father's emotional inconsistency and behavior that led her to expect disappointment from all men. This was reinforced as two men friends forsook her, and her health insurance plan threatened to sever the ties with her analyst. At this time, the provincial health insurance plan threatened to "delist" its unlimited coverage of daily psychoanalytic therapy, but relented under the pressure of mostly feminist criticism. She was able to reverse this regression analytically and to confront an unfair work review with her supervisor.

She began to realize that she had major fears about entrapment in a relationship with a man and spoke of castrating and being castrated as issues that this evoked for her. This was the danger of being the subject of male desire; for example, losing equality, not being recognized, developing a poor self-worth. She missed an extra appointment with me, expressing difficulties she had with self-worth, needing men, and her fear of being her father's kind of indecisive woman. In discussing this, I suggested that what she was overlooking was the need to get her *own* kind of man. Her reaction to this occurred the next day when she heard about a friend's exciting romance and felt something "click—a new spark," encouraging her to activate herself and arrange to meet a new man, Andrew, interested in sports, who had advertised in the personals section of the newspaper.

Now she evinced a new, male-positive mood, centered in the transference, whereas I was idealized in a dream as a boasting, successful analyst and in waking life as an expert writing on analytic concepts of sibling relationships. Identifying with this analytic formulator, the patient articulated her own concepts of her supposed attachment disorder and the split representations of her sister and self into compliant and pseudoindependent polarities. She formulated a new role with men and moved on, detaching her attitude toward her parents while checking out a flood of male personals' letters. She couldn't have done it without analysis, but now she felt concerned that her independent sexuality meant rejecting me, causing my retirement, and possible ill-health.

She now fastened on Matthew, a thirteen years older businessman with whom she shared much, including a pleasure in individual sports. She simultaneously felt gratitude to me and confidence in herself but feared finding a clunker in the boyfriend. That he was about the same age as me, however, suggested to her strength, personal and financial stability, and wisdom.

Fortunately, the patient used her fear of failure in the relationship to pursue a slow, careful course, which permitted her to reflect analytically on her fears of engulfment, sexuality, her lover's penis, and her fear of being crowded by his personality, especially because of his being thirteen years her senior. The process made her feel moody, and these moods included jealousy, provocative teasing, and distracting herself with the future. She came back, however, to deal with the newly verbalized issues around her feelings about her body,[1] her femininity, and what it meant to her to wear a dress. Her parents approved of Matthew, and she progressively began to feel that the relationship was a safe place. It was safe enough to permit complete mutual sexual satisfaction, as facilitated by the analysis of her fears about her own desirability as the sexual subject of her lover. He facilitated this by being understanding about her former gay relationships and appreciative of her new slim 25-pound lighter body. She realized that she could feel and be attractive and intelligent at the same time. She radiated a progressive sense of pride in her body and in her new recognition by his friends, his empathic understanding of her parents, and their plans to live together. She was also busy defending against this progress by regressive dates with a former boyfriend and dreams expressing fears of abandoning her father and the analyst as destructive developments.

I then shocked her by suggesting that it was time for us to consider the termination of the therapy. She could not disagree but wanted to hold onto me by becoming my student. I indicated that this was a reenactment of her not yet relinquished desire for a merger with an idealized mother. In a watershed dream, she rejected Terry's offer of a lesbian reunion. She worked on the issue, mourned, and set a termination date five months hence, expressing fears about a flight into gayness. She also had a wish for a child to cement her relationship in the transference and in the relationship with her boyfriend. Dreams and feelings of triumph over Ginger regarding her boyfriend and symbolically with the mother, highlighted her pride in her bond with him. During our work she had not mentioned a consistent menstrual irregularity, but now she surprised me by reporting that she was having her eighth consecutive

---

[1] If she privately reflected on her vagina as a "black hole" as Siegel demonstrated, she did not share it with me specifically, speaking only in generalities displaced to her body as a whole.

regular menstrual period, concluding that her bodily functions reflected her analytic progress in verbal and behavioral self-expression.

She now began having more realistic dreams regarding the analyst and his wife, mostly stripped of the idealization and bachelorhood, which she had ascribed to me before when her homosexuality still served as a defense against the oedipal transference. She was not competently managing her birth control in association with the intense erotic preoccupation with her partner and her awareness of the details of the different, now vaginal orgasm with which she responded to his attunement, appreciation of her, and frank talks about the thirteen-year age difference. When she heard of a senior local analyst being indicted for having sexual relations with his woman patients, she had an erotic dream about me in which we were engaging in vigorous foreplay. She threw my ring back at me, stating in the dream that she wanted an analyst not a lover. Reflecting on this dream, she spoke of her sadness in having to give me up, after four years, for her boyfriend since I was her first "successful heterosexual relationship."

The intense wishes and poor birth control resulted in a pregnancy that she and her partner decided was occurring too early in their relationship, and the fetus was medically aborted. We explored thoroughly her fantasies about this "expendable germ spot," her anger and grief over the lost child, her age-related fertility risk at 44, and the lost analyst. She shared her grief with her partner and resumed more effective birth control to match her increasingly lustful sexual communications with her partner.

Resuming her grip on the termination process, subsequent to the distraction by the pregnancy, the patient rebooked the termination phase for just after the analyst's summer vacation instead of just before it. As a result, she was able to do additional analytic work resolving the control and competition issue with her mother that she was recurrently working out with her friend Ginger. When I returned from my vacation, she reported that the analytic vacation space was appreciated as a sample of separation and independence, enabling her to try out her enhanced verbal expression of her love for her partner in which she could now feel alternately the sexual roles of both genders.

She was feeling self-recognized and self-authorized and ready to do her own self-analysis. As proof of this, she reported two deep dreams reflecting her residual fears of being the family's irresponsible child or involved in a relationship with a man that would kill her. When she was anxious in the second to last interview, I referred to her termination jitters over taking "the helm" of her life. In the final hour, she bid me a joyous goodbye. She was off preparing a nautical vacation with her new partner.

Approximately three years later, the patient visited my office in order briefly to tell me in person that she and her partner were still together in a mutually satisfying, consistent relationship. As well, her personal career was proceeding as she had planned, but she did not mention the subject of motherhood.

Summary

I have presented the four-year-long psychoanalytic treatment of a therapeutically "separated" homosexual woman who consulted me for psychoanalytic treatment to help her give up a homosexual lifestyle and find and secure a long-term heterosexual relationship. As I have reviewed the work in my notes prior to consulting the current literature, I am impressed with the amount of psychotherapeutic work that had been done on her aggressive issues in regard to the early attachment to the mother, which had been accomplished in her psychotherapy prior to seeing me. It appears to have facilitated not only her determination to separate from and resolve her long-standing relationship to Martha, but also to complete the task, as she saw it, of maturing into a heterosexual long-term relationship with a man. The stormy[2] relationship with the psychotherapist sufficiently mobilized the patient's desire for a transfer of object from the ambivalently held relationship to the mother psychotherapist onto the idealized image of myself first as an ideal, successful, aggressive, and accomplished man at the time of the formation of the therapeutic alliance (see Quinodoz [1989, p. 57] on the selection of a male analyst by lesbian patients).

---

[2]Much of the remembered therapy was characterized by an aggressivized struggle in her transference to the rigidly controlling, "conventionalizing" mother.

This achieved a sufficient consistency that the attachment to the idealized mother could be established. Throughout her life history, there has been a strong theme of ambitious self-development and the early positive effects of the treatment relationship facilitated sufficient success in her career endeavors to remobilize her strong sense of ambition as it had been facilitated for several years in the university study group. When these values were attached to her heterosexual interests, it seemed to provide a strong force that helped her to progress slowly but surely toward a heterosexual lifestyle.

As the analysis progressed, we gradually learned more about the mother's limited capacity for warmth, empathy, and attachment and this made the arrival of her sister traumatic. This resulted in an anxiety-ridden attachment to the mother and presaged her compensatory lifestyle with its high-striving obsession with achievement at work and in her obsessive object choice with Terry.

Significant in her development was the pregenital attachment to the father as an alternative holding, affectionate object, a belief that I think shaped her "butch" role in her initial gay relationships, encouraged aggression, and permitted her to appreciate similar phallic qualities in her ultimate partner. Understandably, it was also her major identification in her high phallic striving in her work and sexual life.

An important object-rivalry theme was perceptible in her life and in her analysis where competing rivals were significant; mother versus father, analyst versus girl friend Terry and finally self versus sister and her recurrent rival, Ginger. These followed from the loss of the exclusive access to the mother's body, revived on one occasion when Terry went on vacation. As part of her reaction, she had a mournful dream in which she felt that she had lost the exciting and soothing qualities of her partner's body to the sister rival. The mother's apparently inconsistent focus on her needs was reflected in a cognitive disturbance that left her with difficulty in maintaining and simultaneously flexibly shifting her mental or erotic focus onto one person. Analytic tracking of the face of a man in one of her particular dreams apparently helped her overcome this cognitive deficit in her object-focusing. This development presaged an improved cognitive performance with very significant object-relational

relevance, first in the transference with me and later in the resolution of her difficulty in finding, fixing on, and consummating a
relationship with a man.

The analysis was rife with separation–individuation themes,
particularly from the inner mother, as emphasized in the final stage
of mourning her long-term attachment to the first lesbian partner,
Martha. Curiously enough, this facilitated a rapprochement with her
real contemporary mother.

Displaced transference enactments enabled us to see how her
rivalrous friend, Ginger, through manipulation and verbal aggression, could unsex her as the mother had done. In other words, not
only did mother not consistently facilitate or positively mirror the
patient's young femininity, at times she was capable of "castrating
her" when theatened by the patient's closer relationship to the father. It was the patient's newly developed capacity to observe herself that permitted this to become the focus of analytic reflection,
insight, and practical application in the management of her relationship to her challenging close friend, Ginger.

Among the deeper issues emerging in the termination period
was a late focus on separation issues with the unfocused mother
and the image of the self as a tragic, helpless child. The clarification
and application of this insight and experience had a strong role in
firming up her sense of personal identity and agency. This in turn
opened up her characterological defense of her self-defeating, self-
sufficiency against mother's inconstancy and fickle behavior. This
led to greater responsivity to my interpretive interventions. Included
in this was a remark in which I advised (and authorized?) her to
find "your own kind of man." She did so by incorporating the
analyst's functions of meaning-seeking and formulating, used to
form her own theories/myths/language that helped explain both her
inner and outer identity issues. This seemed like a kind of cognitive
incorporation of the analyst (Siegel, 1988; Dorpat, 1990).

This enhanced cognitive capacity enabled her to focus on and
attach herself to Matthew and set a deliberate courting course while
concurrently participating in the analysis of corelated fears with
me. These included a second-class feeling about her body, devalued
in the sibling and positive oedipal transference to the mother. This
combined with unconscious gender confusion secondary to faulty
gender mirroring by the parents and their emotional deprivation

caused her to engage in a cycle of overeating which compounded her problem of self-disgust.

Finally among the termination issues, object loss and an interfering baby rival, recreated and obliterated in the service of and attachment to her new partner, was the dominating event. In addition, she showed sexual progress both in body awareness, body differentiation, and bisexual communication. She regained her grip on the termination process, felt able to dream and resolve some of her deeper fears self-analytically, and leave me.

Conclusions

I find myself most in synchrony with the evolved perspective of Elaine Siegel, particularly with regard to the disturbances of the pregenital bonding with the mother, and separation and self-differentiation, especially with regard to sexual self-awareness. The specific fragments that I am able to reconstruct from the earlier therapy with this patient would tend to support the concept of an incomplete sense of a sexual identity associated with a lot of confusion about sexual bodily investments and attributes. Her undifferentiated sexual self-definition was aggravated both by her mother's coldness and the ironic effects of the attachment to the warm father who mirrored her phallic masculine traits where mother failed to encourage her female development, including doll play (Dorpat, 1989; Jacobs, 1990).

The notion of a developmental arrest both in the vaginal awareness and the correlated inner space, compounded by a primary identification with the father's penis, seemed to affirm Siegel's concept of a chronically disturbed parental relationship characterized by a needy mother and a father who failed to teach the girl about being a young woman. This develops bisexuality as an attempt to manage the arrest in the sexually undifferentiated stage. She waited and then tried more actively in her twenties to establish a heterosexual attachment that was probably thwarted by the disturbances in body image and sexual self-image.

It seems that it was primarily in the preoedipal maternal, father, and sister transferences and their analysis that the patient was able to restore herself first through an idealized maternal transference. She then transferred to a more optimistic father transference and moved on to a more developmentally facilitating and secure positive oedipal transference. This enabled her in the alliance to make me her first "heterosexual relationship." The final analytic introject phase enabled her to renounce homosexuality as a defense against a full oedipal transference and identify with the analyst and his meaning seeking function. This facilitated the residual analysis of her genital fears and the efforts necessary to find, secure, and consummate a heterosexual attachment to a suitable heterosexual partner.

References

Acosta, F. X. (1975), Etiology and treatment of homosexuality: A review. *Arch. Sex. Behav.,* 4(1):9–29.

Decker, B. (1984), Counselling gay and lesbian couples. *J. Soc. Work & Hum. Sexuality,* 2(2–3):39–52.

Dorpart, T. L. (1990), Female homosexuality: An overview. In: *The Homosexualities: Reality, Fantasy, and the Arts,* ed. C. W. Socarides & V. D. Volkan. Madison, CT: International Universities Press.

Jacobs, L. P. (1990), Preoedipal determinants of female homosexuality. In: *The Homosexualities: Reality, Fantasy, and the Arts,* ed. C. W. Socarides & V. D. Volkan. Madison, CT: International Universities Press.

Quinodoz, J.-M. (1989), Female homosexual patients in psychoanalysis. *Internat. J. Psycho-Anal.,* 70:55–63.

Schafer, R. (1959), Generative empathy in the treatment situation. *Psychoanal. Quart.,* 28:347–373.

Schuker, E. (1996), Toward further analytic understanding of lesbian patients. *J. Amer. Psychoanal. Assn.,* (Suppl.) 44:485–507.

Siegel, E. (1988), *Female Homosexuality: Choice without Volition.* Hillsdale, NJ: Analytic Press.

CHAPTER 7

A Note on the Resolution of Separation-Individuation Transference Phenomena in the Analysis of a Homosexual Woman

SELMA KRAMER, M.D.

I should like to focus on the influence of working through in analysis of separation–individuation transference phenomenology in a patient who showed evidence of more and deeper pathology than is encountered in the "normal neurotic" patient.

The patient, a 29-year-old homosexual woman, came to treatment because of work inhibition, severe recurrent depressions, and problems in relating to her lovers. She was born in Europe to very young teenage parents who had to marry because of the pregnancy. From reconstruction, and later verified by her mother's diary, it was apparent that the 15-year-old mother was depressed and angry at her well-endowed infant for whom she could not modulate tension. The transference material suggested that the young parents showed little regard for the needs of the infant, but that the infant received attention from many relatives, her grandparents in particular, and an elderly uncle who rocked her. I feel that gratification of symbiotic–libidinal needs probably saved my patient from more serious pathology, but problems in object relations resulted because, among other reasons, there was not one main libidinal object (Mahler, 1968, 1975; Mahler, Pine, and Bergman, 1975).

Material that emerged in treatment, and the diary, suggested that the early practicing subphase, although not especially joyous,

209

aroused some pride in the parents. In the practicing subphase proper, the father left their country to establish himself in the United States, leaving the patient and her once more depressed mother to remain in a relative's home where the child's explorations were markedly curtailed.

Now the depressed mother turned to her daughter for comfort, clinging to her. This too great closeness, too great an encroachment on the child's separation and individuation, continued into her pre- and postoedipal life. The father was not available to help the child separate from her overly binding mother. When they joined him in this country, his daughter, just past 4 years in age, considered him an ogre. At first he seemed to compete for her mother's attention, and she could not vie with her mother *for his* attention at this critical gender-formation period. The father, in a hurry to pursue a new career, soon encouraged his wife and daughter to keep each other company, and gradually actively assigned to my patient the responsibility of providing emotional support to her depressive mother.

Physical separation from the mother did not take place until the patient went to a college far from home. Mutual emotional separateness was not effected, and both mother and daughter were depressed and lonely. The patient soon entered her first homosexual relationship. Her many homosexual partners were older women from whom she sought mothering, although initially in the office and to the world she presented herself as a "Dyke." When depressed she wished to be rocked, as we discovered she had been by an uncle in infancy; then she fantasied herself as little "Raggedy Anne." When in close contact with a mothering object, she fantasied herself as "Raggedy Andy," a soft, spineless, cuddly and not yet phallic male. In a successful business career much like her father's she fantasied herself as phallic and indestructible—"The Six Million Dollar Man."

The anamnesis and reconstruction in the analysis of early preoedipal experiences showed that the libidinal involvement of other family members, and the patient's excellent endowment, protected her against the most noxious effects of her early traumata. She did not achieve libidinal object constancy and repeatedly had to seek a homosexual partner when fear of abandonment and loneliness overwhelmed her. But she also could not remain attached to these objects because dread of loss of self gave rise to overwhelming anxiety.

I shall briefly report on the treatment, focusing especially on the analysis of the transference, through which it has been possible to facilitate the resolution of conflicts from early preoedipal stages as well as of negative oedipal and oedipal conflicts. I wish to make it clear that there was not an orderly sequential process in the analysis, that is, the material did not follow orderly stages of development. At first, needs for negative oedipal gratification coexisted with needs for earlier gratification. Dyadic and triadic transference coexisted.

The formation of a therapeutic alliance took a long time, manifestly because my patient could not trust me, a "straight" woman. She was certain that I could not understand her, and that I would disdain her for being gay. Separations were very painful and caused her to get depressed. She fantasied that they meant disapproval, which sent her self-esteem plummeting.

After a time, evidence of existing and stabilizing basic trust progressively emerged. The patient, on entering or leaving the office, searched my face, and during the sessions listened to my voice for cues. She felt that she perceived a lilt in my voice and fantasied a happy look in my eyes when I was about to make an important remark. I considered this a significant and welcome positive transference manifestation. She felt a sense of acceptance and empathy.

Early in treatment when she could not trust that I would be reliable, it became clear to me that the patient had a coterie of friends with whom she discussed her affects, dreams, and fantasies. I pointed out that in doing this, she was showing her need for so many others; I added that much, however, was lost to treatment. She cried and shouted, "But you're not here for two days each week!" It was at this time that the patient revealed in a "by the way" her insatiable need to be rocked by her homosexual partner, and fantasies that I could rock her and she could even get inside me.

Soon she dreamed about being very tiny, a mouse or flea on the shoulder of the Jolly Green Giant. But the little animal was plucked off and discarded. The mood in the dream, pleasant at first, changed to one of sadness and depression, the way she felt on weekends. She associated to an old favorite song, "I've got you under my sin," but she sang it as, "You've got me under your skin.'' To the mood change, she associated her feeling that I would object to her as a patient if I knew how close she wanted to get—not sexually—just close.

Further associations to the dream were of pleasant kinesthetic sensations of comforting rocking movement. But she found herself angry at me for I didn't give her what she wanted, that is, to feel better. If I would not do this every time, I should not begrudge her the comfort she got from her friends.

I interpreted this dream, not in terms of some of its sexual content which later surfaced, but in terms of her feeling that she had experienced as a child and wished for now in the transference: comforting by those who were not in a main (parent–child) relationship because the main relationship was not enough.

After a period during which the patient was less conflicted, she began to travel for her business. She became very uneasy, reminding me of a rapprochement child, and on some occasions phoned from across the country with desperation and anger: ''What made you think I could do this?'' or, ''You should have told me to stay home.'' On her return she was relieved, yet blamed me, and said that if not for her appointment with me, she could have gone off in a new homosexual liaison. She then dreamed of a tea party. She, her mother, Raggedy Ann, Raggedy Andy, and Elizabeth Taylor sat around a nursery table pretending to have tea. There were sounds in the background that interested her. Someone said, ''Sit down and pay attention.'' It was a little like Alice in Wonderland. Her associations were to the many tea parties she and her lonely mother had with her dolls. To Elizabeth Taylor she associated her attraction to beautiful older women who were bitches, as in *Who's Afraid of Virginia Woolf?* In that play, Taylor couldn't have children and her marriage was bad, as is everyone's heterosexual marriage. The patient associated to her parents' violent battles and her wish to get away. The background sounds seemed to be of children playing. ''Sit down and pay attention'' recalled both parents' admonitions, mother's that she should stay home with her, and her father instructing her to take care of mother.

I pointed out the difficulty that she and mother had about separations; that she liked to play with mother and the dolls, yet part of her wanted to go off. I connected this with recent transference material. The patient said, ''You and I sit around here and play with my

Raggedy Ann and Raggedy Andy selves. And you can go off if you want to, but you don't let me.'' She railed in an impassioned rage that I directed her life. Then she returned to the fact that she did not stay away from treatment to go off with the new homosexual partner. She admitted that she had been relieved for she had been afraid of the woman she called ''Super-Dyke.''

Dreams of negative Oedipus emerged soon. The background to a dream was a poem entitled ''Mother Love.'' Also, the patient wanted to return to graduate school to study law and business. She had fantasies of being rich and powerful and was not sure I would approve. (She was proud that I, a woman, earned a good living and furious that she had to pay my fee.)

The dream was as follows: she was dressed in yellow pajamas. They were baggy and not attractive. She had a dildo stuck in her in such a way that it made a 30-degree L as on a Greek vase. It was pleasant to have the dildo. It was done to her by her. She was a girl, but ''there it was.''

Associations: her father used to parade around in floppy PJ's with the fly open. He thought he was hot stuff. She didn't think so, but sometimes mother did. If she (the patient) were hot stuff, she'd have something to stuff into her female lover. I would think better of her; I would not go away or ignore her. I commented that she must have felt when she was very young that mother would love her more if she had a penis and that when so close to mother, she fantasied taking father's role in sex. I cautiously extended this into the transference, for, although she could accept transference inter-pretations of her dependency, interpretations of her sexual feelings toward me caused great anxiety, shame, and guilt. Although the patient was furious with the implications of penis envy, she was less tense and hostile. There were many dreams and much transference material indicating that she would be loved and admired by mother and me if she were a male. At the same time, she derided men and openly and successfully competed with them in business.

Soon thereafter she had a dream of running, shouting over her shoulder, dragging Raggedy Anne. She associated to an earlier dream of making love to a new female partner. She had awakened in a panic. Other associations were to the fact that she always had toy guns as a child. And father had taught her how to shoot a real gun to protect her mother while he was away. She revealed teenage masturbatory fantasies of being a young man saving mother. Regression followed. She felt orally insatiable and felt orally teased and deprived, but later dreams reminded her of secret oral pleasures which angered her father.

Afterward, the analyst was less the rejecter, more the comforter. Also, the patient was able to comfort herself as she studied modern dance, and rhythmic exercises, living out a combination of rocking, bodily comforting, and gratification, as well as practicing subphase activity awakened by the transference experience. She began to feel freer in making business trips, after which she would show me souvenirs of her trip, with shades of the affect shown as the practicing subphase and then rapprochement subphase child shares things with mother.

Rapprochementlike crises were soon seen in the transference, ambivalence heightened, and she again became angry with me. As heretofore, quiescent genital–oedipal feeling emerged, again she felt that a "straight" woman could not help her. She hoped and feared that I might be tempted by her to be gay. She hated my husband and fantasied him to be tyrannical and abusive, and she recalled primal-scene exposure.

Exaggerations and ambivalence emerged in the transference. She was certain that I would be angry with her for having friends, for enjoying the wheeling and dealing of business, for having homosexual affairs. The crisis gradually diminished; the patient became more productive and creative in her work; the quality of her friendships improved, and life was better. Later the patient confessed with chagrin that a change had occurred in her sexual dreams and fantasies—her sexual partner was male and was not abusive or murderous. The patient became softer, more feminine as beginning positive oedipal material emerged.

In a dream she made love to a man, then she tried to wrap tiny baby mice in pieces of soft flannel. Associations led to her awareness that she'd like children. She also associated to her fear of rats, a fear that caused chagrin because it was "so typically female." Also, rats gnaw, are vicious, and carry rabies. The desired fetus was a dangerous, clawing, dirty, gnawing thing, her own anger at her mother projected on her fantasied fetus.

Oedipal, triadic material gradually became more consistent. About a year later the patient reported that if she submitted a bid, she was certain that an older woman from a competing company would receive the order, and was angry at the thought of having to capitulate. She associated to a question she had pondered in childhood, "Did her father have enough love for both her and her mother?" She connected this question with her fear of competing with older women in business, fearing she would lose mother's love if she did all right with father. She now recalled childhood masturbation fantasies about her father, but denied having been coy or seductive with him; she remembered his reading poetry to her as well as teaching her masculine things, and thinking he looked like Errol Flynn. But she couldn't compete with any woman for any man.

This denial soon gave way as she fantasied again about my husband. Suppose she met him in business and something happened (sexually). Since she would not know he was married to me, it would not be her fault. She imagined my rage and then reminded me that it was inevitable that she would have had fantasies about her father, for he was only 17 when she was born. She called him a "handsome bastard" with some warmth and added that she was no longer furious at men.

Further analysis resulted in increased separateness, especially from mother, and decreasing anger at father. She reported that she had better relationships with both parents, having established with mother that they were separate; she and father were friends at last. The patient now had to take a business trip and knew she would miss me but would get along. There might be men on the trip. She was getting along better with them all the time. She wore skirts now for all encounters with men, and they liked it.

She knows from their responses to her that she must be sending "vibes" to them. Her positive oedipal feelings revived her fear of her father's sadism. Her anger at father eventually centered on the fact that if he loved her at all, and he may have, he did not respond sufficiently to her seductiveness, nor did he make her more important than her mother.

Throughout her analysis, while there were adumbrations of earlier phases of development, there was a powerful developmental thrust, which aided the analytic process and encouraged the process of what traditionally is considered "working through." I wish to state that I in no way feel that the early stage material appearing in the analysis duplicated in an exact way, what actually occurred in the early preoedipal years (Blum, 1978).

Summary

Greater knowledge and integration of developmental concepts and of the frame of reference of separation-individuation, add to the analyst's richer insights and to his more complete interpretations and reconstructions.

Freud recognized the complexity of preoedipal development and the importance of the object and of object relations. Contemporary contributions have enabled us to proceed beyond the preoedipal conceptualizations, and since Freud, to better understand ego and drive regression and evidence of fixations or ego distortions which may appear parallel to "normal neurotic" findings.

I question whether we encounter different patients today and suggest that we understand our patients better, thus making our analytic assessments and practices so different from fifty years ago. Separation–individuation theory encompasses and organizes findings from many sources, research and clinical, and permits us to perceive and process material in a multifaceted way. It must affect the timing and content of interpretations and reconstruction of psychopathology as well as normal development.

References

Blum, H. P. (1978), Reconstruction in a case of postpartum depression. *The Psychoanalytic Study of the Child*, 33:335–363. New Haven, CT: Yale University Press.

Mahler, M. (1968), *On Human Symbiosis and the Vicissitudes of Individuation*, Vol. 1. New York: International Universities Press.

——— (1975), Discussion of "Healthy parental influences on the earliest development of masculinity in baby boys," by R. J. Stoller. *Psychoanal. Forum*, 5:244–247.

——— Pine, F., & Bergman, A. (1975), *The Psychological Birth of the Human Infant: Symbiosis and Individuation*. New York: Basic Books.

CHAPTER 8

The Psychoanalysis of a Homosexual Woman

HOUSTON MACINTOSH, M.D.

Introduction

This paper describes a homosexual woman and the course of her analysis. Psychoanalytic literature on female homosexuality is reviewed, and the patient is discussed in light of it and the multiple meanings and functions involved (Waelder, 1930).

When she first consulted me, Ms. A was a slim, attractive, professional woman in her late twenties. She had become depressed and suicidal after being left by a woman with whom she had been living for three years and with whom an overt homosexual relationship had terminated a year earlier. Although she had always striven toward self-reliance and independence, she felt she could no longer handle her problems without help.

She was the youngest daughter from a middle-class, strictly religious family. Her older sister was married and had children. Her parents came from a poor lower class background. Her father, a strong-willed and opinionated man, was now retired from a never-too-successful career. He was an outgoing, generous man with a sense of humor, yet somehow bitter and complaining of how people had taken advantage of him. He was argumentative, and Ms.. A. would "meet him head on." Although a religious skeptic, he had not completely broken with his religion.

Her mother was a model of a proper "passive," obedient wife and mother: a pillar of religious morality whom the patient both identified with in religious devotion, and yet constantly rebelled against. She felt her father dominated her mother, and she resented her mother for taking it. She described herself as a spoiled child who did things to embarrass her mother. One night, after she had gone off to college, she realized she hated her mother.

During college she lost her religious faith, feeling religion was illogical. Because of the importance of religion to her mother, she continued to feel guilty over this decision. She believed becoming an atheist would be deeply hurtful for her mother, causing her to feel she had failed in her motherly responsibilities. This guilt contributed to her forming a homosexual liaison. Because she would never have to marry, she could conceal her religious rebellion from her mother.

Her decision to give up her religion occurred during her sophomore year at college. Not long after, her mother had a mastectomy for cancer. Ms. A, however, assumed she was cured, until there was a recurrence a year after Ms. A graduated from college. Mother died the following year. This was two years after the start of the homosexual relationship and a year prior to starting analysis.

At college she did average work, but disliked competing with other women academically. She dated several men, but for the last two years of college, she went out mainly with one, Tom. When she first saw his penis (toward the end of her junior year) she felt uncomfortable and "surprised how large it was." This reaction also angered her as she felt she was "delighting his male ego." They first had intercourse during the fall of senior year. She rationalized that by not moving, and feeling nothing, she remained a virgin.

About the middle of her senior year, she attended a party where there was a lot of drinking. She became attracted to a different male student, Sam, who reminded her of her father. They went to his apartment, but she immediately began to have abdominal pain, so he took her home.

The following day she went on a vacation trip with a female student, Ann, who was a year younger than she. One night they got drunk and this woman told the patient that she loved her. Additionally, she added that she had a fatal disease and would be dead in ten years. When they returned to school, Ann stopped speaking to her for a month. This silence made the patient increasingly anxious and guilty. (During the analysis, similar feelings over my silence were traced to her mother's silent disapproval.) She blamed herself for Ann's homosexuality, as she had "kidded around" with her. Finally she decided she must love Ann. Otherwise, how could she be so upset? So she went to Ann and made love to her, somehow feeling she was rescuing her. They became roommates and started sleeping together regularly. At first her orgasms were intense and focused around her clitoris. After a few months sex became less stimulating and was unsatisfying. She liked mainly physical closeness: to be held, caressed, and comforted. Sometimes she would fantasy her partner was male and she would have a little girl by her.

When graduation approached, her male friend asked her to come live with him in another city. She wanted to be rid of him, but she feared leaving college and living alone. The relationship with a woman thus "solved" her conflict with her male friend.

She and her partner continued living together, but she was constantly anxious lest someone discover their clandestine sexual relationship. After a year, they stopped further genital contact at her partner's request, although they continued living and sleeping together until shortly before the patient began her analysis. She had come to think of Ann as a "sister."

Past History

Ms. A's father had courted her mother for twenty years before they were married in their late thirties. This arrangement was said to have been necessary for financial reasons. Her mother was 45 when Ms. A was born by C-section. A hysterectomy was done following the delivery (a sister had been born a few years earlier).

When Ms. A was 2 months old, her mother was hospitalized for asthma. Her aunt cared for Ms. A until age 5 months. She was said to have been a "good baby," rarely crying. At age 2 years she was hospitalized for a tonsillectomy. She cried continuously when she was separated from her mother. Later that evening, the hospital staff insisted she be sent home, and the procedure was never done.

Her earliest memories were of her father holding her stomach while wiping her perianal area. She also remembered lying in a crib with her mother close by and feeling content. She was told she sat on her father's lap while he read to her, but she could not recall this. A photograph taken at age 3 shows her happy and smiling. Another a year later shows her somber. At age 4 she compared urination with a boy the same age. A year later, she and the boy tied up a little girl and "tortured" her (meaning they said "bad things" to her). They also tortured a dog.

She remembered her mother affectionately when she gave her cookies and milk, or when she took care of her when she was sick. (She especially liked Ann to tuck her into bed, years later, when she was sick, thereby reenacting a positive aspect of her relationship with her mother.) When she accidentally wet herself at age 6, her mother was kindly and accepting. However, her mother was also a "frustrated nurse," who was interested in picking and squeezing blisters, splinters, and pimples. When her bowel movements were not prompt and regular, her mother administered suppositories. She hated these intrusions and tried to escape them whenever possible. When she was bad, her mother quietly and determinedly punished her with a paddle, or when she made mistakes playing the piano at age 5, her mother hit her hands with a ruler.

She attended an all-girls religious school from first grade through high school. Her teachers were women. They taught that sexual pleasure was wrong, and always to put others' interests ahead of her own. Between ages 6 and 10, her father did not attend religious services. Her mother quietly, but obviously, prayed for him every day. Ms. A picked a rose from a neighbor's garden when she was 6 and brought it to her mother as a gift. Her mother humiliated her by displaying the rose and telling friends and family that Ms. A had stolen it, in order to "teach her honesty." At age 7, she became obsessionally preoccupied over religious guilt. She announced her increased interest and dedication to religion, hoping for her mother's approval. However, her father and sister teased her about this. She also became prudish and embarrassed about sex. Her father teased her and made her squirm by saying the word *underwear*. She read about religious martyrs and wanted to become one herself. When she was 7 and 8 years old she had a recurring fantasy of being a prisoner in a Communist country, where she was tortured, but did not give in. The fantasy enabled her to fall asleep and possibly defended against masturbation wishes. She recalled tugging on her labia around this time. Then, to her horror, she noticed that one side was longer than the other. She imagined she had caused it to be lengthened, that she was permanently damaged, marked for life, and that everyone would know what she had done. At age 8, a boy pinned her down, and spat in her face, thoroughly enraging her.

When she was 6 she realized she was "Daddy's Girl," and that he was the most important person in her life. She considered herself spoiled and would play mother and father off against each other. Once she heard her mother quietly crying in her room and she felt intensely guilty, imagining mother and father had been fighting over her. Her older sister was mother's favorite, but she eventually believed she won the position of father's favorite. However, father also wanted a boy. He once brought her a baseball glove, but she was always a terrible athlete. Nevertheless she loved her older sister, who was pretty and popular with boys. Her sister had a female friend who was pretty, shy, and athletic. When Ms. A was 13 she developed a crush on this girl, but was rejected. Later she realized that Ann had been very similar to her sister's friend. She remembered vaguely feeling that she had been repeating something with Ann in order to make up for the earlier rejection.

Her menarche also occurred around this time. Her mother's instructions were brief and uneasy. She recalled a fantasy that boys, too, bled each month from their penises. (In this fantasy she denies a difference between the sexes, and perhaps expresses castration wishes as well.) She was afraid tampons would hurt her, but she used them, saving the used ones in a shoe box. Eventually she buried the box.

Around age 14, she vacationed with some relatives on a farm. While sleeping with a female cousin, she wet the bed. She also recalls excitedly reading comic books with her male cousins. Mother had forbidden reading comic books.

She became increasingly sensitive to interpersonal hurts and slights, causing her to withdraw from social relationships, with both sexes. In spite of superior intelligence her grades dropped to barely passing and she spent all of her time reading. This pattern continued until she left home and started college. She then changed her hair style, got contact lenses and new clothes, and started to actively socialize with both men and women.

Course of the Analysis

During her analysis she overcame much of her guilt and anxiety regarding sex. She met and married a man who divorced his wife and married her. Her fantasy of my strong disapproval of her marriage was traced to her mother's religious disapproval of divorce and a feeling that her father disapproved of her having a serious interest in any man. She came to love the man she eventually married. He treated her in the way she desired: with utmost respect and empathy for her wishes; and she tried to do the same for him. He had come from a similar background, but was no longer religious. She came to enjoy sex. Her orgasms were deeper and more satisfying than any she had previously experienced. She steadily advanced in her job and was promoted to a supervisory level. She found she could enjoy her father's company, and no longer felt compelled to argue with him. She became well satisfied with her marriage and her work. Toward the end of the analysis she received a promotion, which came by being favored over a female friend. Her guilt over this victory was subsequently traced to her childhood belief that her father had favored her over her mother and sister.

At the start of the analysis, she experienced considerable anxiety in the analytic situation. She wished I were an older man feeling that would make it easier for her to talk to me. She shamefully and guiltily described more details of the relationship with Ann and her horror of lesbianism. Yet, there was a sense of pride when she described Ann's beauty and how their relationship was like the Garden of Eden: closeness, intimacy, and communion—and not just in a physical sense. She had looked down on Tom and all the men she had previously known, except for Sam. She was afraid of marriage. Her values of empathy and sensitivity were precious to her, and she feared she would lose them through analysis. She associated to rationalizing she was still a virgin. She would not fall in love with her analyst, because she knew that is what she was supposed to do.

Her first dream occurred after a few weeks of analysis. The night before she had been at a party, drinking and smoking hash. A woman whom she knew from work (and who was living with several men) suggested that Ms. A would be more suitable for her husband than she herself. Ms. A panicked. Then the woman put her arm around another woman. This also frightened Ms. A, but less so than the original proposal. When she left the party she wondered if police were following her. When she got home she recognized indications that her female roommate had been in her room, perhaps, she imagined, looking for evidence of her homosexuality. She fell asleep and dreamed, "I was kissing my dog, and I didn't like it." Then she awoke. She associated to fearing she was a lesbian and could not change, and then to further details of her experiences with Ann. During her sophomore year in college, at the suggestion of a girl during sorority rushing, she had started to sleep with a stuffed dog. She talked about her mother and wondered if hating her mother had something to do with her strict conscience. She declared, "Sex is so animalistic." I commented that it's all part of her. She ended the hour by expressing interest in meeting men, and maybe a college course would be a good way to do so.

A few analytic hours later she guiltily confessed that she has masturbated.

The dream cited above suggests oedipal conflict involving incestuous wishes toward her father, hatred of her mother for disapproval of those wishes, and a defensive regression to a homosexual attachment to a woman (mother substitute) which, although frightening and guilt inducing, was less frightening than the heterosexual incestuous wish. She had witnessed sexual behavior between other people at the party the previous evening, so there is an allusion to a primal scene. The dog could stand for father and also for his penis. A dog is also associated to sorority rushing (competition with sisters), where she had met Ann. At the time of the dream, she was taking care of a dog for a married couple. Thus, the dog is also associated to care taking and substitute mothering. During childhood she had tortured a dog suggestive of sadomasochistic conflicts. The torture had taken place originally in partnership with a little boy. She had also compared urination with this boy, so the dog could also be associated to urination, penis envy, and competition with males. However, she did not like kissing the dog, suggesting a reaction formation against oral sexual and aggressive wishes. Doing something she did not like, in addition, suggested imposing a punishment on herself. Moreover, she had slept with a stuffed dog while in college; the latter and possibly also Ann, represented a transitional object (Winnicott, 1953; Pomer, 1976). On the other hand, the dog is not a human object, suggesting the kind of situation Deutsch (1944) described in which a woman is conflicted between making a heterosexual and a homosexual object choice (originally between mother and father) and gets stuck in a narcissistic position, which is neither heterosexual nor homosexual. This, in fact, seemed to be Ms. A's predicament at the time of her dream. The dream, thus, suggests primarily oedipal level conflicts and preodipal conflicts which have been reactivated through a defensive regression.

During the fourth and fifth months negative mother transference and resistance to positive father transference began to emerge. She became increasingly spiteful and rebellious toward me and imagined I would disapprove of what she read. To spite and provoke me, she read the popular book *Games Analysts Play*. I pointed out that her mother had disapproved of what she read, especially if it had anything to do with sex. A few weeks later she began to ask me questions about "transference." She felt that the way she had been acting toward me recently was similar to how she acted toward her mother: irritable, angry, and bitchy. She thought it had to do with some comments I had made about a man she had been dating recently. She felt as if I were controlling her; she knew I was not, but it was a strong feeling. She felt as though she were using me. All day she feels good, comes to see me, bitches for an hour, goes home, and feels good. She felt she could trust me and say whatever came to mind because she is not really responsible for what comes out. I asked, if she isn't, who is? She meant that there is no other situation where she can say whatever comes to mind, but it's hard when she doesn't see me. There is no reassuring approval. She didn't like feeling bitchy toward me. It's a feeling to be avoided. I commented, "Better to be understood." She tried to recall when she started feeling angry at me, and she thought of how embarrassed she had felt when I had not charged her for a canceled hour. (I had done a consultation during the time.) She also had become aware that my clothing had become more stylish (which was true), and this also made it harder for her to talk.

The first hour of the following week started with five minutes of silence. Then she said she had dreamed about Joe (a man at work and her future husband). She didn't realize she liked him so much. He came to her. She can't let it go on. He's married, she's met his wife and she likes her, but she'd like her better if she didn't feel this way about her husband. I asked her to describe the dream. She said, "I was in a cottage, a cabin in the mountains. The walls were white with polished wood [like my office], bright and sunny. People were talking, but I didn't care. I was so happy. He held me and kissed me." She commented that she doesn't dream much, and then thought of the various men she has dated since Ann. She couldn't go back to a woman now. She hates Ann. She must be bisexual, but why is sex with a woman enjoyable, but not satisfying if she is bisexual? I said she was implying that there are no differences between a man and a woman. She laughed and recalled that when she started out with Ann, it was satisfying, but it gradually became more frustrating. She felt hung up. Then they stayed away from each other until one night when they were stoned, but they never talked about it afterwards. Their physical relationship was a way of communicating. Ann held her when she was upset and that comforted her. She had the dream after waking up cold and putting a blanket over herself. The last time she had seen Ann, she had just spent a week at a cottage with another woman. She got stoned and paranoid and thought people were talking about her. When Ann left, she had wanted her to hold her. At this point she was near tears. She struggled to pull herself together, laughed a little and said, "Things have gone full circle. I guess I want a mother." Then she was silent. I commented on her trying not to cry. She said that she loves too much. She shouldn't want to be loved. I asked why, and she replied that she wants too much and that's not healthy. I said that it's not healthy to be afraid to love. She replied that she had, in fact, loved Ann.

She became increasingly preoccupied with Joe. She was falling in love with him. They were both so much alike, but she was afraid he would reject her. She wanted him to divorce his wife, but the idea of displacing his wife caused her great guilt. She tried to stop from thinking it. She was sure I disapproved of her wishes. She associated her father's disapproval of his daughters' boyfriends, and to her mother's disapproval of divorce. As this material was interpreted as transference, she began to view me as a reassuring presence, except when it came to talking about sex. She was afraid to let herself be dependent. Others would discover how great were her needs, and they would reject her. As her relationship with Joe intensified, he began to press her for intercourse, but she feared that if she did not feel anything, it would confirm that she was a lesbian. She also reported intense dislike to the idea of being "pinned down" during intercourse, which she associated to being pinned down by a boy at age 8. After several months they did have intercourse, and it turned out not as good as she had hoped, but better than she had feared. However, the day after, Joe developed an acute illness which was possibly crippling. He withdrew from her and became less certain about leaving his wife. She was crushed.

A few weeks later, they were back together. She said she is attracted to people who are both strong and weak, as is her father. She recalled his sulky silence after fighting with her mother. She remembered two fights: one over her father's mother, the other over his sister. I commented that father and mother were fighting over a rival of mother's for his attention. She replied she was a "Daddy's Girl." She had a "father fixation," that she had done everything with him, and that he was the most important person in her life.

Her romance with Joe continued. She would become passionate and aroused when with him, but her feelings turned off when they went to the bedroom. After intercourse she was surprised and repulsed by semen dripping out; it seemed like going to the bathroom. In fact, she would sit on the toilet after intercourse. This also interfered with her enjoyment.

The following week she reported material that suggested a negative mother transference and the presence of a critical maternal superego that interfered with her enjoyment of adult heterosexual relations. She also seemed to be reenacting an oedipal rebellion against her mother in her affair with Joe. The material also suggested ambivalent father transference and competition with men, possibly based on penis envy.

She told me how angry she was at me, and that she hated to admit that she feels better after she sees me. She felt that I force her to come and that I force her to talk. I asked how I did that. She replied that I really didn't, but it *feels* that way. She feels she has to. It's like eating spinach. If she talks about Joe, she feels ashamed, as she is still thinking of him. "You told me he rejected me," so she should stop thinking of him and find someone else. I said that wasn't so easy, because he occupies an important place in her mental life. She then reported having dreamed: "I'm in my room at home having intercourse with Joe or Tom. My sister comes in and tells me mother says I should stop it. The man goes to the toilet and sits down to urinate, and I laugh. I go downstairs and argue with my mother. I tell her off for interfering with my sex life. I'll do what I want.'' Then there was a second dream: "I was at a fair. There was an amusement ride. I got on with a man and we started equal, but soon I'm precariously hanging out, attached to a rope, but he's safe and unconcerned." She associated that it must say something about her mother and the effect she had on her feelings about sex. The mother was a combination of mother and grand-mother—but neither—a fat, ugly witch. "Why did she get angry at me?" I pointed out the similarity of her feelings toward me and toward the mother in the dream. She replied that I was just like her: calm, patient, and silent. I get her to come around to my way of thinking. I'm like father, too, when she feels as if she has to be very rational and justify everything. If she cried, he would get disgusted. She had talked to Joe that day. He was just not as upset or concerned about her as she is about him. It was just not fair. She doesn't want to be rejected, but she doesn't know how to feel about him. I commented that the idea of fair was in the dream and the uncon-cerned man could be Joe, father, or myself. She agreed and said that if she comes long enough, she'll say everything.

In the following weeks she became less interested in Joe, and more argumentative toward me, complaining that treatment was boring and that I was cold. She felt antagonistic and wanted to fight me. I wondered where her feelings were coming from. She said that she won't be like everyone else: she won't fall in love with her analyst, as she expected she would be rejected. If she fell in love with me, she'd want sex, but that would terrify her, because it would be just like having sex with her father.

Primal scene material was then suggested when she became afraid her roommate in the next room would hear her having sex with Joe. When she thought of sex she turned on, but when she got to the bedroom, her excitement left her, and this was a humiliating failure. She was afraid to grasp Joe's penis for fear she would injure it with her long fingernails. She told me the details of what she did with Ann and with Joe. Talking to me about sex was torture.

After a vacation break she started the second year of her analy-sis. Joe had left his wife. She distrusted my neutrality, and believed I disapproved of him because I had confronted her with the possible unpleasant realities involved in living with a man with his medical problems. His health had improved and she was willing to take a risk. Maybe the diagnosis was wrong, and maybe he would not have another attack. She had never met a man so empathic and sensitive to her needs. She began to think more about her sister and having children. She had displaced her sister as father's favorite daughter. She manipulated him with her looks and her brain. She wanted to conceal herself from me, lest I manipulate her. She had tried to make herself appear like her mother and father's sister to her father, because those were the women he liked, but she did not respect her mother, whom she thought of as a dumb housewife who always kept quiet to avoid trouble with father. So she hid her real self in order to please him.

During the next month she spent more time with Joe. Intercourse was becoming more satisfying. She began to experience orgasm in a new way: occurring during intercourse, and felt deeply in her pelvis. However, she was anxious lest she pass flatus during intercourse. She associated to her mother's keen interest in her bowels, and remembered with embarrassment her mother's passing flatus.

She dreamed she had a penis, and it was covered with "dirty stuff, like printer's ink." This suggested a regressive expression of penis envy in the form of an illusory anal penis. It probably also alluded to the "dirty stuff" she was involved in with Joe, as well as her keen interest in reading, especially books of which her mother would disapprove, as they were "dirty."

She began to feel depressed when she did not spend a night with Joe. She worried that this meant she was becoming dependent on him. Both of her parents would have disapproved of Joe because he was divorced. On the other hand, father was beginning to worry that she would end up a spinster. She had several dreams about her sister, which she related to her feelings about marriage and children. She considered marriage a trap: an endless, mindless, trivial, suburban routine. Children were constantly demanding, and she felt she would have to give in to their every demand or she would feel intolerably guilty for being selfish. She feared she might have to make a decision about marrying Joe sooner than expected. She viewed me as being like her grandmother: intrusive, and disapproving of her curiosity, when I reflected her questions rather than answering them; or like her father who disapproved of her boyfriends. Sibling rivalry was evident in connection with my other patients.

The following month (fifteenth in the analysis) she moved in with Joe. The next night she dreamed she had left him. She became depressed and complained of headaches. She talked frequently of his possible illness, and complained he was not aggressive enough with his former wife or boss. She liked tenderness in people, and this trait is more common in women. She is attracted to weak people. She compared Joe's illness to her mother's. Toward the end she wished for her mother's death and she was afraid she would feel the same about Joe. Yet he and she fit so perfectly together, she would never be able to find anyone else as good as he. She associated my questions about Joe's illness to her father who was always trying to get her to do things "for her own good."

Several months later material reflecting sadomasochistic conflicts became more evident. She recalled that at age 5 she and a little boy had tied up and tortured a little girl. They had also tortured a dog. She denied any masochistic wishes, but said that it was much better to be a masochist than a sadist. She began the following hour by reporting a dream: "It's vague in the beginning. I don't know how I got there—a pro forma marriage. The man I'm marrying is big, blond, beer-bellied, and brutish—a sadist. I talk with my parents and say, 'I'm not that kind of person.' My sister is also getting married with me. My wedding dress is dirty and out of style. There are some flowers there to try to cover up things and make it look okay. I try to rationalize: just live in the present; but I can't. I run away and crouch in a closet. He opens a trap door above me, I see his legs and awaken in terror." She associated to her relief that Joe was not in the dream. It must have something to do with masochism. She thought of the kind of marriage her sister has. She has all kinds of trouble with it, but she seems to like it. She associated living in the present to her attitude about Joe's illness. I asked her about "I'm not that kind of person." She thought of when she was a child and making promises. Her word was her bond. It gave her a virtuous thrill to think of carrying out a promise no matter what. She thought of suffering and punishment. Mother had lived a life of suffering because she thought it was moral and virtuous. Suffering caused people to want to rescue you. Joe is just the opposite of a sadist: kind, reasonable, and empathic. I commented that a marriage to Joe seemed to offer an opportunity to both gratify and ward off masochistic wishes.

In the twentieth month Joe proposed to her and she accepted, although she wished he had waited longer. Now she would have to treat her father with kid gloves on the issue of her marriage. In fact she was treating me with kid gloves. She fantasied she was a fairy princess (Walt Disney, "Tinkerbell" style), all in white—a virgin like Queen Elizabeth. Marriage and children were a trap. She wished to be like Peter Pan and never grow up.

Over the following months negative mother transference was evident. She struggled with me over "Freud's theory of penis envy" and "the rule of free association." She was afraid I would think that it's normal for a woman to want to have a baby, or that I would coerce her into a "passive, masochistic, narcissistic position." She wanted to place any discussion of babies or Joe's medical problems off-limits. She recalled that when she was 7 she had resolved not to be like her mother, or to let her mother mold her into "a docile, obedient, passive, masochistic and religious woman." This had happened to her sister and she would not let it happen to herself. She battled her mother by not letting her know what she was thinking; otherwise, she would have become "hopelessly dependent." She was sure that I was a "Freudian sexist" who would eventually show my true colors and trap her forever in analysis because she was "abnormal," as she did not want to have children. She had felt in a constant struggle with her mother and tried very hard to be the opposite of her and yet she found she was treating herself the way her mother had treated her: scrupulously, suspiciously, and searchingly. On the other hand, when she was sick her mother had treated her with kindness and indulgence. Perhaps there is some connection with her constant complaints of physical symptoms. She feared becoming a "chattering, scatterbrained woman" as were mother and sister. She must not be dominated and submissive as was mother. She declared that the basic rule of analysis was devised by Freud to dominate women and to make them submissive.

She also defended against positive father transference, becoming more concerned lest she have sexual desires toward me. That would make her unfaithful toward Joe. I remarked she was not distinguishing between wishes and deeds. She tried to reassure her-self that I had no sexual interest in her, but if she allowed herself to desire me, she would "have to" carry it out, as she had with Ann. This was because "it would be the logical thing to do." She considered that having a wish and not trying to fulfill it was humili-ating.

After a vacation break, the third year of the analysis started. She angrily realized she felt dependent on me when I was away. She connected her fantasy that as a "Freudian" I wanted her to have children with her mother's wish for her to have children. On the other hand, father considered the idea of her having children as "ridiculous." She had decided when she was 7 not to have children. She feels the opposite of her sister, who is "totally identified with mother," having four children and wishing to be dominated by her husband. On the other hand, she wanted to be like father: intelligent and a good conversationalist.

The time of her marriage to Joe was approaching and she was surprised and disappointed that her father seemed indifferent. When her sister had married, he was indignant, complaining. "She went to college, so a man can tell her what to do?" She felt there was no reason to delay the marriage further, as she knew she would eventually marry Joe anyway. Besides, it demonstrated that he cared for her. She dreamed of caressing Ann's breasts, "just for fun," but the idea frightened her as it could interfere with her relationship with Joe.

At this time she told me about her favorite childhood story, *The Secret Garden*. She remembered it as follows: a little girl lives in India and hates her mother. Her mother dies of cholera, and she is sent to England to live with an uncle who has a crippled son. The uncle has blamed his son for his wife's (the son's mother) death because he was in the garden at the time a branch fell from a tree and killed her. (The girl always thought this judgment was unfair.) There is a friendly, nonintrusive nanny who lives in the village. One day the girl finds keys to the garden and goes there to play. She is not pretty, but independent and self-sufficient. (This detail was quite appealing to her.) She takes the crippled boy to the garden and teaches him to walk. The uncle discovers the boy is no longer a cripple. The garden is reopened, as the uncle realizes his mistake in having locked up the garden.

In this story, Ms. A identifies with the little girl who hates her mother and also the crippled (i.e., castrated) little boy who is responsible for the mother's death. The broken branch refers to castration, and the lame child who learns to walk refers to a fantasy concerning restitution of the penis. The "secret garden" refers to the discovery of the vagina, which frequently occurs at this age and is kept secret (Bernstein, 1976). The friendly, nonintrusive nanny refers to a good preoedipal mother with whom she longs to be reconciled. This is something she later attempted to act out in a homosexual relationship, possibly as a regressive defense against oedipal conflict. There are homosexual elements in the relationship between the boy and his father.

Reporting the story at this point suggests that she unconsciously wished that her marriage would heal and repair how she had felt crippled by her early relationship with her mother. Her earlier homosexual relationship with Ann was probably a similar attempt. In addition, the material is also consistent with her homosexual relationship reflecting a defensive regression from oedipal conflict (including a strong castration complex) in search of a kindly, nonintrusive preoedipal mother[1] (Peller, 1958; Almond, 1990).

After she returned from her honeymoon, she continued to struggle with me over saying what came to mind. We worked through considerable negative mother transference, where I was viewed as coercing, intrusive, controlling, and demanding that she submit. She associated to her mother's use of suppositories to produce bowel movements, if she failed to cooperate sufficiently. Also to speak freely continued to mean that she was a "dumb, chattering female."

At the start of the fourth year, she arrived for her session one day and spent several minutes silent. Finally she began to talk about

---

[1]As Friedlaender (1943) has noted, reading provides children and adolescents with direct instinctual gratification. Parents sense this and they prohibit reading the "wrong" books just as they prohibit masturbation. This leads to reading books "in secret" and interferes with normal desexualization of the ego function of reading, which is necessary for adult reading to obtain information. The patient's mother openly interfered with her reading and much of her reading then became secret. During early adolescence she read books in secret with male cousins, and the activity also probably took on an unconscious masculine meaning for her and helped to support a masculine identification. Conflict with her mother over what she read, first made its appearance in the transference not long after she had guiltily confessed to me having masturbated.

the movie *Forty Carats*. The male in that movie was the epitome of desirability: handsome, very sexy, extremely empathic and sensitive, but in charge, directing and taking care of things. She realized that she wished to be dominated by a man, like a father and a little girl. She depressively thought she had married the wrong man, as he is so unassertive. The man in the movie reminded her of her father. She never thought she would want to be like mother. It makes her think of ending up on her knees as a scrub woman. She'd struggled so long against being dominated, and it's an important part of her. Sam had been more like father than any of her boyfriends, and after her marriage she had dreamed of him.

A few weeks later she brought up termination. She was afraid that if she left it up to me that this could go on for years. Therefore, I should tell her; she has a right to know. I commented that it's best to work toward a consensus, and then asked her how it concerned her who raised the question. She said that she certainly wouldn't stop until she was very sure it was what she wanted to do, but then I would only question her motives, as I always did (and as did her mother), and she would then feel put down as she did when she was a child. I asked her if that feeling reminded her of anything, and she thought of her mother who didn't like her asking questions that were none of her business, because she was too young. On the other hand, her father would always answer her questions if she asked in a rational, unemotional way. Then she reported a dream: "Joe had fallen in love with another woman. We were talking very reasonably. He couldn't make up his mind." It reminded her of her feeling that she can't get angry at people by asking if they act reasonably. She asked me what I thought of the dream. I responded by asking what else comes to mind about the dream? She thought of a similar episode with Tom, but then it was just a game. The other girl got hysterical, but she defeated the other girl by remaining cool and calm. I suggested that Joe leaving her stood for her stopping her analysis, and she anxiously anticipated feeling helpless without me. "Perhaps," she answered; but if she needed more help, she would just have to have a primal scene. I asked what she meant by that, and she referred to Janov (author of *The Primal Scream*), whose writings had interested her during the early part of her analysis. I pointed out her slip and asked if she were familiar with the psychoanalytic term, *primal scene*. She replied that she hadn't seen it, but she was surprised, as she had been reading so much psychoanalytic literature. I explained the meaning of the term, and she replied that her parents never did anything sexual, but they did have a bedroom right next to hers. I then told her that I thought in her dream, Joe stood for her father and the other woman stood for her mother, and in the dream, she was expressing the competition she felt toward her mother, for her father's love. In addition, this competition could have been intensified and made more painful by her overhearing the sounds of their love making in the next room. She remained quiet for a short time, then said, "I think you are right."

She became increasingly preoccupied with ending her analysis and she succeeded in doing so over the next four months. She resented the time it took away from being with her husband. Yet to terminate was an embarrassing admission that she had stopped striving for perfection. Her conflicts with her mother regarding separation, independence, and authority were intensified in the transference. She viewed me as intrusive, controlling, and demanding perfectionist work from her, never satisfied with her performance, and preventing her from freeing herself from me. Yet she also wished I would be a benign, protective, all-knowing authority, who would advise her how to make perfect decisions and to live in a risk-free world without conflict. The idealizations of myself and her mother were eventually substantially decreased.

She finally began to feel that she was voluntarily attending her analytic hours. It felt like growing up. To her surprise and pleasure, she found that she could now, for the first time, enjoy father's company and not get into arguments with him.

She announced she had become "a convert to saying what comes to mind" during the analytic sessions. She associated leaving analysis to giving up her religion. She had feared and avoided her religion (mother), but there was a strong attraction: to be sucked up, to be separate, yet part of a whole, where there was comfort with no conflict or tension. She realized that she had attempted to marry a mirror image in order to avoid conflict, but she was very satisfied with her husband who was kind, gentle, and tolerant—sort of an ideal parent.

She began to think more of having a child, and she reported a fantasy she had once had: when she terminated analysis, she would be reborn—perfect and completely equipped. The idea of having a child, perhaps in a few years, became appealing. One day she asked if Houston were a family name. If she had a son she would name him after me (and then in a slip, suggesting penis envy) and if a girl, they would name *him* after her husband's grandmother.

There remained little incentive for further analysis other than to fulfill a perfectionist ideal of maximum self-development. This value became subordinated to one of comfort and happiness. She recognized the uncertainty of life and the value of additional analysis in the future if she became unable to handle her problems on her own. She had arranged her life in a way that seemed to provide her maximum security and freedom from conflict by achieving a stable, well-paying job and choosing an undemanding husband.

During the forty-third month and the final weeks of her analysis, she experienced decreased narcissistic vulnerability with fewer demands on herself for perfection and fewer expectations for magical help from me. She continued to attempt to deny separation anxiety, but indicated some ability to recognize her conflicts and to risk facing them. Her transference was neither strongly positive or negative and she seemed emotionally able to accept transference interpretation.

Three weeks after we had stopped, I received a check and the following note:

> Dear Dr. MacIntosh.
>   Things are going much more smoother than all my fears on leaving would have ever led me to expect. I want to take the opportunity to again thank you for all ~~this~~ [crossed out in her letter] the assistance you have given me in the past three and a half years. You helped me discover so much and, through you, I hope I have learned that not facing things is the worst thing one can do. Thank you again.
>   D.A.

Five years after she had finished her analysis, I received some indirect information that she was living with Joe, and she appeared to be happily married.

Literature Review

In the *Three Essays on the Theory of Sexuality* Freud (1905) described sexual deviations as the result of the continuation into adult life of infantile component instincts. Where there was a substitution of the infantile for the adult sexual aim, he referred to perversion. Where there was a substitution of the normal heterosexual object, he referred to inversion.

In "A Child Is Being Beaten" (1919) he formulated perversion as representing a regressive expression of the Oedipus complex. Freud (1920) described three months work with an 18-year-old woman whom he called homosexual. He stated:

> The task to be carried out did not consist in resolving a neurotic conflict, but in converting one variety of the genital organization of sexuality in the other . . . making access to the opposite sex (which had hitherto been barred) possible to a person restricted to homosexuality, thus restoring his full bisexual functions. After that it lay with him to choose whether he wished to abandon the path that is banned by society, and in some cases he has done so. . . . It is only where the homosexual fixation has not yet become strong enough, or where there are considerable rudiments and vestiges of a heterosexual choice of object, i.e., in a still oscillating or in a definitely bisexual organization, that one may make a more favorable prognosis for psychoanalytic therapy [p. 150–151].

According to Freud, his patient chose a feminine love object and developed a masculine attitude toward that object. She had passed through a "normal female Oedipus complex" (p. 155). However, comparison of her genitals with her brother at age 5 or younger had left a strong impression and had far-reaching aftereffects. The homosexual love object was a substitute for her mother, and her homosexual libido was "probably a direct and unchanged continuation of an infantile fixation on her mother." Moreover, her "Lady's slender figure" (p. 156) also reminded her of her brother (p. 155), thus also serving as a substitute for him. Her homosexual object choice combined both her feminine and masculine ideals (p. 156), thus simultaneously satisfying homosexual and heterosexual tendencies. Her mother had acted with favoritism toward her brothers, treated her as a rival, limited her independence, and kept her from any close relation to her father (p. 157). She thus "had little cause to feel affection for her mother" (p. 157). Her homosexual love, therefore, was a mother substitute, reflecting "a yearning for a kinder mother" (pp. 156–157).

When her father impregnated her mother (her unconsciously hated rival) with the baby she had wished for from him, she hatefully and vengefully turned away from father and all men (p. 157). Her homosexuality in this instance represented an act of vengeance and defiance on her father for failing to gratify her oedipal wishes (pp. 159–160). Thus, she "changed into a man and took her mother in the place of her father as the object of her love" (p. 158). This was accomplished "through a process of identification" (p. 158) on her part with the lost love object, which was "a kind of regression to narcissism" (p. 158) thereby making easier the choice of a new love object of the same sex as oneself.

Because of her original ambivalence toward her mother, she could revive her earlier love for her mother, using it for an "over-compensation" (reaction formation) for her current hostility toward her (p. 158), but "since there was little to be done with the real mother" (p. 158), she sought for a substitute in her homosexual love object. She also secured her mother's love by giving up hetero-sexuality, thus stepping aside as a rival with her mother for men. Freud called this the mechanism of "retiring in favor of someone else" (pp. 158–159). He considered it one of the causes of homosex-uality. Her "Lady's" attraction also stemmed from her bad reputa-tion, which served as a opportunity for her to act out a rescue fantasy, something Freud said referred to a masculine type of loving (p. 161).

Furthermore, she had "brought along from childhood a strongly marked 'masculinity complex' . . . often inspecting her older brother's genital organs, she had developed a pronounced envy for the penis, and the thoughts from this envy continued to fill her mind. She was, in fact, a feminist; she felt it unjust that girls should not enjoy the same freedom as boys, and rebelled against the lot of women in general" (p. 169). (Thus, one might infer Freud also recognized a cultural influence in forming female homosexuality.) She also found the idea of pregnancy and childbirth disagreeable, which Freud felt reflected a narcissistic fear of bodily disfigurement.

He summed up his formulation by stating that her homosexual behavior was the result of a strong mother fixation, combined with the effect of maternal neglect and observation of the genital differ-ences between her and her brother.

After three months work with his patient, he terminated her analysis, as he had concluded that her "repudiation of all men" (including a negative father transference) was sufficiently intense that she would "render futile all [his] endeavors . . . by clinging to the illness." He advised her parents that "if they set store in the treatment, it should be continued by a woman doctor" (p. 164).

In later writings (1930, 1933), he elaborated on the importance of the preoedipal stage, the nature of the girl's attachment to her mother (ambivalent), and the factors he considered important in the oedipal shift to father from mother. On the one hand they were constitutional, and on the other hand they stemmed from the girl's disappointment with her mother, for various reasons. He restated his ideas that a particularly strong masculinity complex, partly accounted for on constitutional grounds, could lead to manifest homosexuality. He cautioned, however:

> Analytic experience teaches us, to be sure, that female homosexuality is seldom or never a direct continuation of infantile masculinity. Even for a girl of this kind it seems necessary that she should take her father as an object for some time and enter the Oedipus situation. But afterwards, as a result of her inevitable disappointments from her father, she is driven to regress into her early masculinity complex. The significance of these disappointments must not be exaggerated; a girl who is destined to become feminine is not spared them, they do not have the same effect. The predominance of the constitutional factors seem indisputable; but the two phases in the development of female homosexuality are well mirrored in the practices of homosexuals, who play the parts of mother and baby with each other as often and as clearly as those of husband and wife [Freud, 1933, p. 130].

Anna Freud (1965) listed factors that favor homosexual development. The following are relevant to female development:

1. [T]he bisexual tendencies which are considered as part of the inborn constitution. They endow all individuals with psychological characteristics not only of their own, but also of the opposite sex and enable them to take as love objects, or offer themselves as love objects, not only to the opposite but also to their own sex. This innate bisexuality is intensified in the preoedipal period by the identifications with both male and female parent and remains the constitutional basis for any homosexual inclinations which arise later.

2. [T]he individual's primary and secondary narcissism, i.e., the libidinal cathexis of his own self. So far as object choice in later childhood follows this original narcissistic pattern, partners are chosen to be as identical as possible with the self, including identity of sex. Such homosexual, or more strictly speaking narcissistic relationships are characteristic of the latency period and certain stages of preadolescence and adolescence.
3. [T]he anaclitic object attachment of the infant, for which sex is of secondary importance. This is of special significance for female homosexuality since the girl may become fixated to this stage as to a ''homosexual'' one.
4. [P]enis envy which provides the normal basis for the girl's masculine identification.
5. [T]he negative Oedipus complex which represents a normal ''homosexual'' phase in the life of both boys and girls [pp. 145–146].

On the other hand, she said the following developmental factors discouraged homosexuality: (1) anything which promoted heterosexuality; (2) reaction formations against anal wishes; (3) tendencies toward ''complete development'' and ''biological reasonableness'' which ''makes individuals prefer normality to abnormality.''

In further reviewing the psychoanalytic literature on female homosexuality, I have identified forty-six factors that various authors have associated with this particular sexual organization, and no doubt there are more. In this patient, I have observed thirty-six. There is no general agreement or attempt on the part of the authors to indicate which factor(s) are the most important. Some attempt can be made to ascertain this, however, noting the frequency a particular factor is reported. Thus, I have arranged the factors in order of frequency. Some categories are at different levels of abstraction, and may, therefore, overlap; for example, ''oedipal factors'' and ''incestuous wishes.'' Furthermore, as this review covered most of the twentieth century, using this quantitative approach will produce a result that, to many, may seem dated in its emphasis. Some of the more recent ideas concerning preoedipal trauma and object relations will appear less important than the emphasis given them in current theorizing (i.e., Socarides, 1978, 1988; Siegel, 1988; Dorpat, 1990; Jacobs, 1990; Moore and Fine, 1990).

1. *Castration complex or penis envy:*
   Abraham, Bacon, Bergler, Blos, Brenner, H. Deutsch, Dorpat, Fenichel, A. Freud, S. Freud, Jones, Lampl-de Groot, McDougall, Rado, Schafer, Siegel, Socarides, Weigert, this patient.
2. *Preoedipal factors:*
   Bacon, Bergler, Blos, Brenner, H. Deutsch, Dorpat, Fenichel, A. Freud, S. Freud, Jones, Kestenberg, McDougall, Serota, Siegel, Socarides, Weigert, Weiss, this patient.
3. *Oedipal factors:*
   Bacon, Bergler, Blos, Brenner, H. Deutsch, Fenichel, A. Freud, S. Freud, Jones, Kestenberg, McDougall, Serota, Socarides, Weigert, Weiss, this patient.
4. *Masculine or father identification:*
   Abraham, Bacon, H. Deutsch, Dorpat, Fenichel, A. Freud, S. Freud, Jones, Lampl-de Groot, Jacobs, McDougall, Radó, Schafer, Socarides, this patient.
5. *Narcissism—defense of or object choice:*
   Blos, H. Deutsch, Dorpat, Fenichel, A. Freud, S. Freud, Kestenberg, McDougall, Radó, Serota, Siegel, Socarides, Weiss, this patient.
6. *Bisexuality or biological factors:*
   Bergler, Blos, Brierley, H. Deutsch, Fenichel, A. Freud, S. Freud, Jones, Lampl-de Groot, McDougall, Schafer, Socarides, Weiss, this patient.
7. *Hatred (or depreciation) of her father:*
   Bacon, Blos, Brenner, H. Deutsch, Dorpat, Fenichel, S. Freud, Jacobs, Jones, Lampl-de Groot, McDougall, Schafer, Socarides, this patient.
8. *Mother fixation (or developmental arrest):*
   Bacon, H. Deutsch, Dorpat, Fenichel, A. Freud, S. Freud, Jacobs, Jones, Lampl-de Groot, McDougall, Siegel, Socarides, Weigert, this patient.
9. *Hatred of her mother:*
   Bacon, Brenner, H. Deutsch, Fenichel, A. Freud, S. Freud, Jones, Lampl-de Groot, McDougall, Schafer, Socarides, this patient.
10. *Defense against loving or incestuous wishes for her father or brother(s):*

Bacon, Brenner, H. Deutsch, Fenichel, A. Freud, S. Freud, Kestenberg, McDougall, Schafer, Socarides, Weigert, Weiss, this patient.

11. *Defensive regression from oedipal conflict:*
Bacon, Bergler, Blos, H. Deutsch, Fenichel, S. Freud, Jones, Kestenberg, McDougall, Serota, Socarides, Weiss, this patient.

12. *Homosexuality represents a reactive defense against hatred of her mother:*
Bergler, Blos, Brenner, H. Deutsch, Dorpat, Fenichel, S. Freud, Jacobs, McDougall, Schafer, Socarides, this patient.

13. *Preoedipal factors:*
Bacon, Bergler, Brierley, H. Deutsch, Dorpat, Jones, McDougall, Siegel, Socarides, Weiss, this patient.

14. *Excessively strong aggression (or aggressive drive):*
Bacon, Bergler, Brierley, H. Deutsch, Dorpat, Jones, Jacobs, Siegel, Socarides.

15. *Homosexual partner represents a mother substitute:*
Bacon, Bergler, H. Deutsch, Fenichel, S. Freud, McDougall, Socarides, Weigert, this patient.

16. *Homosexuality as a compromise formation:*
Brenner, H. Deutsch, Fenichel, S. Freud, McDougall, Serota, Socarides, Weigert, this patient.

17. *Homosexual partner represents a wished for "Good Mother":*
H. Deutsch, Dorpat, S. Freud, Jacobs, Radó, Socarides, Siegel, Weigert, this patient.

18. *Masochistic conflict:*
Bergler, H. Deutsch, Fenichel, Jacobs, Radó, Socarides, Weigert, this patient.

19. *Acting out of mother–child relationship:*
Bacon, H. Deutsch, Dorpat, Fenichel, S. Freud, Jacobs, Socarides, this patient.

20. *Emphasis on oedipal conflict (vs. preoedipal):*
Bacon, Blos, Brenner, H. Deutsch, Fenichel, S. Freud, this patient.

21. *Excessively strong guilt:*
Bacon, Bergler, Jones, Radó, Socarides, Weigert, this patient.

22. *Emphasis on preoedipal factors (vs. oedipally):*
    Bergler, Dorpat, Jacobs, Jones, Siegel, Socarides.
23. *Cultural influences:*
    Abraham, Bergler, Blos, S. Freud, Socarides.
24. *Insufficient separation-individuation:*
    Dorpat, Jacobs, Siegel, Socarides, Weigert, this patient.
25. *Sacrifice of heterosexuality to gain her mother's love:*
    H. Deutsch, S. Freud, Schafer, Socarides, Weigert, this patient.
26. *Clitoral erotism:*
    H. Deutsch, Jones, Kestenberg, Radó, Socarides, this patient.
27. *Rivalry with her sisters:*
    Blos, H. Deutsch, Fenichel, Weigert, this patient.
28. *Defense against primal scene:*
    Bacon, McDougall, Radó, Socarides, this patient.
29. *Defensive flight from male:*
    H. Deutsch, Jacobs, McDougall, Socarides, this patient.
30. *"Struggle against identification" (or faulty identification) with her mother:*
    Dorpat, McDougall, Siegel, Socarides, this patient.
31. *Disturbance of gender identity:*
    Dorpat, Jacobs, Siegel, Socarides.
32. *Emphasis on negative father transference:*
    Brenner, S. Freud, Socarides.
33. *Acting out of rescue fantasy:*
    H. Deutsch, S. Freud, Schafer, this patient.
34. *Symbiotic conflict:*
    McDougall, Socarides, Weigert, this patient.
35. *Ego defect:*
    McDougall, Serota, Socarides.
36. *Homosexuality represents a defense against psychosis:*
    McDougall, Siegel, Socarides.
37. *Transitional object:*
    Dorpat, Pomer, Socarides, this patient.
38. *Denial of differences between sexes:*
    Abraham, Dorpat, Socarides, this patient.
39. *Father fixation:*
    Bacon, Jones, this patient.

40. *Emphasis on negative mother transference:*
    McDougall, Schafer, this patient.
41. *Homosexual relationship is an attempt to repair faulty female body image:*
    Siegel, Socarides.
42. *Unstable object relations:*
    Dorpat, Socarides.
43. *Father critical of her heterosexual interests:*
    Bacon, this patient.
44. *"Eternal virgin" fantasy:*
    Kestenberg, this patient.
45. *Fear of pregnancy or childbirth:*
    S. Freud.
46. *Defective superego:*
    Dorpat.

Discussion

Although I have indicated that hatred, disappointment, or rivalry with her father were present in Ms. A, I was not impressed with its intensity. Negative father transference occurred mainly in the earlier parts of the analysis. Far more negative transference was observed in connection with her mother. A frequent pattern could be observed in which analyzing negative transference would lead to emergence of positive father material. This is more in line with the observations of McDougall (1964) and Schafer (1973), who emphasized the importance of recognizing negative mother transference to a male analyst. This contrasts with the observations of Freud (1920), Socarides (1968), and Brenner (1976), who emphasized negative father transference in the analysis of female homosexuals.

On the other hand, I was impressed with the strength of the positive father transference, and much of the hostility in that area seemed to be a reactive defense (Brenner, 1976). Paternal jealousy and disapproval of her boy friends similar to what Bacon (1956) observed was present. Disappointment, feelings of rejection, and wishes for revenge toward her father were not a factor. Some mild sadistic teasing by him did occur during latency, however. Penis envy and rivalry with males was present also, but did not seem to account for considerable negative transference. Identification with her father (as noted by many authors) was evident. As her father was intellectual, verbal, and favored rational solutions to problems, this was helpful to the analytic work and encouraged positive transference and therapeutic alliance. Her emphasis on rationality, however, created a resistance to free association.

To "chatter irrationally," moreover, seemed too much like her hated mother and sister. She "struggled against [this] identification" (Greenson, 1954). Socarides (1975) also noted this phenomenon in homosexual women. To identify with her mother was also dangerous, because it meant to be masochistically controlled by the demands of her children. She highly valued her work and her free time (which she typically preferred to spend reading). Her conscience and sense of guilt were such that she was certain that, should she have children, she would have to give up her job and much of her free time, and devote it to child care, which she was unwilling to do. This seems to be a type of conflict between narcissism and masochism that Deutsch (1944) has described. It also seems similar to Kestenberg's comments (Panel, 1962) concerning the "wasting of motherhood." Also in line with Kestenberg's comments, is her fantasy of being a virgin, even though she had experienced intercourse.

As maternal transference developed, her mother appeared more and more as a rigid, controlling, intrusive, and sexually prohibiting figure. This is similar to the descriptions of Freud (1920), Deutsch (1932), McDougall (1964), and Socarides (1968, 1978, 1988). She longed for reconciliation with a good mother, and Ann was supposed to serve this purpose. She wished to create a "Garden of Eden" with her. By carefully respecting her autonomy, and analyzing what *her* wishes were (regarding intellectual curiosity, choice of husband, marriage or not, and children or not), I was able to work through much negative mother transference.

She split her ambivalence for her mother with her sister who represented her idealized mother (McDougall, 1964). Ann represented this version of her mother via displacement through her sister's friend whom she had admired as a teenager. Ann probably also represented an ideal version of herself. Thus, the choice of a homosexual partner, and to a lesser degree, the choice of her husband, was narcissistically made (Freud, 1914, 1920).

Handling transference around the issue of Joe's illness was especially difficult. I felt it necessary to confront her with the reality of the unpleasant life she could very well encounter should she enter into a marriage with a man with his potential medical problems. I pointed out to her such a situation, in some ways, could be appealing to her out of masochistic wishes and a need to suffer, because of guilt, both conscious and unconscious. Marrying a ''crippled'' (castrated) man could also help to deny the anatomical differences between the sexes (Abraham, 1920). These confrontations made it more difficult to analyze transference aspects of both her mother's and father's disapproval (and later the Church's) of her heterosexual desires. On the other hand, she *had* fallen in love with Joe prior to the onset of his illness, so the above mentioned factors were probably of lesser importance in determining her original choice of the particular man. She was partly defending against sexual wishes for myself in the paternal transference. However, the quality in Joe which she repeatedly emphasized as making him special, unique, and worth risking future hardships, was his empathy, sensitivity, and similarity to herself. This suggested a wish to recreate a blissful symbiotic unity with her mother, but it being with a man, helped to defend against fears of being swallowed up or losing her identity in such a symbiotic relation (McDougall, 1964; Socarides, 1968). She, in fact, was consciously aware of such wishes and fears in relation to a religious life. Her religion represented a mother substitute as did her homosexual partner.

Several authors (Panel, 1962; Socarides, 1963, 1968, 1978, 1988; McDougall, 1964) have observed that homosexual women frequently come for treatment in a state of suicidal depression after having been rejected by a female lover.[2] This has been attributed to severe conflicts in the oral stage and failure to develop past the separation–individuation phase with consequent fixation on the mother at this stage. A homosexual relationship then both gratifies and protects against frightening wishes for fusion. It has been theorized that loss of the homosexual relationship results in terrifying fears of disintegration, engulfment, or severe depression, frequently of psychotic proportions. On the other hand, Serota (Panel, 1962),

---

[2]This was true with Freud's case (1920) as well, although the acute depression had lifted by the time she had begun treatment with him.

and later Socarides (1978, 1988), suggested that fixation points can also occur at later stages of development, and it is with these cases the best therapeutic results can be obtained. This seems to have been more the situation with this patient. Although she, too, came to the treatment because of a suicidal depression following the loss of a homosexual lover, there was no indication of psychosis, and the most important conflicts seemed to be oedipal. Some degree of difficulty around separation–individuation problems did exist, however, and it is interesting to speculate to what extent her mother's illness, and the resumption of her mothering role when the patient was at the height of the symbiotic phase (Mahler, Pine, and Bergman, 1975), produced a traumatic fixation which interfered with the later separation–individuation process. Stoller (1975) has suggested that trauma at this stage leads to increased masculine identifications, which he has observed in homosexual women. The depressive relations which she experienced during the course of the analysis seemed to be more related to the type described by Sandler and Joffe (1965) and Joffe and Sandler (1965) in which she failed to live up to perfectionistic demands of her ego ideal of ideal self.

Factors which seemed to influence a favorable outcome of her analysis included good ego strength (intelligence, perseverance in the face of frustration, intact sense of self), primarily conflict at an oedipal level, self-referral, conscious guilt and shame regarding her homosexual behavior (inhibited), heterosexual interest, physical attractiveness to men, and a basically loving relationship with her father, which enabled her to develop a positive transference to her analyst.

Summary

An analysis of a homosexual woman in which a favorable outcome occurred is reported. Relevant analytic literature is reviewed and discussed. This woman's homosexual behavior is formulated primarily as a result of oedipal conflict, including a defensive regression to preoedipal conflict with her mother. There is also some suggestion of developmental arrest as a result of separation from her mother during the first year of her life. Later conflict with the mother involved intrusiveness and overcontrol in regard to her body and its functions, especially sexual. As she grew older this control was extended to what she read. Her mother's control resulted in hatred for her mother, which was combined with, and accentuated by guilty incestuous wishes for her father. Penis envy and rivalry with males also played a role, but was less important.

References

Abraham, K. (1920), The female castration complex. In: *Selected Papers of Karl Abraham, M.D.* London: Hogarth Press, 1968, pp. 338–369.

Almond, B. (1990), The secret garden: A therapeutic metaphor. *The Psychoanalytic Study of the Child*, 45:477–494.

Bacon, C. (1956), A developmental theory of female homosexuality: In: *Perversions: Psychodynamics and Therapy*, ed. S. Lorand & M. Balint. New York: Gramercy.

Bernstein, I. (1976), Masochistic reaction in a latency age girl. *J. Amer. Psychoanal. Assn.*, 24:589–608.

Brenner, C. (1976), *Psychoanalytic Technique and Psychic Conflict*. New York: International Universities Press.

Brierley, M. (1932), Some problems of integration in women. *Internat. J. Psycho-Anal.*, 13:433–448.

Deutsch, H. (1932), Homosexuality in women. *Psychoanal. Quart.*, 1:484–510.

——— (1944), Homosexuality. In: *The Psychology of Women*, Vol. 1. New York: Grune & Stratton, pp. 325–254.

Dorpat, T. (1990), Female homosexuality: An overview. In: *The Homosexualities: Reality, Fantasy, and the Arts*, ed. C. Socarides & V. Volkan. Madison, CT: International Universities Press, pp. 111–137.

Freud, A. (165), *Normality and Pathology in Childhood*. London: Hogarth Press, 1966.

Freud, S. (1905), Three Essays on the Theory of Sexuality. *Standard Edition*, 7:123–143. London: Hogarth Press, 1955.

——— (1914), On narcissism: An introduction. *Standard Edition*, 14:67–102. London: Hogarth Press, 1957.

——— (1919), ''A child is being beaten'': A contribution to the study of the origin of the sexual perversions. *Standard Edition*, 17:175–204. London: Hogarth Press, 1955.

——— (1920), Psychogenesis of a case of homosexuality in a woman. *Standard Edition*, 18:145–172. London: Hogarth Press, 1955.

——— (1933), New Introductory Lectures on Psychoanalysis. *Standard Edition*, 22:1–182. London: Hogarth Press, 1964.

Friedlaender, K. (1943), Childrens' books and their function in latency and prepuberty. *Amer. Imago*, 3:129–150.

Greenson, R. (1954), The struggle against identification. *J. Amer. Psychoanal. Assn.,* 2:200–217.

Jacobs, L. (1990), Preoedipal determinants of female homosexuality. In: *The Homosexualities: Reality, Fantasy, and the Arts,* ed. C. Socarides & V. Volkan. Madison, CT: International Universities Press, pp. 139–160.

Joffe, W., & Sandler, J. (1965), Note on pain and individuation. *The Psychoanalytic Study of the Child,* 20:394–424. New York: International Universities Press.

Mahler, M., Pine, F., & Bergman, A. (1975), *The Psychological Birth of the Infant.* New York: Basic Books.

McDougall, J. (1964), Homosexuality in women. In: *Female Sexuality: New Psychoanalytic Views,* ed. J. Chasseguet-Smirgel. Ann Arbor: University of Michigan Press, 1970, pp. 171–212.

Moore, B., & Fine, B. (1990), *Psychoanalytic Terms and Concepts.* New Haven, CT: American Psychoanalytic Association/Yale University Press.

Panel, C. (1962), Theoretical and clinical aspects of overt female homosexuality. Reporter: C. Socarides. *J. Amer. Psychoanal. Assn.,* 10:579–592.

Peller, L. (1958), Reading and day dreams in latency, boy–girl differences. *J. Amer. Psychoanal. Assn.,* 6:57–70.

Pomer, S. (1976), Prepared discussion of a paper by C. Socarides. Presented at the American Psychoanalytic Association Fall Meeting. New York.

Sandler, J., & Joffe, W. (1965), Notes on childhood depression. *Internat. J. Psycho-Anal.,* 46:88–95.

Schafer, R. (1973), The idea of resistance. *Internat. J. Psycho-Anal.,* 54:259–285.

Siegel, E. (1988), *Female Homosexuality: Choice Without Volition.* Hillsdale, NJ: Analytic Press.

Socarides, C. W. (1963), The historical development and theoretical aspects of female homosexuality. *J. Amer. Psychoanal. Assn.,* 11:386–414.

———— (1968), *The Overt Homosexual.* New York: Grune & Stratton.

———— (1975), *Beyond Sexual Freedom.* New York: Quadrangle.

———— (1978), *Homosexuality.* New York: Jason Aronson, pp. 119–142.

———— (1988), *Preoedipal Origins and Psychoanalytic Therapy of Sexual Perversions.* Madison, CT: International Universities Press.

Stoller, R. (1975), *Perversion: The Erotic Form of Hatred.* New York: Pantheon Books.

Waelder, R. (1930), The principle of multiple function. In: *Psychoanalysis: Observation, Theory, Application.* New York: International Universities Press, 1976, pp. 68–83.

Winnicott, D. (1953), Transitional objects and transitional phenomena. In: *Through Paediatrics to Psychoanalysis.* New York: Basic Books, 1975, pp. 229–242.

PART III

Transvestitism

CHAPTER 9

The Analysis of a Prehomosexual Child with a Twelve-Year Developmental Follow-Up

GEORGIE BABATZANIS

Early History

Peter H was 8 years old and entering grade 3 when he was referred by a psychoanalyst for assessment. After an unhappy experience at camp the previous summer, Peter was reluctant to go to school, preferring to stay at home close to his mother. He first exhibited this behavior at age 2 when he was sent to nursery school; he would cry so much when separated from his mother that she eventually gave up her job to stay home with him. Peter also had a periodic sleep problem and would often fall asleep in his parents' bed. He also had difficulty making friends, particularly ones his own age. He feared change and consistently refused to go anywhere alone; for example, he would go to the corner store only if accompanied by his sister.

In the final assessment session, the parents revealed that Peter liked to take off his pants and dance in the nude, pretending to be a girl, wear his mother's clothes, and play with his sister's dolls. The unhappy experience at camp had been caused by his inability to participate and act properly when involved in boyish activities. The parents had not initially imparted this information because they were apparently in conflict over it: the father was deeply concerned that Peter was effeminate, and the mother protectively described her son as a fine, decent, and sensitive lad.

Mrs. H was a beautiful, charming woman. At the age of 13 months, her mother abandoned her, and she was left with distant relatives, until the father remarried. Mrs. H described her stepmother as a cold woman and a strict disciplinarian. She was often unhappy during her teenage years and at times considered suicide. She married her husband abroad less than a year after they met as she was pregnant with their first child, and they immigrated to Canada. Dr. H was a tall, handsome man with a Ph.D. in archaeology and was considered brilliant in his field. Mrs. H was unhappy and lonely during her first years in Canada.

Catherine, a year and a half older than Peter, apparently resembled her father in appearance. She was protective of Peter, looking after him on the bus or keeping him company at recess when other children would either ignore him or hit him. Nicolas, five years younger than Peter, apparently also resembled the father and was described as "intelligent and masculine." Peter was extremely jealous of his brother and often teased and hit him.

Mrs. H was well during her pregnancy with Peter and delivery was short and uncomplicated. She said Peter was a beautiful baby; when she first saw him she noticed a resemblance to her mother and maternal grandfather. Dr. H described him as a "carbon copy" of his wife. Mrs. H did not breastfeed any of her children, because she "had no milk." Milestones were normal, and Peter was easily toilet-trained. As a toddler, he always stayed very close to his mother.

At 12 months, Peter became preoccupied with small pieces of fluff that he would pick off blankets and roll between his fingers or rub against his nose. In conjunction with this he would often suck his thumb; this behavior had a highly sensualized and ritualized aspect to it, and it would leave him restless and perspiring. At age 2, he insisted on taking flowers to nursery school every day as a kind of security blanket. His separation anxiety caused bed-wetting, which lasted for one to two years and was cured by a loving, firm housekeeper while the parents were away. Separation anxiety and difficulty participating in group activities persisted throughout his school career and culminated the summer before he started treatment.

When Peter was 4, he began taking off his clothes and dancing wildly in an effeminate manner. He began to wear his mother's clothes, and the sleep problem began about this time as well.

From the developmental history, it was clear that this boy had a disturbance in the development of his sensual arousal patterns if not a disorder of gender identity. Examination confirmed a gender identity disorder. Peter was a very verbal, intelligent boy who constantly rolled his eyes or gazed out the window or at the ceiling. He talked freely and could articulate his preoccupation with sexual matters. Of great concern to him was the fact that other children called him "gay." He was disgusted that other boys at school looked at *Playboy* magazine, yet, with a little support and reassurance, he also acknowledged that the boys might not be so wicked after all. He admitted that he had at times been interested in pictures of girls and had become stimulated by them. At first it seemed that he might simply be playing a submissive role in his response to the questions. However, it was evident that there was considerable plasticity in his sexual interests, albeit tremendous fear of heterosexuality.

His dancing occurred when he was sexually or sensually aroused and seemed to be a defense against masturbation but also a method of finding substitute sensual gratification. He described this quite clearly in words. When he danced, he became more sexually aroused and in fact had an erection at times, although his parents had not mentioned this. He also described the pleasure he took in the act of changing clothes, particularly when dressing in women's clothes. Peter's preference was to assume an effeminate role, but he was also quick to respond to questioning of this behavior, insisting that he was going to change and assume more boyish manners.

For purposes of classification, he was given the designation *Anxiety neurosis,* which minimized the degree of his disorder. This benign label was used because the examiner wished to emphasize Peter's psychotherapeutic potential. Psychoanalytic treatment was recommended for Peter as well as counseling for the parents. It was felt that the mother might benefit from treatment, but she rejected this suggestion. Peter was treated three times a week. Mrs. H came biweekly for counseling, and, when required, Dr. H joined her.

First Year of Treatment

Peter was brought to the sessions by his father and picked up by his mother. He came immaculately dressed in fashionable European-style outfits selected by Mrs. H. He was always careful not to soil his clothes, saying, "My mother will get mad." When relaxed, Peter had a warm smile and easily became animated, but his handsome appearance was often marred by a perplexed if not lost expression. He related well to adults and had an inquisitive and precocious manner.

He engaged readily in treatment and looked forward to his sessions as a place where he could talk about his "psychology" problems. He referred to some of his symptoms as "disease" and felt that they could be cured in a hospital. He communicated easily, both verbally and by simultaneously talking and drawing or playing with toys (puppets, doll house, and animals). He displaced some of his maternal attachment to the therapist during the first sessions, and a positive transference began very early.

One of the early themes in his play with dolls or puppets was a family whose members resembled his own family: parents, brother, sister, and baby brother. He identified mostly with the baby, giving him great powers and calling him the "bionic baby." He often destroyed everyone except the mother, who had great authority, whereas the father was weak and ineffectual. Peter exhibited a strong feminine identification with his mother and a weak masculine identification with his father. Interpretations were made, including an emphasis on the defenses used by the "bionic baby," who was omnipotent and destructive, the passive, absent father, and the all-powerful mother. Occasionally Peter played himself as the brother and exhibited his fierce sibling feelings by destroying the baby and flushing him down the toilet. At these times, play disruption occurred.

He also talked extensively about his fantasies, the "Fembots" (from femme = girl and bot = robot) and "Wonder Woman," sometimes imitating them in histrionic fashion. The "Fembots" were powerful, machinelike creatures that could be invisible but could be switched on and off only by Peter. He used them as a defensive fantasy when he was afraid of the disproportionate intensity of his own aggressive impulses or when he was being threatened or in his manipulation and control of others.

Another symptom emerged: derealization and depersonalization states which Peter coined "whoingitis" (*who* I don't know who or where I am, and *ingitis* from meningitis). He considered this a disease to be cured with his other problems. This state usually occurred when he was changing from masculine to feminine roles; this interpretation helped him come to some understanding of it. He could change roles quickly and suddenly and chose the role of a girl, frequently in order to avoid expressing aggression (he feared he might explode). He also engaged in what he called "gay-tis" activities, such as making flowers compulsively or swaying his hips like a woman, which was interpreted as a defense against his destructive wishes and fantasies. The interpretation that he acted like a girl when he was afraid of being a boy (aggressive) was a fruitful insight for him.

Peter himself enumerated lack of friends and loneliness as one of his problems. He related best to younger boys and girls. When with children, he usually took a submissive role, acting like a baby, or he used obscene language or demonstrated chaotic behavior. His peers were either frightened by his uncontrollable outbursts or felt provoked by his bossy and intolerant behavior. Although he fantasized about being aggressive, he was unable to respond with aggression when he was teased, and would regress to oral and anal levels as a defense under stress. Another defense was projection of his own aggressive feelings and/or envies on his peers or on his environment; he would say other children were jealous of him and wanted to hit him; people in the bus wanted to kill him; Nicolas was a "bad boy" because he said "those awful bad words." When confronted with his disappointments, he used denial, saying that he did not care about school or if other children teased him or rejected him.

When playing X's and O's, Peter often cheated and would go into a rage when he lost. He often felt omnipotent and had terrible outbursts when failures threatened his omnipotent self-image. Although he was often overconfident in solitary activities (drawing), only a few of his activities involved object relations. Little pleasure, however, was derived from this cathexis of self. On the contrary, he gave the impression of being dissatisfied and helpless.

Through interpretations of his defenses and resistances, Peter gained some insight into his problem of omnipotent control and interpersonal manipulation techniques, especially after he brought in the "role reversal" game which he introduced as "the Mrs. Babatzanis game." He pretended to be the therapist, sat in her chair behind the desk, and acted like a benevolent, understanding person asking her 8-year-old patient, Peter, about his problems. The therapist, pretending to be Peter, maneuvered to prolong the session, refused to clean up, and talked about his fears. At times, Peter the Therapist introduced new material, saying, "Are you scared, Peter, to go on the bus alone because someone might give you poison?"

As treatment progressed, several environmental influences continued to be prevalent, most significant of which was Mrs. H's seductive attitude toward Peter; they would lie side by side when he was in distress or unable to sleep. Mother's babying of Peter at the time suggested overindulgence at infancy so that age-appropriate expectations were inconsistently demanded. Also noted was the mother's obsession with cleanliness and Peter's observance of this. Her need to compensate for her own deprived childhood was seen in comments such as, "I always wanted to be a good figure skater; that's why I had him take lessons." Peter's parents argued frequently and this triggered anxiety that he would be sent to boarding school if his parents separated. This threat was sometimes used if he engaged in girlish behavior. And it hardly seemed fortuitous that Peter's dancing had started at the time his mother was pregnant with Nicolas.

Peter had only precariously arrived at the phallic stage of psychosexual development. His mother was the most valued person in his life. His relationship with her was highly sexualized, and his battle (oedipal struggle) at this stage had regressed him to earlier stages. This was being reinforced by the mother who enjoyed his closeness and infantile, if not symbiotic, dependence that he in turn induced by his apparent helplessness and fears. Peter was not identifying with his father who was seen simultaneously as remote and as a rival.

Libidinal fixations at the anal and oral stages were also contributory factors as a large amount of libido had remained arrested and therefore unable to contribute to normal development. Anal fixations could be inferred from Peter's references to feces and his outbursts of rage. His frequent complaints of nausea, excessive clinging, and demands could be related to oral fixations. His wish, which he often carried out, to bite his brother because "his bum is so nice and soft" and his use of swear words could be categorized as oral aggressive impulses.

Peter had not reached adequate achievements in latency despite his good endowment and ego skills. There was no doubt that Peter had superior to very superior intelligence, but his school performance had always been much below ability level. It was impaired by emotional or motivational factors including his obsessional concern with sex and fantasies and his defense of passivity or laziness. Although he was dissatisfied with himself, he was unable to cope appropriately with any change. He was not utilizing his sublimation potential fully because of the interference of his sexual and aggressive drives. He had developed only his artistic skills but was not able, without a great deal of effort and then only after therapy started, to participate in sports and games.

Although Peter was proud to be a boy, he often enjoyed displaying girlish behaviors; at the same time, he felt guilty about the pleasure and sensual gratification he derived in assuming a feminine role, dancing in the nude, and using obscene language. He also feared punishment; he felt he was going to be harmed, killed, or might die from some terrible disease—probably because of his incestuous longings toward his mother.

Peter's defenses were immature for his age and were far from adequate to cope with excessive sexual and aggressive conflicts; the result was anxiety and symptom formation. His superego was so perfectionistic that whatever he did was not good enough and left him displeased and insecure with himself. Despite this, Peter showed a drive to change and improve himself. He was concerned about his girlish behavior, lack of friends, and frightening dissociated states. He recognized that his way of coping was inadequate, and he was in search of a better method of contending with what often seemed a threatening environment.

By the end of the year, the "bionic baby," "Fembots," and "Wonder Woman" were themes of the past. For several months, Peter had been repeatedly drawing subway lines. In doing this and analyzing his fantasy that people stared at him on the subway, he was able to conquer his fear of crowds and closed spaces. Peter started to come to his sessions alone on the bus, which led to sparing attempts to go on bus trips with his sister and with other children.

Peter had also started talking about his fears. His fear of planes was associated with leaving home and meeting new people. The family was planning a trip to Europe that summer to visit Mrs. H's relatives and he viewed this with trepidation. The trip was used to work through his fears stemming from separation anxiety. His constant efforts to prolong the duration of his sessions were interpreted as both his difficulty in separation and his need to control the therapist's time.

Noticeable progress was made in the area of effeminate and babyish behaviors that had almost disappeared, both outside and within the analysis. Only rarely did Peter sway his hips when imitating a "gay boy," but he would quickly laugh after doing so. He seemed to have fully accepted the interpretation that the "girl part" (passive feminine identification) was a protection against some danger, especially when he felt defenseless in relation to other boys. Peter started to take small steps both physically and verbally to protect himself (his motility seemed freed somewhat from his defensive restrictions). Ego functions and activities came to be employed more in the service of the reality principle than the pleasure principle. He was in better control of his impulses, thus able to modify wishes and delay gratifications. He was starting to take a keen interest in hockey and power skating, which were used for the direct sublimated release of his drives.

Although he started identifying more with his father, he still saw his father as a threatening figure. Emphasizing the assets of masculinity even further was a goal that would be undertaken both in the treatment sessions and by counseling the mother. Other objectives included obtaining proper gender identity by resolving the oedipal conflict, and at the same time enabling Peter to develop healthier relationships with peers. In his need to be omnipotent, he belittled others. Therefore, another important aim was to help Peter gain control over his tension, sexual fears, and uncontrollable outbursts. Peter's feeling of omnipotence had been the main cause of all of his unresolved developmental issues and was continuing to delay their resolution. "School phobia" was no longer an issue, but he was still underachieving. Strengthening the ego through conflict resolution, helping Peter recognize his strength and gain confidence, would hopefully weaken his helpless view of himself and facilitate more active coping strategies.

Parent Counseling

Mrs. H's sessions consisted of her bringing news of Peter's activities at home and family developments. She volunteered this information readily, and it often shed light on topics discussed or played out in the treatment. Mrs. H. suffered from severe bouts of depression and also discussed her own problems frequently, including her unhappy childhood, her marital conflicts, and her strained relationship with her in-laws.

Sessions with Mrs. H focused on developing more appropriate expectations of an 8-year-old with Peter's problems. She was encouraged to let Peter be less dependent on her; for example, her method of comforting him by lying next to him in bed, which she admitted she also enjoyed, was to be achieved by a different method: verbal reassurances. She was also encouraged to find healthier substitutes for her needs, outside her relationship with Peter. When discussing Peter, she had a tendency, however, to interpret the therapist's statements as critical of her. She reacted, at times, with feelings of failure and guilt about Peter's problems but continued to reject the idea of therapy for herself. She did try to change some of her attitudes, to be more tolerant of Peter's getting dirty, but remained conflicted; she'd allow him to wear clothes like his peers' for a short time and then he'd come to sessions again in his "Sunday Best"; a couple of weeks later, he'd again be wearing more boyish clothes. His winter boots caused him a great deal of embarrassment, and he started to express his anger toward his mother; "I hate her; they laugh at me because I have girls' boots."

Dr. H had a passive personality, rarely involving himself in decision-making issues concerning the children. He connected his wife's inability to get along with his parents to her own deprived childhood, but he responded passively to suggestions that his wife might benefit from therapeutic help. However, he also made efforts to improve his behavior toward Peter and followed all advice to interact more with his son and promote boyish sports. An avid skier himself, Dr. H was pleased to report that Peter was not only interested in this new activity but had the makings of a good skier. He also started playing table games with his son but was unable to handle Peter's explosive behavior when Peter did not win.

Both parents acknowledged improvement in Peter's behavior after the first year of treatment. They were aware that Peter lacked aggressiveness, and they were both encouraging him to "fight back," although Mrs. H said, "I can't believe it's me telling Peter to punch them." The parents continued to be very cooperative, but the most important task remained to help Mrs. H realize, without making her feel guilty and resentful, that Peter's effeminate behavior had been her own unconscious preference for him.

Second Year of Treatment

Peter entered grade 4. When sessions resumed after the summer break, Peter was visibly happy to see the therapist. He then reviewed all the prominent themes from the months of analysis prior to the vacation and concluded the session with: "This is just to refresh our memories."

While playing games, Peter, now more aware of his need to be omnipotent, sometimes made fun of his own behavior. He mastered new games quickly; however, his bossy behavior continued and he still found it difficult when he lost. This was seen in the transference situation. He would give orders: "Give me the ruler" or "You clean up. I have to finish this picture." His consistent refusal to clean up both in his sessions and at home was another of his controlling devices. Several times he told the therapist "I hate you," when she won a game. In the transference the therapist represented his all-powerful mother. His reaction to failure, pursued for a long time, was experienced as a narcissistic injury and narcissistic rage was exhibited.

Peter drew "preoedipal phallic women," which he called "dinky woman." Whereas "Wonder Woman" had been powerful but not frightening, Peter found these five-breasted creatures terrifying, and yet still envied their power. Defenses against these "dangerous" people resulted in regression, acting like a girl, becoming confused, and calling on magic.

This precipitated the introduction of the "Explosion Birds." These were creatures, either male or female, whose birth was an "accident." The "girl" bird was born first and her tail was "explosive." Then the "boy" bird was introduced with "a not-so-explosive tail." The "accident" was that they were neuters and could look alike, in his words, "the same way girls are sometimes born with dinkies and boys can have tits." The interpretation offered—that if there were such accidents at birth one would not have to decide—could not be pursued. His defense of regression to the stage that boys think they can have breasts was also interpreted. He was able to accept the reality that males and females are sexually different and that indeed he had himself always known this because he had invented the concept of neuters.

The repetitive drawing of railway tracks, crossings, and various types of switches began, but to a greater intensity and quantity than any other repetitive drawing. His preoccupation with railway tracks and switches bordered on obsessional. Many of these drawings unconsciously took the shape of a female body. Interpretation was met with resistance.

Map drawing then entered the analysis. Usually, he drew Peter Country, which was an island divided into different lands. Peter Land occupied the largest portion with the neighboring Babatzanis Land second in size. Other sections were named after his parents, siblings, friends, or teachers. Death Land, which originally bordered on Peter Land, finally broke off and was separated from the mainland by deep waters and fierce tidal waves. Tidal waves were interpreted as representing a powerful woman: both his wish and fear of being engulfed by the mother. On the one hand he wanted to be immersed in the womb, and on the other he was frightened at this strength and tried to break away and be autonomous through the transferences.

After Christmas, one of the few maps Peter drew had Peter and Babatzanis Lands as the largest lands, side by side, at the southern tip and therefore of temperate climates. Death Land, which had been an island, disappeared, sinking into the bottom of the sea; "It's terrible there and frightening—no boat will go there even if they had a seaport. The planes will also crash." Peter then added to the mainland a Land where strangers lived. This seemed to represent his inside world repressing frightening thoughts and simultaneously coping with unknown entities.

Peter then began to bring his homework to the sessions, saying he either had no paper or time to do it at home or that he was lazy. This was interpreted as an attempt to control the sessions, and another way to exhibit his infantlike omnipotence. It was decided that focus would be placed on character rather than content: to confront Peter's character behavior and his defense against character traits. In using the defense "I'm lazy," he was denying responsibility for his own unhappiness. Another character trait, his narcissistic attitude, was also discussed. He took interpretations, at times, as criticism that was painful. He was showing some negative transference reactions toward the therapist and showed intense anger against his mother. He continued to comment on his boots; "I hate them. My mother buys me girls' things" and complained that his mother never bought him toy soldiers and Lego. This was seen as the beginning of progress and a more appropriate manner for dealing with his anger. He was starting to lose his fear of his mother, or to be aware that his anger would not destroy her.

Peter started making drawings of women with penises in which breasts and penises resembled each other. His identification with the phallic mother continued. It could be that he was depicting the "fusion" of man and woman or recalling primal scene material. His wish to be both boy and girl was also implied.

For the first time, Peter drew a boy during therapy. Much later he added a girl to the picture for company. This was seen as Peter being able to accept the two sexes separately, in a mutually non-threatening situation. Peter also gradually became less active in therapy and accused the therapist of being bored—a projection of his own boredom and a healthy sign of independence. Other times he would get angry at the therapist's interpretations and say "Stop your mental stuff." Around this time, Peter saw the therapist for the first time outside her office, by coincidence, and deliberately crossed the street on a red light to avoid talking to her.

He started drawing tracks again in order to cope with his anxiety and male–female conflict. He was preoccupied, said that his peers called him "gay," and that he had nobody to play with at recess. He was depressed because grandiosity used defensively was not helping to obtain friends. When his bossy behavior was mentioned, he said, "I'm so nice and I give them things to play with me but that doesn't work." He was teased about the girlish way he threw a ball and allowed boys to hit him. The therapist used reconstruction to present reality to him: "When you were younger you thought boys did angry, nasty things to girls and you felt like you were going to be punished for boyish feelings—or being a boy."

The most traumatic experience and the peak of Peter's persecution by his fellow students occurred about this time when four boys tried to carry him from the boys' bathroom to the girls' bathroom. He admitted his castration anxiety when he stated he was afraid to retaliate: "I want to be a nice boy and not hit anyone." The interpretation was repeated, that boys were tough and girls were not; perhaps he was afraid of losing his mother's love if he was not a good boy. He began to perceive his conflict of dependence versus independence—that he was still dependent on his mother for protection and frightened of losing his love object. At the same time, he longed to be in a peer group and to be independent.

Peter then introduced the "Problem Tree" which became a repetitive theme of how Peter viewed his problems, anxieties, and defenses as represented by different branches. These were related and interwoven with his long-term compulsive track drawings which depicted his primary male–female conflict and the working through of it.

Peter started talking about how he acted like a girl because he was afraid to be a boy. His defenses dropped and he felt helpless. His castration anxiety was undefended. There were signs of his oedipal anxiety; in secret he was trying on his father's clothes. He said he would probably be coming for treatment for at least another year. Thus, some of his oedipal fantasies were portrayed. He was afraid to lose his mother, and his castration anxiety was prominent when he said he hated his mother for setting out his clothes every morning.

The use of a tape recorder then entered the analysis and was used extensively for two months. Peter said he wished to preserve his thoughts. Mostly monologues, he talked about feeling lonely ("I'm out in the cold alone and they're nice and warm inside") and about how other boys called him "gay" and hit him. When the tapes were played back, he was able to see that his voice would become girlish when he was frightened. It was also suggested that the girlish talk was defensive and used when he did not get his way. Peter would sometimes mock himself while listening to the tapes, deriving some type of masochistic pleasure from this. Self-mockery also lessened his anxiety.

In the last session but two before the summer vacation, Peter asked to tape the session. He started by describing a drawing he had seen of a boy about 5 sucking his mother's breast. He wished he could do this with his mother but, besides her not having any milk in the last year or so, she did not allow him to see her naked. (Mrs. H through counseling had gradually started to discourage Peter's oedipal advances.) He described how excited he used to get and how he now got his "excitements" when he saw his sister, Catherine, naked.

He then confessed sexual activities between Catherine and himself saying that, from time to time over the past couple of years, they had been lying naked in bed feeling each other's bodies. She would pull his penis and he would suck her breasts, put his finger in her vagina and try to insert his penis. This took place concomitantly when their parents were "necking." Catherine appeared to displace his mother. Peter said they had decided to stop a few days ago although all his friends still did it with their sisters. They did not want to commit "adultery" which, according to Peter, meant to have intercourse when you were not married. Another reason they stopped was that he did not want to get his sister pregnant. Peter concluded by saying, "I'm glad I got that out of my system—it's too bad that we have only two times left." Peter's relief at exposing his sexual secrets was interpreted to him and was related to his fear of loss at separation. He wanted to make peace with himself and the therapist before the temporary parting. It appeared that he wanted to make these concerns interpersonal rather than intrapsychic. Externalization or projection were defenses often used by this child patient.

Ambivalence was expressed when he later lamented the loss of his sexual play with his sister. "I used to get so excited—my dinky used to get hard." He described the following fantasy: when he was young his parents had him between them in bed. They would kiss him and then start to "neck." Then he recalled primal scene material: "When I was young and sleeping in my crib I started to cry because I thought my father was killing my mother—I was so scared." Thus, sexual activity was seen as dangerous to females. At the same time heterosexuality was seen as dangerous for males; if they were sexually aggressive they might lose their penises. His oedipal anxieties were also indicative of heterosexual anxieties. Perhaps he was trying desperately to show that he was a boy by acting like a grown-up man and thus camouflaging his feminine wishes.

Also, by displacing his positive oedipal desires from his mother to his sister, he was displacing that his prevailing sexual feelings were heterosexual. By interpreting his continual defense of enacting the role of an adult, he came to understand that it was difficult for him to feel comfortable with another person. This material was another determining factor in the conclusion that his 'gay'' behaviors were primarily defensive.

In the last session, Peter brought his "favorite" therapist a thank you card for their "year together" and this was viewed as a possible indication of his heterosexuality. He then drew a plane with the therapist sitting in first class. He wanted to know the airline and departure time as he wanted to come to the airport. He felt like crying but rationalized, "We have two more years together so I can wait." He was looking forward to attending private school in the fall where he hoped to find friends who would not taunt him. As he was leaving he pocketed his "transitional object"—a paper bus. Peter's conflict still prevailed although in a more age-appropriate manner. He had difficulty leaving, a recurrent feature at the end of a session.

Peter had started to verbalize his disappointment in and hate for his parents: the way his mother dressed him, his father's indifference. He had become more provocative toward the therapist who had, at times, become the transference object by displacement from the mother. The therapist was also an object of externalizing the part of himself that wished to be free of his mother. He started to be aware of the containment in the treatment and tried to keep his intense feelings in the treatment room and in the transference. He was becoming more insightful of his relationship between his present behavior and conflict and past causes.

At the onset of therapy this child patient and his mother had a very intimate, almost incestuous relationship which was beginning to fade even though she had often even encouraged his oedipal advances. In this phase he came closer to identification with the male. His dominant sexual orientation was becoming heterosexual without the previous intense guilt about the male being dangerous to the female. It was possible that the original diagnosis of gender identity disorder was not applicable in view of his oedipal advances to his mother and his confessions of sexual activities with his sister.

His homosexual behaviors may have been a defense against castration anxiety, and not a total submission to the father.

Parent Counseling

Sex play with his older sister and with another boy was reported by Mrs. H during this period and was very upsetting to her. In both instances Peter would be seduced, become frightened, and take a passive role. At times Mrs. H felt Peter was incurable and would become a homosexual, and other times she denied that he was any different from most boys his age. She thought that Peter should perhaps be allowed to decide about his own sexuality because if he was forced to change "he might be unhappy all his life" and she gave him the book *The Best Little Boy in the World* about homosexuality. The ambivalence expressed by her doubt that Peter could grow as a normal man was interpreted; she associated normal development with unhappiness and concluded that Peter might be happier as a homosexual or transvestite.

It was difficult for Mrs. H to desist from some unsuitable handling. In her efforts to help Peter, or herself, she sometimes encouraged activities which were not age-appropriate: for example, they would watch adolescent movies together; "It's good for him to watch teenagers and their lovemaking—Peter always has an erection." She made her son watch the movie *One Flew Over the Cuckoo's Nest* to show him "what happens to people who behave differently." She vacillated between being overly protective and very permissive. Therefore, as Peter progressed through treatment he received conflicting messages from his most precious, loved object. She often identified with Peter and tried to give him the freedom she never experienced as a child. Her guilt was, at times, a hindering factor in the patient–therapist relationship, as she was inclined to act in an opposing way.

Mrs. H compared Nicolas who was "all boy" to Peter at a similar age. She bought Nicolas guns and soldiers, which she admitted she had never done for Peter. She could see the difference in the two children because of her changed attitude, but she felt that Peter was born with a boy's body and female characteristics, and only reluctantly bought him clothes like those worn by his male peers. Although Mrs. H was no longer as seductive with Peter, she still enjoyed his special attention; "I am very romantic—I like it when he plays my favorite tune on the piano." She became very sad when she realized that she had difficulty freeing herself from feelings of wanting him.

Peter had not done well in school during this second year of treatment due to, according to his teacher, lack of interest and disruptive classroom behavior. Mrs. H decided to send Peter to a private school, convinced that he would not be persecuted by peers there.

After two years of treatment, Peter's controlling behavior had diminished and his outbursts had almost disappeared. Improved object relations were seen in his ability to depend less on imaginary people and interact better with peers. Peter had begun swimming lessons and was trying to swim with boyish movements. He also wanted a man's bathing suit and to select all his own clothing so it would not be "gay."

There were, however, still important areas that required work, including his intense rivalry with his brother, Nicolas, and his overfondness for his mother. He craved exclusive possession of his primary love objects. Another important aim was to involve Dr. H more in the counseling with a view to developing a closer relationship between father and son.

Third Year of Treatment

Peter entered grade 5 at the private school. When he came to his session after his first day at his new school, he immediately asked if it was all right to cry and then proceeded to do so for the first time in front of the therapist. A sign of progress, he was more realistic and not using grandiosity as a defense. However, he still exhibited fear of new situations and, at his new school, Peter tried to make friends using his old methods of inciting negative attention. His disappointment was exacerbated by the fact that Peter had believed his mother that the boys at his new school would be less cruel than the ones at public school.

This period also revealed his ambivalence toward the analysis. He liked coming but also wanted time to be with friends. Old repetitive themes returned; drawing tracks or playing with Lego. Peter expressed his boredom and was afraid this would make the therapist dislike him. At times, he was very sad: "I am not gay now but I was." His depression seemed to have been caused by the loss of his effeminate behavior.

As his ambivalence was worked through, his anxiety and the conflict with the superego diminished. Gradually, he was able to verbalize his anger at his loved objects. "My mother calls me a 'faggot' when I'm not as she wants me to be. I tell her off." This was viewed as a more normal way of reacting. He also started taking an interest in his father's work and they would go home together. As functioning was freed, Peter started to take advantage of the accessible age-appropriate sources of pleasure and self-esteem.

Peter asked if he could reduce the number of sessions from three to two a week. After all, the main problems were solved now, only little ones were left. The therapist agreed with this, adding that in the next year they could also consider eventual termination. He went on to say that he had not "done it with Catherine" since last summer. He "felt like it though." In the same session Peter drew a complex structure. He drew the center part first and as he was finishing he said, "Before I make the outside, I have to dig deeper." The next day, he seemed depressed as he made the bottom part. Then he said, "This is getting to be like a person; before you go out, you dig inside." The "outside" was made last and Peter left happier than when he had arrived. The drawing was interpreted as the phases of analysis. When Peter first started analysis, his behavior and manifest symptoms had been rooted in early experiences. Problems could not be analyzed until there were insights in lower levels, material of which he had not been conscious. Working through this material had enabled Peter to become "conscious of the unconscious." This enabled him to adapt to reality and then try to find different ways of coping with it. He was going "from downward to upward; from regression to progression." He was seeing himself outside the analysis, in an upward direction (progress).

He continued to work through his grief and anger at his mother and his hatred of Nicolas was a prominent theme. His parents loved Nicolas because he was boyish; it wasn't his fault that his mother wanted a girl and made him act like one. He started to show anger at the therapist and once exploded when he saw a Lego man hidden behind the books. He suspected, and was right, that it was left there by another child patient. He dismantled it and shouted, "Why should that brat have it and not me?'' The therapist said that he was not really angry at her but at his mother. The feeling was similar to the one that he had experienced when he first saw her with Nicolas in her arms. He had felt inadequate, neglected, dirty, and that the new boy was taking his place because he had not been good enough. His fear of being rejected and displaced by another patient and the fantasy that the therapist had lost interest had the same significance. His depression was separation depression. He was angry at his mother and the therapist, and he was becoming independent of both. This was one area that needed further work: his reaction to breaks, separation, and being left alone.

His continued resistance to change was analyzed. It was risky to change as he would lose gains. Primary gains were relief of anxiety, and secondary gains were obtained through playing ''sick.'' He said, for example, ''I'm a girl, I'm not anxious of losing my penis.'' Also, ''If I am too boyish there's competition with father.'' Although he had wanted to start coming twice a week, he began to wonder if he would have enough time for his problems, particularly his renewed feelings of hostility toward his father. Perhaps anger at his father was the only way he could preserve the relationship with his mother whom he loved and whom he was afraid of harming.

It was a very important stage of development, and Peter's need to remain attached to the mother was interfering with an oedipal resolution and contingent goals (or attain goals) consistent with ego capacities of the latency period. The necessity of a parameter was discussed and it was mutually agreed that a meeting with Peter, the therapist, and the father would take place in an effort to improve the relationship between father and son. Because of Peter's fear of the unknown and unexpected, he postponed this meeting for a month and a half. He had to plan the hour thoroughly, and referred to it as ''group therapy.''

When this meeting did take place, Peter was extremely nervous and he regressed in his father's presence which, in turn, corresponded to his father's attitude toward him. One of the father's inappropriate ideas was to bribe other children with chocolate bars to play with Peter. However, he mentioned that his wife was wrong to buy Peter a pair of girl's shorts and this made Peter feel that his father was an ally and he told his father to get rid of the shorts which symbolized his mother's unconscious wish for him to be a girl. Rather than compete with his father, he was relating to him as a male.

Parent Counseling

During this treatment period, the parents had also felt one of Peter's main problems was the way he treated his father. Mrs. H said, "He speaks awful to his father and the worst thing is his father takes it." In Dr. H's opinion, Peter's fights with him took place mostly after he and his wife had argued: "He explodes like his mother and always takes his mother's side in conversations."

When discussing the bad relationship between Peter and Dr. H, it was difficult for Mrs. H to see that when she made derogatory remarks about her in-laws, which she often did, she was putting her husband down in Peter's eyes and distancing the father. On the other hand, she could admit that Peter's perception that she was stronger than her husband was reinforced by Dr. H's silent and passive role during their many arguments. She was able to accept, although not readily, that at times Peter might be displacing his anger from her to his father. "He's better to me although when he's real angry, he calls me bitch." Mrs. H attributed some improvements in her relationship with her husband to her counseling sessions and effort on both sides, for Peter's sake, to argue less.

Both parents felt the private school had been a good choice. It was strict and Peter had started to become competitive. They reported his academic progress and success in gymnastics. He was not as depressed or isolated (this coincided with the times that he was bringing the depression in the transference). Dr. H was also proud to announce that Peter was the tallest boy in his class, had quite a boyish physique, and was a daring skier. He was encouraged to find more time to be alone with Peter.

However, as Peter improved, Mrs. H unknowingly reverted to her old methods. For a year she would not buy him boy's boots (and never did). She said, "If he feels inside of him secure, he wouldn't need boy's boots." Her conflict was evident when she said, "Nicolas is getting punished at school for being too aggressive. It's better than being called gay. It's my fault." Her ambivalence was ever present. On the one hand, she felt she was encouraging grown-up behavior by allowing Peter to try smoking and not getting angry when he took Nicolas to the store without her consent; on the other hand, she wanted to know everything he did and failed to encourage individualization or age-appropriate manners. It was difficult for her to treat him as a latency child, to allow him to learn as an independent person.

Final Phase

As the presenting symptoms had disappeared, by mutual recognition of the parents and therapist, the ending of the therapeutic process was discussed. It was agreed that the date would be decided solely by the patient and therapist. When his reactions about termination were elicited, after some reluctance to think about it and several changes in dates, Peter decided the last session should be combined with the holiday break. This way it would be similar to past separations. A summer trip was being planned for Peter and his sister to go alone to Sweden to visit relatives, and it was agreed that analysis would be terminated just prior to this vacation.

The sessions became very intense. Peter was frightened and was defending against the end of analysis. His parents had enrolled him at a private school closer to home and Peter would discuss his inability to cope at a new school. The therapist was consistent in saying he was overlooking his strengths but Peter persisted in trying to convince the therapist not to abandon him. He reenacted many of the past themes by drawing women with penises and drawing flowers. He recapitulated the whole treatment, his family life, and conflicts. His concern of being abandoned and lonely was prominent. He recalled how he felt about going to school for the first time and about the arrival of Nicolas. The fact that he was leaving rather than being left was repeated many times. He was ambivalent: he wanted to stay with the therapist but also wanted to go. In one session, he staged a mock farewell party, hoping to ease the pain by practicing. Working through this phase was a turning point in the terminal process.

In two of the next sessions, he wanted to leave the therapy room and go to the cafeteria with the therapist saying, ''I want to act to you as I act to my mother, so then you'll know'' and, ''In any case, my mother will be my therapist.'' He split the ambivalence: his mother became the therapist while the therapist would not exist.

Peter had often felt disloyal to his mother because of his relationship with the therapist. Now, the identical conflict was reappearing and he felt guilty about leaving the therapist and implying she was of less importance to him. At the same time, it was important for him to react to the therapist as a separate person. This would make it easier to retain her in his mind. He was reinforcing his reality testing which was threatened by the anxiety of termination.

Peter drew one of his "Problem Trees," which had only four branches named "lazy," "afraid to be a boy," "Nicolas," "fights with mother." For the first time, he added roots that were divided from the surface by a line called "below the ground." He said, "If you cut off bad roots, you get a good tree; but you can't cut off a good tree above the surface only, the bad roots would stay." To him, being mentally healthy meant getting rid of the deep unconscious conflicts and thus the suffering they cause. It was interesting that the four problems he named were areas he had focused on in his final phase, and he was beginning to consciously recognize and accept their origin.

In the penultimate interview, he asked, "What present would you like?" When this question was returned, he said, "A picture of you to remember you, not that I would forget you." Following this, he made one of his elaborate maps and the only one of this period. In this map, Babatzanis Land and his Parents Land were no longer bordering on Peter Land. In his representational world (inside), Peter was separating himself from his parents and the therapist. This was interpreted as, although he had started to separate himself from the therapist in his inner world, he still wanted to maintain her, the good mother object, internally and keep her there protected and indefinitely as an ally (confidante). He had not as yet internalized the therapist. He wanted to establish a more realistic picture of the therapist and not the distorted one he sometimes recalled. The most important fact, however, was that Peter, like most children, was afraid of forgetting.

When he arrived for his final session he said, "Your sister is outside waiting" and pointed at a lady in the waiting room not unsimilar to the therapist. The interpretation was made that Peter wished the therapist had a sister (part of herself) who would be outside and would remain waiting for him. He was eager for the therapist to unwrap her present as he wanted to do the same with his. He gave the therapist a picture of a monkey and beside it was written, "At last I have found a solution to all my problems, but I've forgotten the problems." In his thank you card were two turtles happily parting from each other. The therapist gave him two pictures of herself, one taken inside the therapy room and the other outside the office. It was obvious he liked the first one.

He then interrogated the therapist about the details of her personal life. It seemed important for him to remember and acknowledge her, and in separating from her as a therapist to make her part of his ego ideal, as he had his parents, and perceive her as a real person. He had saved all his unanswered questions to ask in the last hour and he felt they should now be answered. It had been three years and that was a long time. He then reminisced about this time, starting with his first day of therapy. He tried to recapture some of the memories and looked around intently as if afraid he might forget. He attempted to escape the pain of separation by fantasizing about coming with his parents the next week or coming again in the fall for two sessions.

Just as he was leaving, he dissolved into tears and came back to sit down. Peter was not handling loss by denial but was reacting appropriately to a sad situation. While trying to stop crying, he asked the therapist, "When you were a little girl, did you come here?" The therapist answered, "I have been through this as a big girl and I understand." As he calmed a bit, he asked how other children felt when they stopped, and would the therapist start with a new child. This was possibly the anniversary of the time he first saw Nicolas (an anniversary reaction on a deep unconscious level). He decided that instead of leaving the therapist by himself he would call his father to come and get him, inside the therapy room. When Dr. H arrived, Peter smiled but his eyes flooded again. His father reassured him that he was now more capable of solving his own problems and that he could always ask for help if he needed it. And thus, the father with his arm around his son, they left. Peter did not look back.

Both parents came for the final interview. Peter's improvements were reviewed: his effeminate behavior had disappeared, he was doing well in school, had some friends, and was enjoying and performing well in some sports. Dr. H had been spending more time with Peter and had been amazed to discover how knowledgeable and interesting his son was. They reported that following the decision of a termination date, they had had a difficult time with Peter who had obstinately refused to go to camp. During one explosive fight Peter had said he would go and live with the therapist. He had also reverted to wanting to sleep in their bed, saying that he was frightened. They coped with it well and related it to the fact that he was ending his treatment. The fact that Peter and Catherine were going alone to Sweden that summer was a big step for Peter who not that long ago had refused to go to the corner store alone. They were most appreciative of Peter's treatment and the help they had received in coping with their son. Mrs. H announced that she would like to come about every three months for a follow-up. Like Peter, she too had difficulty terminating.

Conclusions at the Termination of Treatment

I briefly examine here the changes in the symptomatology and personality structure that took place during analysis. In the early part of the treatment, focus was placed on his internal conflicts (masculine-feminine). It was important to extensively alter Peter's defensive organization so he could come to see the unconscious conflicts (for which his symptoms had supplied an uneconomic compromise). The interpretations which then connected the real life situations with the past experiences and with the transference situation enabled him to realign his defenses as he found more age-adequate solutions.

At the end of treatment, Peter was almost 11 years old. His manner of dress was boyish. He walked with confidence; his self-consciousness and "perplexed" expression had disappeared. He had completed grade 5 as one of the top students, and had received an award for gymnastics. He had become quite independent as revealed in the planned trip to Sweden with his sister.

He had friends in school with whom he shared boyish secrets, such as looking at *Playboy* magazine, and he belonged to a "gang" in his neighborhood. His behavior toward his peers was quite age-appropriate. He no longer sought out younger children as partners and had a normal appreciation of girls. He accepted his sister as such and not as a sexual partner. He was taking more of a "big brother" role with Nicolas and was helping him to learn to read.

Peter's perception of himself was much more realistic, and he had redeemed a more realistic ego ideal. He could accept his limitations—for one, he was still rather awkward in making friends and had to work a it. Peter expressed interest in becoming an architect, a profession that could combine his superior intellectual capacity and artistic skills. He also expressed interest in his father's work, archaeology.

The therapy confirmed that there was an unresolved oedipal conflict. At the termination of therapy, Peter's libidinal position was in latency. Although his mother remained the most important person in his life, he reacted to her more realistically. He was not afraid to show her hostility and became more accepting of the manner in which she could show love. His relationship with his father had improved, he was now identifying with him, and was able to compete with him in a more age-appropriate manner. He was conscious of rules and no longer cheated at games. Anal fixation seen in early treatment—references to feces and outbursts or rage—had abated and practically disappeared. His nausea and excessive clinging no longer existed. He no longer used obscene language, had urges to act like a girl, or got pleasure in assuming a feminine role by dancing in the nude. With less guilt, his ego was now more able to coordinate instinctual impulses and reality.

Peter no longer suffered from depersonalization or derealization states. His reality testing was good. He was using his endowment and ego skills at school and at home and was motivated to do well at school and in sports. He liked himself better, was coping quite well with new situations, and was now more able to enjoy life.

Peter now displayed a more adequate degree of frustration tolerance and was much better equipped to cope with aggression which he now directed toward the service of sports, or toward his peers in a fight. His ego no longer was alarmed of being dismantled. Also, the abatement or disappearance of some of his defenses (the defensive fantasy of "Wonder Woman" or a "Fembot") had removed some of the obstacles that had prevented the positive use of his aggression. Omnipotent thinking and projection were used less often. His sublimation potential was now utilized more fully. He was now better able to cope with anxiety and did not run to his parents for help. Peter had, over the three years, tried to improve himself. He was responsive and faithful to his treatment and through it had adopted more age-adequate solutions in coping with the no longer so threatening environment.

Working with the parents was extremely important. Mrs. H had to be carefully approached as she was experiencing considerable guilt, fearful of being accused of wrongdoing, and the therapist had not wanted to be a threatening figure. Although the structural changes in the parents were minimal, they did overtly try to help Peter in his endeavors to become more independent and to pursue boyish activities. They trusted and helped the therapist further by disclosing their own problems and feelings, as well as events at home and at school.

I hope that psychoanalytic treatment had brought about a dynamic change in Peter's personality and had not merely freed him from his symptoms. At termination, not only had Peter given up his effeminate behaviors completely and was acting boyish, but he also felt like a real boy, with sexual urges toward girls. Although the treatment enabled Peter to return to the mainstream of mental development, one still had to regard him as a highly neurotic boy, and one could speculate that he might return for treatment or a review in two or three years. However, it was hoped that he had gained enough experience to act with awareness and that this would be an asset in his continuing development.

Follow-Up Over a Twelve-Year Period

Over the course of the next twelve years, Peter's parents would call occasionally when they felt Peter needed help, and he would drop by to talk informally. He usually came three or four times over a short time period, and then would not be in contact for another year or so. He often asked for help but neither he nor his mother ever followed up on referrals to psychoanalysts and psychiatrists. Only when he reached a crisis in his early twenties did Peter seriously attempt to obtain treatment again.

Mrs. H's primary concerns when Peter was 13 and 14 were that he did not have many friends, was often depressed and preoccupied, and avoided intimacy with girls. She thought there were two or three girls Peter liked, but he said he would not date them because he did not want to hurt them later. Peter won an argument with his mother about changing to a public school and said that he was still happy at the private school except that one of his teachers called him gay. He said he did not want to be gay, felt he could protect himself against such comments and added: "I'm not gay. I like girls, but I'm not in a rush."

At 16, Peter was tall and looked very "masculine." He talked about two of his friends, both homosexuals, and a newer friend, Mark, whom he believed to be a homosexual. He was feeling a great deal of conflict because he did not want to be a homosexual, and yet he had a crush on Mark. He said, "Girls don't like me, whenever I ask them out they laugh at me, and Mark doesn't like me." Peter felt rejected by both men and women. When Peter did once take a girl to a dance, he became jealous when he saw Mark with a girl. He discovered Mark was not gay and yet desperately wanted to express his feelings to him and once told Mark that he loved him and asked him to try to be a homosexual. He realized that when he felt angry at his mother, he felt more attracted to Mark and thought this was because he was doing something his mother did not like. When Peter met with oppositional behavior from his mother (negative feeling for his mother), his frustration with a feminine figure made him seek masculine figures. This parallel desire for male and female is a narcissistic aspect of homosexuality. Peter, however, showed no sexual interest in his two friends who were homosexuals. He pursued Mark, who was heterosexual, and this may have been one of the reasons he liked Mark.

The next two years were a period of confusion for Peter, and his contradictory feelings preoccupied him. His marks at school dropped. He would refer to himself as a "fag," and then negate that firmly by saying "I am not gay." He changed his hair style, but also wanted to buy new boots to look more masculine. He was still infatuated with Mark, but would insult him because he felt rejected by him. Peter was also unhappy at home. His mother, whom he often said he hated, was in a state of depression. Sometimes in an effort to comfort him, or herself, she would take him to her bed when the rest of the family was not home. Dr. H, whom Peter had described as passive, spent most of his time with Peter's younger brother, Nicolas. He continuously encouraged Peter to achieve academically, not noticing that Peter's level of achievement was actually declining. Peter felt lonely and in turmoil. When I asked if he wanted me to find him an analyst, he said, "No, I want you."

My reason for referring Peter elsewhere, to an adult therapist, was twofold: (1) my training and experience to date were mainly in child analysis, and (2) Peter did not seem ready to modify the good child/adult therapeutic imago that was sustaining him. In Peter's mind, his parents were unavailable, which left me as the only option. This was seen as an effort to understand his problems and perhaps find an answer in his past behaviors.

During one of his visits, Peter talked about getting old and dying. He said, "I'd like to die if my mother died. And I'd like to have a family." In particular, he wanted daughters. "If I have a girl, my mother will be reborn in my daughter." His relationship with his mother was close and pathological; there was a symbiotic identification. In talking about his mother, himself, and a daughter he was unconsciously talking about a continuation through him, never mentioning a wife. His mother would return in his daughter.

During his final year of undergraduate studies, Peter went to a great deal of effort to trace me. We had not been in contact for over a year, and I had since moved my place of work. He said he was hoping to go to graduate school and that he was now closer to his father and sometimes helped him with his work. His mother was still often depressed. Peter was particularly eager for me to meet his girl friend Susan. He had deep feelings for her but thought that she needed help as she suffered from depression. He asked me to find her an analyst as well as one for himself, preferably female and middle aged, but neither one of them followed up on the names I provided.

Peter said he still felt attracted to men sometimes. He had never had intercourse with a man he said because of his fear of AIDS and because he wanted to have children one day. I noticed that the effeminate manners he had exhibited as a child had completely disappeared. However, the emphasis he placed on the fact that he had a girl friend led me to think that the emotions he revealed on the surface did not necessarily correspond to his inner struggle.

That spring, Peter called to say that he had finished exams and had received a research scholarship for which there had been a great deal of competition. However, he was disappointed because he had done extremely well at university but his parents were unable to attend his upcoming graduation.

A Turning Point: A Struggle for Gender Identity (Indeterminate Sexual Orientation)

A year and a half later, Peter began to call and visit more frequently. In one of these visits, he brought up the topic of his two girl friends, Susan and Alexandra, and why he had not been able yet to have a successful relationship with a girl. He had met Susan in junior high school and they had embarked on a relationship in high school, which included sexual contact. Susan was insecure and suicidal. Peter had also known his only other girl friend, Alexandra, from high school and she was also depressed and unstable. They had a close friendship but minimal sexual contact. They drifted apart after Peter became obsessed with a young man. Like Peter's mother, Peter's girl friends had been depressed and very needy of Peter who, in turn, had played the role of ''provider.'' Peter's choices for heterosexual relationships had been women with emotional disorders and consequently he had had little success in this area. This may have played a role in the redirection of his interest toward males.

That fall Peter has reached a turning point about whether to submit to his homosexual tendencies. On the bus one day to a summer job, Peter noticed a young man (Steven) whom he found attractive. Peter started taking the same bus everyday and following Steven, and became more and more obsessed with him. He also became more interested in improving his own looks.

After two months, Peter worked up the nerve to give Steven a note saying that he was interested in him. He asked him to call within three days if he was interested. Those three days were miserable for Peter; he had trouble sleeping, cried often at night, and masturbated frequently. He could not believe that Steven did not love him. A week passed, and one day Peter saw Steven with some friends. When Peter approached him and asked him about his note, Steven became embarrassed and did not answer. Steven's lack of response and the fact that Peter thought Steven's friends were all laughing at him caused Peter tremendous anguish. A few weeks later, when Peter and his mother were at an art gallery, Peter spotted Steven in the lobby. Peter pointed Steven out to his mother but she did not find Steven handsome.

Another day, Peter met Steven by coincidence outside the office and felt it was fate. When Peter asked Steven directly how he felt, Steven replied, "'Isn't it clear? I'm not interested." After that Steven was friendly and introduced himself, but did not disclose his surname. A month later, Peter saw Steven again. This time it was not a coincidence as Peter said he had been following him for the past month and knew a lot about his schedule. They noticed each other but did not speak. Steven was with a girl and this upset Peter, but he said he would have been more upset if he had seen him with another man. A week later, he saw Steven again on the bus and purposely paid no attention to him. Seeing him again disturbed Peter and that night he was not able to sleep well.

Peter wished he could stop thinking about Steven and he made concerted efforts to do so, but felt he could not control his thoughts. Consequently, his productivity waned; sometimes he would start to cry while he was working and he could not focus his attention. He sometimes felt a desire to find someone else, but he was not really keen to do that either. He said the episode with Steven had devastated him; he liked his life better when he had been alone; with neither a man nor a woman, but he still wished that Steven were a homosexual.

This course of events triggered a feeling of panic and set Peter off once again on a desperate search for help. A psychoanalyst and two psychiatrists he consulted were not willing to take him for intensive treatment or psychotherapy because he would not take medication, which they felt he needed during his acute anxiety state. He tried medication once for two days but felt it would not be good for him. As a last resort, he made an appointment with a gay group. He postponed this appointment several times in, I believe, the hope of finding a psychoanalyst and avoiding the gay group.

In the course of our conversation that month, I felt that Peter had improved in the last couple of months. He was seeing that, in one way, circumstances had made the decision for him: Steven was heterosexual, and he therefore did not have to embark on a homosexual relationship. He consistently said that he had been happier not having to make a decision before meeting Steven.

In one of our last meetings, I told Peter I had found a psychoanalyst who would not prescribe medication. He asked many times if this doctor would understand his problems. He finally went to see him but, because Peter was unsure where he would be attending school the next year, he could not make the firm commitment the psychoanalyst required. Peter was later accepted at a university in his hometown, but it is not known whether he returned to the psychoanalyst. However, since he had the opportunity for the indicated treatment—psychoanalysis—it is hoped that Peter showed the same motivation and self-awareness he had always exhibited, that he pursued treatment and would derive long-term benefits.

Discussion

It is thought that Peter would not become a bisexual as he would experience too much guilt. His eroticized obsession with Steven was all-consuming; however, when Steven said he was not interested, Peter became calmer. With both Mark and Steven, Peter did not pursue the right partners for a homosexual relationship, revealing his possible ambivalence about actually embarking on such a relationship.

Peter remained fixated at the oedipal level, where the sexual object was his mother. He was struggling with his unconscious inner conflicts for the resolution of the oedipal complex that was opposed by existing environmental influences. He was struggling to overcome his love for his mother and reach the secondary identification stage. To do this he needed to replace the mother with another female object while maintaining a normal object relationship with the mother. Also, his rivalry with his father needed to be replaced by identification with the father wherein the father would become more a model and less a rival. These two conflicts had to be overcome in order to obtain oedipal resolution.

In terms of external environmental influences, Peter was struggling with his parents' reactions to him which were similar to when he was a child. The family dynamics continued to perpetuate and reinforce psychopathology. His mother remained very seductive, repeatedly blurring the boundaries. She sometimes slept with him and still bought him clothes. When Peter tried to separate from his mother, his sexual object, she prevented it. He was therefore trapped in a vicious cycle of narcissistic object relations.

Simultaneously, Dr. H did not address his son's overall psychosexual development. When Peter's grades were declining in high school, his father ignored the underlying causes and simply continued to encourage his son to achieve more. The message "concentrate on your work" reduced Peter's castration anxiety by not having to deal with both the reality and mental representation of sexual objects—genitalia (disavowal). His father was unavailable and unresponsive to Peter's needs during his teenage and young adulthood years. In adulthood, he overtly avoided his son. Although he wished Peter would pursue his own line of work, he refused to publicly acknowledge his son's accomplishments in the field. Consequently, Peter often felt rejected by his father, feeling his father was ashamed of him. This prevented Peter from identifying with his father or with other masculine figures.

Dr. H did not interfere in, and passively tolerated, Peter's relationship with his mother. He may have felt guilty about not actively encouraging his wife to seek help, and improve their marital relationship, as he never attempted to follow my suggestions for Mrs. H to obtain help. Peter's analysis as a child sustained both the child as well as the mother during her periods of depression. At that time, Mrs. H was involved in supportive therapy and had an outlet. Dr. H may have been aware that since that time his wife had deteriorated noticeably.

Peter's expressed interest in his analysis as a child revealed his hope that, by looking at the past, he might discover how he arrived at his conflictive situation. At the same time he was afraid of discoveries about himself that might shed light on his current condition. His rejection of all male psychoanalysts revealed a conflicting relationship with authoritative male figures. He felt that he knew more than they did—even about medication. It was also a repetition of his relationship with his father: he had been rejected and therefore rejected them. Peter, however, wanted to pursue a career in the same field as his father.

Relationship between Therapist and Peter

The question of why Peter continued to seek my help must also be examined. It could be that he held me responsible for his problems because he did not get enough help as a child, or that he had regressed and felt that I could help him again. Another possibility may be based in a neurotic attachment to me in which he idolized me; I was not a frightening seductive figure as he was not afraid of incestuous tendencies as he was with his mother. Therefore I may have represented a more ideal mother figure that he wished for in times of confusion. Because of this, he may have developed a positive attachment to me and had a good working transference. He felt he could talk freely to me, knew that I was familiar with his background and his problems, and believed I would sincerely try to help. In this case, I was a nonsexual object with neither the traits of his mother or his father. I represented the self-reflective part of him and I helped him in his self-reflective efforts. Self-examination of his feelings and responses alleviated some of his anxiety. He therefore continued to seek psychoanalysis as an adult.

CHAPTER 10

Transvestite Behavior in a Preschool Boy: Reflections on Analytic Treatment

PURNIMA MEHTA, M.D.

The condition of transvestitism is complex. There have been three main approaches to this topic—biological, intrapsychic, and developmental/learning. However, there are fewer psychoanalytic studies of transvestitism, especially of children. Moreover, transvestite sororities exist on a national scale with chapters appearing in different cities in the late twentieth century. This permits the maintenance of transvestite practices. From published psychoanalytic reports, various psychic components have been delineated; the desire to merge with the object, anal components, the castration complex component, and the role of aggression (Glasser, 1979). According to Fenichel (1939), the transvestite has not been able to relinquish the fantasy of a phallic woman and desires to identify with her. Sperling's (1964) report of Tommy's analysis—a prelatency boy—emphasizes the bisexual wish in the transvestite's behavior rather than a defense against homosexuality.

I intend to present detailed analytic material of a preschool boy in order to elaborate further on the various fantasies and conflicts that have been discussed; more specifically, the dilemma of the analysis of young children and the importance of parent work, as well as the therapeutic nursery setting in which such a treatment can take place. Kliman's (1975) work on the application of child analytic techniques in a therapeutic nursery is the pioneer work related to this topic.

The Patient

Ryan is a 3½-year-old male child who was referred by the mother's psychiatrist for parental concerns regarding Ryan's behavior. Ryan has a brother who is 18 months younger. The parents are in their early forties, and it is significant that Ryan was born after eight years of infertility, and that the mother had fibroids that were misdiagnosed. I will now give separate reports on what I gathered from the mother and the father, who were seen in a combined session and on separation occasions.

History from the Mother

Ryan's mother presented with complaints about his behavior, stating that she was concerned that Ryan wanted to wear girls' clothes. She felt this behavior had escalated over the last few months, and that he had shown considerable interest in girl characters in cartoons, for example, Cinderella, Belle (*Beauty and the Beast*), and Mary Poppins. She also heard Ryan quite openly state that he wanted to be a girl. The mother said that she had been estranged from her son since he was 4 months old. More recently, she had felt closer and warmer toward him since Ryan was responding well to her. She stated that from 4 months until 2½ years he preferred the company of his father, who had been significant as a primary caretaker. Currently, Ryan prefers the mother. She felt that she had been left out of early caretaking responsibilities, but recognized that it might have been due to her own wishes to keep her distance. She was quite pleased about his recent attachment to her. Currently he seemed comfortable with his three times a week school schedule and two days a week in home day care. There had also been some description of occasional hostility and aggressive outbursts toward the brother.

As the mother vividly described Ryan's interest in *Beauty and the Beast* and *Cinderella,* she also noted that he would mimic many roles from both, playing them out in perfect detail. Initially the mother had felt pleased with this ability, but lately she had begun to feel concerned. He had begun to be preoccupied and obsessed with precise enactions of the details. It was actually at the insistence of the mother's psychiatrist (whom the mother had been seeing twice a month for the past eight years) that the parents had decided to have Ryan evaluated. The mother described Ryan's self-care functions as fairly reasonable and felt that he was eating independently and sleeping quite well. She also reported frequent nightmares with crying spells.

She described a great deal of excitement at being pregnant after eight years. She worked throughout the pregnancy and was pleased to have the child born through a C-section. The second pregnancy was 18 months later, very spontaneously, and she became depressed shortly after that for about six weeks and was treated with Ativan. Ryan's mother stated that Ryan was a beautiful baby who "was in touch with his surroundings" and "wonderful to hold." She stated, however, that at 4 months, when she started part-time work, Ryan became attached to the father who had more predictable hours. She described feeling resentful, but had gradually come to accept that Ryan's favorite parent was his father. However, I believe she used this acceptance defensively; she said that she had been told to be accepting of this fact by the psychiatrist. There were numerous caretaker changes. At 13 months a caretaker came to the home but lasted for only a few months because of her inconsistency. There were several switches with either a concern about quality of day care personnel or a feeling that Ryan could not adjust. She further described Ryan as a very curious, happy toddler, attentive to detail. He also had a great sense of humor. However, he would shame very easily and also displayed a fear that he would be easily hurt. The mother, as an adult, tried to protect him from social situations where she felt that the other children were being aggressive. More recently, Ryan had found a cape just like that of Little Red Riding Hood and Snow White and insisted on carrying it around with him.

The mother described her own relationships with her family as highly disturbed, and stated that she never speaks to her own mother who appears to be a somewhat cold and distant, narcissistic woman. Her father is an alcoholic. She described this in a quiet, contained, intellectual manner and stated that she tries to keep her peace within herself by keeping a distance from her parents. She meets her mother in public occasionally, but they do not talk to each other, sticking to superficialities. She felt that the marriage had gone through stormy times when she could not conceive, but overall

her husband remained supportive. Though she seemed quite emotionally isolated, it seemed that she functioned well in the household
chores and managed her day-to-day activities, including her job as
a home coordinator. She seemed genuinely concerned about Ryan
and also displayed an excessive willingness to please me. She further stated that her husband seemed to be an intense, anxious man
who needed to attend to details in a precise and regular way. He
often became extremely self-depreciating and guilty, which she felt
related to his own childhood background.

History from the Father

The father, who also seemed very eager and engaged in the process
of his son's evaluation, stated that he too had similar concerns
regarding Ryan's wanting to play girls' roles and pretending to wear
girls' clothes. The father had become quite irritable and angry about
Ryan's requests and had insisted that Ryan should "cut this non-
sense out" and be a boy. He too felt that Ryan was a very bright
child and had been pleased at his initial display of interest in details,
and attention to character study. The father described his relationship with Ryan as "instant bonding" from the birth and sometimes
very close, but that recently Ryan had attempted to move away.
While the father outwardly felt pleased, it was interesting to note
that he was injured by Ryan's attempts to move away. This was
implicit in his stating that "He'll soon come back to me. He needs
to have his mother for a little while." The father seemed to be half-
consoling himself. The father described a particular experience at
the time of Ryan's birth, stating that Ryan was immediately attached
to him, recognized his voice by turning his head toward him, and
wrapped his tiny hand around his finger. Apart from this particular
history given by the father, he too seemed very anxious about Ryan's wish to be a girl and felt that there had to be a fairly quick
way to manage it because of his own mounting anxiety about what
this would mean. He then elaborated on worries whether this was
a homosexuality that was genetic, and said that the mother's brother
had homosexual interests.

Evaluation of Ryan

I saw Ryan over two sessions with each of his parents. He was
reluctant to separate from either of them, though his interactions

with both parents were quite different. He was pleasant looking, with blue eyes and fair hair. He seemed to have a certain daintiness in him which betrayed a girlish quality. Ryan was shy and stuck close to both parents during the interview. It was noteworthy that Ryan was much more comfortable with the mother than the father. He stayed close to his mother who seemed to be able to follow his cues, allowing him to play with the toys which he would quickly bring back and share with her. On the other hand, Ryan seemed to have an intensely charged relationship with the father. He sat in the father's lap, refused to get down, and any suggestion from the father was met with aggressive outbursts where Ryan would attempt to hit the father in the face. The father at this time became quite embarrassed and tried to set limits by gently telling Ryan that he should not do that and that he loved him very much. I felt that the father was trying to control an intense rage underneath this very quiet control in my presence.

The father often voiced wanting to provide the best possible fathering. On one occasion during the interview the younger son had rolled down the steps and cut his lip. I could see the father becoming terribly self-depreciating and guilt-ridden at the idea that his younger son had been hurt and that it was his fault for not putting up a gate. The father appeared to be quite conflicted about Ryan moving away from his lap and trying to play in my office. He immediately reacted with several statements of the ''don't touch that'' type. One could easily see an expression of constraint and fear on Ryan's face as he tried to comply with the father while wishing to explore further.

At the end of the evaluation I clearly saw Ryan as having a neurotic disturbance of gender identity. It seemed that early caretaking disturbances might have contributed to this. Additionally, the father seemed particularly guilty about having taken on the primary caretaker role, while the mother, with her own difficulties of her mothering, could not assert herself and feared she would have nothing to offer this child. The symptoms had seemed to become more marked in the last few months, which also coincided with Ryan's moving from the father to the mother. Clearly, preoedipal factors of early separation were significant in this symptom. The child's wish to be a girl most likely also defended against both separation and castration anxiety, which might have been heightened by the father's covert aggression and hostility toward him. Obviously the child represented at this point many important aspects of the parents' personality, particularly as a mothering object and an idealized father. I felt that Ryan was at high risk and vulnerable to future symptoms and neurotic compromise formations. Considering the parents' enthusiasm and concern, Ryan's verbal ability, and clear neurotic disturbance, I recommended analysis for Ryan.

Recommendation and Preparing Parents for Analysis

This process took approximately six to eight weeks. My recommendation for analysis was met with considerable interest. I felt that this quick interest also represented an idealized view of my abilities, feeling that it would instantly cure their son and also allay all their concerns. One of the early ideas was that I would somehow talk Ryan into becoming a boy. When I informed them that analysis would need plenty of exploration and time, and that Ryan was seeking a girl role in order to alleviate genuine suffering, they became a little skeptical about the method of treatment. I also shared with them that the treatment would have no definite time limit but was the treatment of choice for Ryan's symptoms. Desperation motivated these parents and they seemed keen on pursuing treatment despite the initial skepticism. The mother's attachment to her own psychiatrist who had made the referral enabled her to trust me fairly quickly, and she was able to talk meaningfully about her resentments at not being able to take care of Ryan as an early caretaker. However, she was also painfully aware of her own guilt and feared that her lack of maternal availability might have led to Ryan's wanting to be a girl. It was out of this guilt that the parents felt analysis would alleviate Ryan's wish to be a girl and therefore were willing to obtain the best possible treatment. This too proved to be resistance to the actual undertaking and the practical realities for the analysis, for there seemed to be motivation to alleviate the guilt by a rapid move into analysis. As I began to help them look at the requirements of analysis, they began to ask more questions regarding the structure and goals. As we talked, the parents were gradually able to realistically look at the commitment needed for four-times-a-week analysis.

The Beginning of Analysis

Ryan's analysis was initially conducted with either the mother or the father present. It was arranged that the mother, because of practical realities, would bring him for three sessions and father for the fourth. It was immediately evident that the father felt excluded from the situation, but outwardly rationalized this and felt that this would help Ryan's bond with the mother. I had additionally arranged to meet with the parents on a once-a-week basis. Ryan did not separate from the mother during the first two months of analysis, and most sessions were conducted with mother present in the room. From very early on Ryan clearly began to play girl roles. He wore ribbons in his hair and dressed his mother's hair, wishing that we all could play girls. This remained a consistent theme while mother was present. He gradually began to familiarize himself with me. A frequent play theme was related to playing Belle from *Beauty and the Beast*. He seemed very pleased at the idea of being able to come to my office and play girl roles. This seemed to be the initial motivation. Nonetheless, he began to form an attachment with me.

The mother seemed to be quite well contained watching her son slowly move himself from her lap and proceed to explore my office. She seemed to be in tune with his needs and was delighted to see her son being playful. However, what quickly became apparent was that Ryan had much difficulty with any limit setting. For example, any attempt on my part to limit him in trying to dress me or comb my hair while we talked of wanting to pretend (or on one occasion the mother forgot a favorite toy of his), Ryan began to be quite aggressive, loud, and tearful. This was followed by the mother becoming worried, feeling that she was the cause of his unhappiness. This gave me important information about how these parents managed Ryan's behavior (obviously having much difficulty in saying no to this child). There was a particular session where Ryan sat in mother's lap and looked up at her in a pathetic way, while both of them cried looking at each other. This incident had arisen when Ryan had forgotten a mirror at home. The mother took cues from me to be able to tolerate Ryan's intense feelings of anger and hurt, but herself became quite anxious, wishing to drive home to get the mirror. However, the mother was able to delay this gratification as I suggested that Ryan might be able to wait it out. As Ryan was able to tolerate reasonable limit settings, the mother too was able to quickly identify with me in this regard and take on a more adult role. Another particular incident was Ryan's mistakenly breaking a vase in my waiting room while he was examining it. Both mother and child had become terribly anxious and fearful, fearing that I would be retaliatory. While I did reassure them that it was an accident, mother's concerns about the vase not being fixed remained very profound. We were then able to identify that both mother and child had considerable anxiety about breaking, not fixing, and damage. The mother experienced Ryan's affect as dangerous and powerful, seeking to quickly alleviate it by premature gratification.

The sessions with the father were of a different nature. The father was often controlling, fearing that Ryan would venture away too far. The father set limits in terms of play and was very concerned about Ryan messing up the office. (we had certain rules about what could and could not be removed). While we had designated play areas, which Ryan was able to use with my limit setting, the father seemed quite anxious. I managed this by helping the father become aware of some of our conversations with the mother in terms of do's and don'ts, and that Ryan seemed quite receptive to them. On one occasion Ryan refused to come to a session (after I had set limits) crying very loudly at home. The mother called me worried about whether bringing him would traumatize him further. I suggested that Ryan would be more overwhelmed by not coming, and that the clear message to him was that he could have bad feelings and he and I would deal with it. These and many interventions aimed at tolerance of affect both in parents and child in the early part of analysis, helped the parents become quite comfortable with the child's affect. They had in the past attempted to distract him by offering toys or another topic. It began to seem that managing these affects was one of the many motivations that Ryan had in wearing his girl costume (which he associated with making him "happy"). The parents had gladly agreed to make it a favorite pasttime.

As we dealt with more interactions of the mother–child dyad, with increasing tolerance of Ryan's affect (both by himself and by the parents), Ryan began to hint that his mother should sit in the waiting room while he came into the office and played. Mom seemed visibly relieved, but also curious as to how Ryan was doing. This separation became important as Ryan began to attach himself to me and wished to play girl. The girl stuff in the form of cape and shoes and dress were kept in a special box with clear limitations: they might only be used in the office setting. At first Ryan protested, but then was able to accept this limitation without much frustration. What seemed to be important at this point was Ryan's concern about the session ending and numerous thoughts about good and bad witches, the good who bring good feelings and the bad who bring bad feelings. I became a "good witch" in the beginning and a "bad witch" if I would say no or announce the end of the session. Ryan would often react to the end of sessions with anxiety, which was displaced in the form of regression to baby feelings, refusing to get up, and crawling on the floor. Many sessions were spent in dealing with "the end of session feelings," "sad feelings," "missing feelings," and "hurt feelings." It soon became clear that the parents, who had initially viewed separations as injurious or tremendously painful, were now able to tolerate Ryan's concerns about leaving. As a result, Ryan's own anxiety seemed to have diminished considerably.

In parent sessions they were relieved at the idea of limit setting. It soon became clear that aggression was a very difficult issue in this family. They saw limit setting initially as a mean and harsh act, and sometimes became overpunitive out of growing frustration. They were able to make a distinction between assertion and aggression and limit setting, and seemed relieved at the idea of being able to demonstrate some authority as parents.

The Analysis Progresses Further and More Work with Parents Is Done

Shortly after Ryan began to talk of girl feelings, we began to identify boy feelings. This came up as Ryan would play around as a fairy or ballerina with his cape on like a skirt, and would fall and quickly move his skirt to reveal his pants, saying they were "boy parts." We began to identify girl and boy parts, and the fear that I would respond to boy parts in a negative way. In one of the sessions, he appeared with a hoe (a long object). Then, gradually, he began to accumulate many such items in my office. While the parents were quite pleased with Ryan's obvious delight in showing "boy parts," the mother also cautioned him not to "collect too many" items. I

explored these thoughts within the parent sessions and it became
clear that while his parents wanted Ryan to exhibit masculinity,
they both had inner fears about it as well. The father covertly feared
that Ryan would "grow away" if he became a boy, and the mother
feared Ryan's masculine aggression. This became important as
Ryan began to deal with "the end of hour feelings" by becoming
quite loud and aggressive with me. I set limits in terms of action
but also permitted him to feel and talk about angry feelings. The
mother often became worried when she heard loud sounds in the
office, admonishing him to be "nice to me." Much of the parent
work at this time focused on helping them recognize the analytic
situation as unique, which enabled Ryan to get to parts of himself
that were worrisome or frightening. The parents had definite concerns about Ryan's emerging aggression, feeling that he would lose
control and become a tyrant if he was allowed to do anything he
pleased within the sessions. It was with much work that I was able
to help the parents address this realistic concern, at the same time
enabling them to make distinctions in terms of their roles as parents
and mine as an analyst.

Toward the still later part of analysis, Ryan had many omnipotent fantasies in the form of big witches and greedy pigs in his
profound wishes to be a girl or a woman just like me. He wished
to do that by identifying with my dress color or my hair color,
hoping that would magically turn him into a girl or a woman. The
analytic situation had been stabilized, the parents seemed to be
pleased with the progress Ryan had made in terms of much relief
of anxiety in being able to set limits in an appropriate way. Most
of all, Ryan's separation from the mother was facilitated by his
undertaking an attachment with me. The first long vacation helped
us also to address the parents' difficulties in separation, identifying
"missing feelings," their own anxiety about me leaving, and fearing
that Ryan would miss playing girl parts. Ryan too questioned what
would happen to his girl clothes. I responded to this by saying that
they would remain safe in my office. He was able to find an interesting way of bridging the vacation by bringing in two little soldier
figures, keeping them in my office for a couple of days, and then
having me keep one while he took the other. We talked of ways of
remembering each other while we were not with each other.

On return from my vacation, Ryan increasingly played at being a girl with definite themes linked to separation at the end of the hour. Yet there seemed to be an emerging interest in differences between boys and girls. The period began with the parents reporting Ryan's concerns about monsters under the bed, which they would check out quite regularly. In one of the parents' sessions, it became very clear that Ryan was put to bed by the mother lying next to him on an ongoing basis, cuddling up close to him. She would then return to her bedroom where Ryan would end up in the middle of the night (this contrasted with their early history in the course of evaluation during which they mentioned normal sleep habits). When I wondered with the mother whether she felt that there was any connection between monsters and his form of sleeping (i.e., the mother lying down close to him), she immediately felt hurt and offended at any idea that this had any effect on his night life. The father, however, did seem to be concerned about Ryan's watching the mother undress or in the nude, when the mother allowed the child to be with her in the bathroom. There seemed to be conflicting reports and history on this. The mother felt that Ryan never watched her undress, while the father felt that Ryan was always wishing to be with the mother in the bathroom and did sometimes end up there when he existed. This began to cause considerable tension in the marital dyad with feelings of wishing to place the blame of Ryan's symptoms from one parent to the other. I intervened by helping them recognize that many factors played into Ryan's symptom of wanting to be a girl. It seemed that night-time fears were additionally linked to having to be alone. The previously stated history of Ryan's good sleeping patterns was quickly revised in light of the new information about Ryan visiting the parental bedroom in the middle of the night every night. Additionally, the early caretaking history seemed to have been much more chaotic than previously suggested. Much of Ryan's separation fears centered around being left abruptly. This became apparent in Ryan attempting to control our separation by him closing the door on me rather than me closing the door. He would look at me longingly as he made the exit, waving good-bye, and then closing the door. Work on the separation issues, along these lines, gradually helped Ryan to become more assertive with a decrease in nightmares.

While Ryan's anxiety had greatly decreased, the parents began to worry about his excessive phallic exhibitionism (e.g., his becoming loud, displaying more rough and tumble behavior, and, on one occasion, his proudly talking about penises to the children at school). During these sessions, Ryan played monsters and reenacted the night scene regularly. Common themes were that the monsters would gobble him up. It soon became clear that he was fearful of his oral sadistic wishes, wishes to gobble anyone up who caused him frustration, including me. In order to defend against those feelings he was going to be a nice Thumbelina or Belle who did not have such gobble-up feelings. He called them the "good girl feelings." Oftentimes he would bring his mirror and reflect his image in the mirror stating that it made him feel like a good little girl.

In one particular session around the time of his fourth birthday, Ryan spontaneously invited the mother in for a tea party during the session. It was clear that Ryan needed to alleviate the mother's feelings of being left out, which had become apparent to him as she appeared hurt by his enthusiastic wish to visit my office on days that sessions were not scheduled. She began to fear his attachment to me and I attempted to discuss this. She was highly defensive and became even more concerned when she became hostile toward me on one occasion. Retrospectively, I could have better prepared the mother for this. It was around this time that I also changed from wearing a dress to a sari (part of my personal growth and consolidation). Ryan reacted with curiosity (which I had prepared the mother for), while the mother seemed a bit offended at the actual sight of me wearing a sari. With covert prejudice, she felt that this was too shocking. Overstimulation themes came to center stage and such themes at home began to get displaced onto the office setting.

The parents feared that Ryan was becoming too overstimulated, with too much energy and too much talking. Paradoxically, this is what the parents had wished for instead of the shy boy who used to cling to the parents on every social occasion! The father was becoming concerned about Ryan's boisterousness, and the mother was concerned that Ryan became quite charged with energy when he would run into my office. This began to create much resistance in the parents in terms of their concerns about whether to continue Ryan's analysis or not. This was about ten months into analysis when the parents insisted that they wanted a pediatrician involved and utilized the pediatrician's resistance to serve their own. I had many telephone contacts with the pediatrician, and recommended that the analysis was of utmost importance in terms of Ryan's health. It seemed obvious that the parents' ambivalence, particularly the mother's, had been displaced onto the pediatrician. The pediatrician herself, a trusted elder in this family, felt threatened by the idea that anybody else could offer Ryan the help that she could not, since she had watched his symptoms develop. Much splitting began to be utilized by the parents and a disequilibrium in the family emerged with Ryan's improving hold on himself. The parents began to feel uncomfortable that Ryan was openly talking about differences in boys and girls, which he had been thinking about in the sessions. Ryan talked about how boys had "yucky" things called penises and worried about "breaking feelings" (i.e., castration fear). The father had confirmed this by stating that Ryan would not touch his penis while urinating, but would instead hold his scrotal sac up so that the urinary stream was uncontrollable. Ryan would demonstrate this in the session by walking on his tipsy toes and lifting up his skirt in a butterfly manner, which would reveal his straight legs.

An Understandable but Unfortunate Turn of Events

As we made these connections, Ryan began to feel freer to express parts of his body (via boy and girl doll play), and on one occasion to speak about them to the other day care children, which caused considerable upset to the day care personnel. Apparently Ryan had gone up to one of the kids and stated that boys had penises, while girls had vaginas. This was seen as too outspoken by the personnel who felt that this was obnoxious behavior. I attempted to help contain this anxiety, both of the day care workers and the parents, by stating that Ryan was going through a period of "scared boy feelings," and he was pretending (in a counterphobic defense) to be a big, powerful boy to manage those scared boy feelings. I saw this as a "hyperphallic" developmental phase that would soon pass with more analysis. The parents, however, abruptly announced to me that they did not want the sessions continued and that they felt that Ryan's analysis had to come to a halt until they felt comfortable. However, interestingly, they decided to continue parent work with me. Despite all my attempts to convey to them that an abrupt disruption of treatment would be detrimental, I could see clearly Ryan's father's aggression emerge in a very intense way during one of the sessions as he smiled sarcastically while Ryan was crying desperately that he wanted to continue to come and see me. The father patted him in a patronizing way, stating that he loved him very much and that they would take care of this problem. Both parents obviously were responding to Ryan's attachment to me as something pathological rather than a growth in a positive direction. It soon became clear that their vulnerability from their own backgrounds and personalities had definitely supported Ryan's symptoms.

I continued to do parent work, for two months (on a once-a-week basis), inviting the parents to look more at their own fantasies about what they see as Ryan's growth, his separateness, and his suffering. The father is emerging as a very controlling and angry person with separation anxiety and castration fears related to his own chaotic background, including abuse by his father. It is becoming clear that the mother's background is much more disturbed than she had originally conveyed to me, with a very pathologically abusive mother–daughter relationship. The father's anxiety far outweighs the mother's; she keeps the peace in the marital dyad by submitting and hence placating the father's anxiety and, therefore, is unable to protect her son's treatment. The parent work continues with the hope that Ryan's analysis can be reinstated.

Summary

Ryan, at 3½ years of age, presented with wishes to be a girl. His intense pleasure in acting and dressing as a girl has multiple determinants, some of which were analyzed. During the one year of his analysis, separation–individuation issues with a somewhat anxious mother and a covertly hostile father were negotiated. A working through of this allowed for an emergence of a hyperphallic and exhibitionistic boy related to castration fears. Unfortunately, the parents', particularly the father's, vulnerability to the child's aggression and separation prompted them to abruptly remove Ryan from treatment. I think a therapeutic nursery school might have been more ideal and provided more containment to allow for continuation of analysis. Ryan remains very vulnerable to continued female gender identification and parent work is aimed at helping the parents recognize Ryan's separateness and sources of psychic pain.

Discussion

Transvestitism is a distinct perversion with its own well-defined features. Sperling (1964) makes a clear distinction between transvestitism, homosexuality, and fetishism. The love object of a transvestite is a heterosexual one. Moreover the transvestite requires a piece of female clothing, not necessarily limited to one fixed piece of clothing, while the fetish requires a specific fixed article, which can be a piece of female clothing, and is worn by the love object. Ryan's symptoms were definitely of a transvestite nature. The question is how significant was the disturbance. Stoller (1978) describes the significance of manifestations of femininity. While Freud (1905) and Beohm (1939) described manifestations of femininity as common, Stoller with Green (1976) emphasized intensity as the main criterion; that is, how much does the boy desire to be feminine, how often does he express the desire and how persistently, especially in response to efforts by others to stop it. Ryan expressed a mixture of desires—"I am a girl," to "I shall become a girl," to "I want to become a girl." Other criterion of his wish to wear girls' clothes all the time if readily available and his feminine mannerism, grace, build, and talk suggested a perversion. He also preferred to play with girls than boys. He clearly required analytic intervention. Sperling (1964) notes that bisexual wishes are prominent in the transvestite act. The "half and half" fantasy, to be half boy and half girl, defends against the danger of loss and the trauma of the primal scene. While Ryan revealed wishes to be a girl, his bisexual fantasies were not clearly delineated. Rather, the girl "armor" defended very powerfully against an emerging boy self representation. Hence, could the transvestite tendency be a defense (as I suggested in the clinical material) against what it would mean to both parents if Ryan displayed his phallic powers? Both parents had loud, provocative fathers. Ryan's masculinity represented danger and humiliation for both parents. I believe that the castration fears were secondary to discouragement from both parents of his emerging masculinity, which was strongly linked to aggression and somewhat forbidden.

The conflict seemed to be rooted in separation–individuation issues, autonomy related, rather than true oedipal phase related castration fears. The mother sensed that Ryan's autonomy would hurt her directly, while the father feared losing his "beloved son" (especially considering the father's idea of Ryan's attachment to him at the time of his birth).

Of further note is the father's involvement in early caretaking and the mother's absence. Glasser's (1979) description of the core-complex component has relevance. He describes "a deep-seated and pervasive longing for an intense and intimate closeness to the object, amounting to a complete 'merging' or union: it is as if the parent has a memory of primary identification and is trying to regain it." However, the conflict borne by the wish to escape from the union with the object causes fears of separation and abandonment. Hence the undressing at the end of the transvestite act is crucial in obtaining the freedom from the mother–child "envelope." This bears truth in Ryan's dilemma. The maternal absence created a hunger which was evident in the maternal transference—repeated themes of merger and separation in the act of dressing and un-dressing. However, it is also important to note that this was further compounded by the father's intense hunger for his boy. Most litera-ture points to the father's absence, physical and psychological or both in the case of the transvestite or transsexual. In Ryan's case, the father fostered a merging that paralleled the engulfing, fearful mother. His intense attachment to the child is different from that reported in literature. He was in fact part of the evaluation and treatment process. He was an available model for masculinity, but became anxious as Ryan became a separate masculine force. The father's investment in a homosexual compromise appeared to be less prominent, but he could not find sufficient ego resources within him to allow his son to separate within the father–son dyad.

Finally, the question of technique requires comment. Few cases of actual analytic treatment of transvestite children have been re-ported. Sperling (1964) clearly notes that the concomitant treatment of the mother is essential. She mentions dealing with the resistances of the mother before treating the child. Stoller (1978) aims at helping the mother tolerate the depression that occurs as the son's treatment begins to work. Additionally, he speculates that a mother might end a marriage to deal with her devaluation of her husband. The withdrawal of Ryan's treatment occurred in the context of Ryan separating from both parents. The resultant disequilibrium is similar to Stoller's prediction of marital imbalance that can occur as the child improves. I was unable to help contain the parents' fear of losing their child to growth and development. Moreover, added opposition from the pediatrician and the school teachers magnified the parental anxiety. It is with this in mind that I mentioned the need for a therapeutic nursery to help successful treatment of these children. Kliman (1975) has reported interesting analytic work in the classroom with a boy with transvestite tendencies. The presence of such a setting allowed many transient emerging phenomena like hypersexuality, aggression, separation issues, and regressions to be contained without overwhelming the parents. I believe that an analysis of such a disorder, due to profound and intense separation issues, requires more careful planning and anticipation of description. The support of other significant people like teachers and caretakers would be crucial in helping contain transient behaviors and action in the course of treatment.

Conclusion

It is clear that treatment of children with transvestite tendencies is essential and could be helpful. Various indicators of femininity (benign versus malignant) can be reliable markers for treatment. While bisexuality has been considered to be one central fantasy for a transvestite, Ryan displayed a more defensive need to be a girl in order to allay the anxiety about being a boy related to the parents' difficulty in separation issues. Moreover, treatment done in the context of a therapeutic nursery setting can have a better chance of completion. Parent work with involvement of both mother and father is crucial.

References

Boehm, F. (1930), The femininity complex in men. *Internat. J. Psycho-Anal.,* 11:444–469.

Fenichel, O. (1930), The psychology of transvestitism. In: *The Collected Papers of Otto Fenichel,* ed. H. Fenichel & D. Rappaport. New York: W. W. Norton, 1953, pp. 167–180.

Freud, S. (1905), Three Essays on the Theory of Sexuality. *Standard Edition*, 7:125–243. London: Hogarth Press, 1953.

Glasser, M. (1979), From the analysis of a transvestite. *Internat. Rev. Psycho-Anal.*, 6:163–173.

Green, R. (1976), *Sexual Identity Conflict and Adults*. New York: Basic Books.

Kliman, G. (1975), Analyst in the nursery—Experimental application of child analytic techniques in a therapeutic nursery: The cornerstone method. *The Psychoanalytic Study of the Child*, 30:477–510. New Haven, CT: Yale University Press.

Sperling, M. (1964), The analysis of a boy with transvestite tendencies: A contribution to the genesis and dynamics of transvestitism. *The Psychoanalytic Study of the Child*, 19:470–493. New York: International Universities Press.

Stoller, R. (1978), Boyhood gender aberrations: Treatment issues. *J. Amer. Psychoanal. Assn.*, 26:541–558.

Name Index

Abraham, K., 115–116, 166, 167, 245
Acosta, F. X., 187
Adler, A., 112
Akhtar, S., xiv, 63
Almond, B., 232
Arlow, J. A., 5–6, 15, 16, 30, 135

Babatzanis, G., xix–xx
Bacon, C., 243
Bak, R. C., 166
Barahal, H. S., 15
Bergler, E., 15, 34
Bergman, A., 9, 23, 63, 66, 209, 246
Bernstein, I., 232
Bibring, G. L., 15
Bieber, T., 32, 34
Bieber, T. B., 32
Bjerre, P., 136
Blackman, J., xvii, 48, 63, 65
Bleuler, J., 110
Blos, P., 16, 66
Blum, A., 177
Blum, H. P., 62, 166, 167, 215–216
Boehm, F., 301
Böhme, J., 122
Bonaparte, M., 160
Brabant, F., 111
Brenner, C., 63, 135, 243
Brenner, I., 64
Brierley, M., 154–156, 240, 241
Brody, S., 165n
Busse, G., 108
Bychowski, G., 15, 34

Calef, V., 64
Cameron, J. L., 110

Cameron, N., 110
Chodorow, N. J., 166
Coen, S., 167, 178

Dain, H. J., 32
Decker, B., 188
Deutsch, H., 152, 156, 166, 223–224, 244
Devreese, D., 108, 129
Dickes, R., 24, 63
Dince, P. R., 32
Dorpat, T. L., 145, 199, 206, 207, 239
Downey, J., 180
Drellich, M. E., 32

Ehrhardt, A., 63, 180
Eidelberg, L., 15
Eisner, H., 29
Eisnitz, A., 176–177
Eissler, K. R., 20, 27, 28
Englehardt, H. T., Jr., 33
Erikson, E., 66

Falzeder, C., 111
Fast, I., 147–148, 166
Fenichel, O., 9, 12, 15, 287
Ferenczi, S., 5, 12, 118
Fine, B. D., 16, 239
First, S., 16
Flechsig, P., 108–109, 110, 113–114, 120, 128, 129–131, 132–134
Francis, J., 65
Freedman, A., 63
Freeman, T., 110
Frenkel, R. S., 166
Freud, A., 12, 19–20, 22, 181, 238–239

305

Subject Index